CONTENTS

Preface

This Macedonian-English/English-Macedonian dictionary contains more than ten thousand vocabulary entries in both languages in a concise format. The selection of the vocabulary is based on the contemporary Macedonian Standard Language, spoken today by almost 1.3 million people in the Republic of Macedonia as well as in some regions in Southern and Eastern Albania, Western Bulgaria (Pirin-Macedonia) and Northern Greece (Aegean Macedonia). The dictionary is meant to provide quick reference in both Macedonian and English for students, travelers and business people. However, it does not include phrases, and many derivatives and compounds that follow a clear pattern of derivation or combination have been left out as well.

Each entry is printed in bold and is followed by pertinent abbreviations in italics indicating the grammatical categories. The vocabulary entries in the English part are also supplied with a phonetical transcription. In the Macedonian part the nouns are marked with their gender. The Dictionary includes a table of Macedonian symbols with their transliteration and a guide to pronunciation, as well as a table of abbreviations and symbols for phonetical transcription of the English sounds. If an entry is followed by several equivalents in the other language, it is the basic meaning or etymologically the earliest one that comes first.

Judith Wermuth
New York
March 13, 1997

The Macedonian Alphabet

Letters		Pronounciation	Transliteration
A a	*A a*	a in art (but shorter)	a
Б б	*Б б*	b in book	b
В в	*В в*	v in voice	v
Г г	*Г г*	g in good	g
Д д	*Д д*	d in door	d
Ѓ ѓ	*Ѓ ѓ*	gj (no equivalent)	g
E e	*E e*	e in ever	e
Ж ж	*Ж ж*	s in pleasure	z
З з	*З з*	z in zoo	z
S s	*S s*	ds in ends	dz
И и	*И и*	e in equal	i
Ј ј	*Ј ј*	y in yes, yard or you	i
К к	*К к*	k in kind	k
Л л	*Л л*	l in lamp	l
Љ љ	*Љ љ*	lj in "Gigli" (Italian)	lj
М м	*М м*	m in man	m
Н н	*Н н*	n in noon	n
Њ њ	*Њ њ*	nj in "cognac" (French)	nj
О о	*О о*	o in offer	o
П п	*П п*	p in play	p
Р р	*Р р*	r in room	r
С с	*С с*	s in sun	s
Т т	*Т т*	t in table	t

Ќ ќ	*Ќ ќ*	kj (no equivalent)	k
У у	*У у*	oo in moon (but shorter)	u
Ф ф	*Ф ф*	f in fire	f
Х х	*Х х*	h in help	h
Ц ц	*Ц ц*	tz in quartz	ts
Ч ч	*Ч ч*	ch in chair	c
Џ џ	*Џ џ*	j in jazz	dz
Ш ш	*Ш ш*	sh in show	s

Abbreviations/Скратенки

adj.	adjective
adv.	adverb
Br.	British
conj.	conjunction
eccl.	ecclesiastical
f.	feminine noun
fig.	figurative
gram.	grammar
inf.	infinitive
interj.	interjection
interrog.	interrogative
lit.	literature
m.	masculine noun
mil.	military
mod.	modal verb
mus.	music
n.	noun
ntr.	neuter noun
num.	numeral
part.	particle
pl.	plural
polit.	political
prep.	preposition
pron.	pronoun
refl.	reflexive verb
v.	verb

MACEDONIAN - ENGLISH
МАКЕДОНСКО - АНГЛИСКИ

a *conj.* and, but, while, yet
абажур *m.* lampshade
абдикација *f.* abdication
абдицира *v.* abdicate
аби *v.* wear out, get worn out
абитуриент *m.* senior year student
абонент *m.* subscriber
се абонира *v.* subscribe (to)
абортира *v.* abort
абортус *m.* abortion, miscarriage
аванс *m.* advance
авансира *v.* make advance, give advance
авантура *f.* adventure, venture
авантуризам *m.* adventure
авантурист *m.* adventurer
авијатика *f.* aviation
авијатичар *m.* aviator, airman, flyer
авијација *f.* aeronautics, aviation
авион *m.* airplane
авлија *f.* court, courtyard
автентичен *adj.* authentic
автобиографија *f.* autobiography
автобус *m.* bus
автограф *m.* autograph
автомат *m.* automatic machine, slot machine, pay phone
автоматизација *f.* automation

автомобил *m.* automobile, car
автономен *adj.* autonomous
автономија *f.* autonomy
автопат *m.* highway, freeway
автопортрет *m.* self-portrait
автор *n.* author
авторитет *m.* authority, personal influence
авторитетен *adj.* authoritative
авторитетно *adv.* with authority, authoritatively
автострада *f.* motorway
автотранспорт *m.* autotransport
агент *m.* agent, broker, commercial traveler
агенција *f.* agency
агитатор *m.* agitator
агитација *f.* agitation
агитира *v.* agitate, propagate
агол *m.* corner, angle, nook
агонија *f.* agony
аграрен *adj.* agrarian
агрегат *m.* aggregate
агресивен *adj.* aggressive
агресивност *f.* aggression
агресор *m.* aggressor
агрикултурен *f.* agronomic
агроном *m.* agronomist
агрономија *f.* agronomy
ад *m.* hell, inferno
адверб *m.* adverb
адвокат *m.* lawyer, attorney

адет *m.* habit, practice

адјектив *m.* adjective

административен *adj.* administrative, managing official

администрација *f.* administration, management

адмирал *m.* admiral

адреса *f.* address

адски *adj.* 1. hellish, infernal; 2. very

адут *m.* trump

аеродинамика *f.* aerodynamics

аеродинамичен *adj.* aerodynamic

аеродром *m.* airport, airfield

аероплан *m.* plane, airplane

аеротранспорт *m.* airtransport

ажурен *adj.* diligent, precise, punctual

ажурност *f.* diligence, preciseness, punctuality

азбука *f.* alphabet

азбучен *adj.* alphabetical

азил *m.* asylum

азот *m.* nitrogen

азур *m.* azure, sky blue

ајвар *m.* caviar, roe

ајдук *m.* 1. freedom fighter against the Ottomans; 2. robber,

ајкула *f.* shark

академија *f.* academy

академик *m.* academician

акавриум *m.* aquarium

акламација *f.* acclamation

аклиматизација *f.* acclimatization

аклиматизира *v.* acclimate, acclimatize

ако *conj.* if, even if, although, that's all right

акомодација *f.* accomodation

акомодира *v.* accomodate

акорд *m.* accord

акордеон *m.* accordion

акредитив *m.* credentials, letter of credit

акредитира *v.* accredit

акробат *m.* acrobat, tumbler

акробација *f.* acrobatism, acrobatic performance

аксиома, *f.*, аксиом *m.* axiom

акт *m.* act

актив *m.* assets

активен *adj.* active, to be on active duty/ service

активизира *v.* to activate

активност *f.* activity, diligence

актуелен *adj.* current, relevant (to the present or current situation), topical

актуелност *f.* actuality, relevance

акузатив *m.* accusative

акумулатор *m.* accumulator

акумулација *f.* accumulation

акустика *f.* acoustics,

акутен *adj.* acute; (question) urgent, pressing

акушерка *f.* midwife

акушерство *n.* midwifery

акцент *m.* accent, stress, emphasis

акција *f.* campaign, share, stock, action

акционер *m.* shareholder

аларм *m.* alarm

алармантен *adj.* alarming

алармира *v.* alarm

албум *m.* album

алга *f.* alga

алегорија *f.* allegory

алегоричен *adj.* allegorical

алинеја *f.* paragraph

алка *f.* iron ring, (chain-) link

алкохол *m.* alcohol, spirits, alcoholic drinks

алманах *m.* yearbook, almanac

алосан *adj.* injured, mad, crazy, insane

алтернатива *f.* alternative

алуминиум *m.* aluminum

алхемија *f.* alchemy

алчен *adj.* greedy, acquisitive, avaricious

алчност *f.* greediness, acquisitiveness, avariciousness

ама1. *conj.* but, but still, yet; 2. *interj.* what a...

амандман *m.* amendment

аматер *m.* amateur

амбасада *f.* embassy

амбасадор *n.* ambassador

амбиција *f.* ambition

амбуланта *f.* ambulance, clinic for outpatients

ами 1. *conj.* but, but also, and; 2. *adv.* why

амин *interj.* amen

амнестија *f.* amnesty

амнестира *v.* amnesty

анализа *f.* analysis

анализира *v.* analyze

аналоген *adj.* analogous, similar

ананас *m.* pineapple

анархизам *m.* anarchism

анархија *f.* anarchy

анатомија *f.* anatomy

ангажира *v.* engage, to be/become committed, to become involved

ангажман *m.* engagement, commitment, agreement

ангел *m.* angel

ангина *f.* tonsillitis, angina

анексија *f.* annexation

анемија *f.* anemia

анкета *f.* survey

анонимен *adj.* anonymous

антагонизам *m.* antagonism

антена *f.* antenna

антилопа *f.* antelope

антисемитизам *m.* anti-Semitism

антифашизам *m.* antifascism
антологија *f.* anthology
апарат *m.* instrument, apparatus
equipment, gadget, apparatus,
appliance, machine, (radio, telephone) set
апартман *m.* apartment, flat
апел *m.* appeal
апелира *v.* appeal
апетит *m.* appetite
аплаудира *v.* applaud
аплауз *m.* applause
апостроф *m.* apostrophe
апострофира *v.* apostrophize
април *m.* April
апс *m.* custody, prison, detention,
arrest, jail
апсана *f.* prison, jail
апсеник *m.* prisoner
апси *v.* arrest, put in prison/
jail
апсорбира *v.* absorb
апстрактен *adj.* abstract
апсурден *adj.* absurd
аптека *f.* pharmacy
ар *m.* are, 100 square meters
аргумент *m.* argument, reason
арена *f.* arena
аритметика *f.* arithmetic
армија *f.* army, armed forces
арогантен *adj.* arrogant
арсенал *m.* arsenal
артерија *f.* artery
артикал *m.* article, product

артилерија *f.* artillery
артист *m.* actor
артистка *f.* actress
архаичен *adj.* archaic
археолог *m.* archaeologist
археологија *f.* archaeology
архив *m.* archives, registry
архитект *m.* architect
архитектура *f.* architecture
асимилација *f.* assimiliation
асимилира *v.* assimilation
асистент *m.* assistant
асоцијација *f.* association
аспект *m.* aspect
астма *f.* asthma
астролог *m.* astrologer
астрологија *f.* astrology
астроном *m.* astronomer
астрономија *f.* astronomy
атака *f.* attack
атакува *v.* attack
атеље *ntr.* studio
атентат *m.* assassination
атентатор *m.* assassin
атлас *m.* atlas
атлет *m.* athlete
атлетика *f.* athletics
атмосфера *f.* atmosphere
атом *m.* atom
атомски *adj.* atomic
атрибут *m.* attribute
аудиенција *f.* audience
ауто *ntr.* car, automobile
афект *m.* emotion, affect

афера *f.* affair, business, scandal, case, incident
афион *m.* opium, poppy

афоризам *m.* aphorism
аџија *m.* pilgrim
ашлак *m.* hooligan, scamp

Б

баба *f.* grandmother, granny, old woman,
бавен *adj.* slow
багаж *m.* luggage, baggage
багер *m.* excavator, dredger
багрем *m.* acacia
бадем *m.* almond
баење *ntr.* exorcise, lay, conjure (away)
база *f.* base, foundation, basis
бајат *adj.* not fresh (bread, dough, pastry)
бајачка *f.* healer, fortune-teller, psychic
бајрак *m.* flag, banner
бакал, бакалин *m.* grocer
бакалница *f.* grocery
бакне *v.* kiss
бактерија *f.* bacterium
бакшиш *m.* tip
бал *m.* ball
балада *f.* ballad
баланс *m.* balance
баласт *m.* ballast
балерина *f.* ballerina
балет *m.* ballet
балкон *m.* balcony

банален *adj.* ordinary, banal
банана *f.* banana
банда *f.* gang, band, bunch
бандит *m.* bandit, robber, brigand
банка *f.* bank
банкар *m.* banker
банкрот *m.* bankrupt
банкротира *v.* go bankrupt
бања *f.* bath, bathroom, public baths, health resort for hydrotherapy
бар *m.* nightclub, bar
бара 1. *f.* puddle, pool; 2. *v.* seek, look for, search for, hunt for
барабан *m.* drum
барака *f.* shed, barn
барем *adv.* at least
барикада *f.* barricade
барикадира *v.* barricade
баритон *m.* *(mus.)* baritone
барометар *m.* barometer
барут *m.* gunpowder
бас *m.* *(mus.)* bass
басамак *m.* stair, step
басен *m.* swimming pool, reservoir

баснa *f.* fable, (*fig.*) lie, falsehood

бастон m. cane

батак m. mess

баталјон m. battalion

батерија f. battery

бацил m. bacillus

бацува, баци v. kiss

баш adv. just, exactly

башка adv. extra, separately, in addition, specially

бебе ntr. baby

бег m. flight, escape

бега v. run away, flee

бегалец *m.* refugee, fugitive, runaway

бегач *m.* runner

бегло *adv.* superficially, cursory, hastily

беда *f.* misfortune, calamity, trouble, poverty

беден *adj.* poor

бедем *m.* wall, dam, dyke

бежанец *m.* refugee

без *prep.* without, except

безалкохолен *adj.* nonalcoholic, soft drink

безбожен *adj.* godless, ungodly, wicked

безброен *adj.* countless, uncountable, numberless, innumerable

безбро *m.* a host of, any number of

безверие *ntr.* unbelief, scepticism

безвкусен *adj.* tasteless, savorless

безвластие *ntr.* anarchy, lawlessness

безволен *adj.* weak-willed, spineless

бузвучен *adj.* soundless

безгласен *adj.* voiceless, speechless, mute

безграничен *adj.* boundless, limitless, endless, infinite

безгрешен *adj.* sinless, blameless, innocent, perfect

безгрижен *adj.* carefree

бездеен *adj.* inactive, passive, inert, idle

безделник *m.* idler, loafer

бездетен *adj.* childless

бездна *f.* abyss, chasm

бездомен *adj.* homeless

бездушен *adj.* lifeless, heartless, hard-hearted, merciless, pitiless

безжален *adj.* pitiless, ruthless

беззаконие *ntr.* lawlessness, unlawfulness, violence

беззаштите *adj.* helpless, defenseless

безизразен *adj.* expressionless, meaningless

безимен *adj.* nameless, unnamed, anonymous

безличен *adj.* impersonal, without/lacking individuality

безмесен *adj.* vegetarian

безмилосен *adj.* merciless, pitiless, ruthless

безнадежен *adj.* hopeless

безначаен *adj.* insignificant, unimportant

безобразен *adj.* impudent, insolent, impertinent, arrogant, pert

безодговорен *adj.* irresponsible

безопасен *adj.* safe, secure, harmless

безработен *adj.* unemployed

безразличен *adj.* indifferent

безразлично *adv.* indifferently

безредие *ntr.* disorder, untidiness, mess

безропотен *adj.* humble, obedient, resigned

безукорен *adj.* faultless, irreproachable, impeccable, perfect

безумен *adj.* mad, insane

безумие *ntr.* madness

безусловен *adj.* unconditional

безусловно *adv.* unconditional, without reservation, absolutely

бел *adj.* white

белег *m.* scar, mark, sign, characteristic, feature

белезица *f.* bracelet, handcuff

белетристика *f.* fiction, belle letters

белешка *f.* note, remark

белка *f.* egg white, albumen, protein

бензин *m.* benzine, petrol

бербер *m.* barber, hairdresser

бере *v.* pick, gather

берза *f.* stock market, stock exchange

бес *m.* rage, wrath, madnes, fury

бесвесен *adj.* unconscious, senseless

беседа *f.* talk, lecture, speech, discourse

бесен *adj.* mad, furious, violent

беси *v.* hang

бесконечен *adj.* endless, infinite

бескраен *adj.* endless, infinite

бескрупулен, бескрупулозен *adj.* unscrupulous

бесмислен *adj.* absurd, meaningless, senseless, foolish, silly

бесмртен *adj.* immortal

бесплатен *adj.* free (of charge), gratis

бесплоден *adj.* unfruitful, unproductive, sterile

беспокои *v.* disturb, worry

беспокои се *v.* worry, be upset

бесполезен *adj.* useless, unprofitable

бесполезно *adv.* vainly

беспомошен *adj.* helpless, feeble, defenseless, powerless

беспорен *adj.* undisputable, unquestionable

беспоштеден *adj.* merciless

беспределен *adj.* limitless, boundless, unlimited, infinite

беспредметен *adj.* pointless, objectless, senseless, useless

беспризорен *adj.* homeless

беспринципен *adj.* unprincipled

беспристрасно *adv.* impartially

бесрамен *adj.* shameless, indecent, impudent, brazen

бессилен *adj.* powerless, weak, impotent

бессовесен *adj.* unscrupulous, shameless

бессонен *adj.* sleepless

бестрашен *adj.* fearless, reckless, intrepid

бесцелен *adj.* aimless, purposeless, useless

бесчовечен *adj.* inhuman, cruel, fierce, brutal

бетон *m.* concrete

библија *f.* Bible

библиографија *f.* bibliography

библиотека *f.* library

библиотекар *m.* librarian

бивол *m.* buffalo

бие *v.* hit, strike, fight

бизон *m.* bison

бик *m.* bull

билет *m.* ticket

билтен *m.* bulletin

бина *f.* stage

бинт *m.* bandage

биографија *f.* biography

биолог *m.* biologist

биологија *f.* biology

биро *ntr.* office

бирократија *f.* bureaucracy

бисер *m.* perl

бит *m.* customs, way (manner) of life, way (style) of living, conditions of life, living standards

битие *ntr.* being, existence, genesis

битка *f.* battle, fight

бифе *ntr.* buffet, refreshment bar

благ *adj.* gentle, kind, kindly

благо *ntr.* good, welfare, prosperity

благодарен *adj.* grateful, thankful,

благодарност *f.* gratitude, thankfulness

благодат *f.* blessing, boon

благодатен *adj.* beneficial

благопријатен *adj.* favorable, propitious

благороден *adj.* noble, high-minded

благородник *m.* nobleman

благосостојба *f.* prosperity, well-being

блазни *v.* attract, allure, entice, tempt

блед *adj.* pale

блеска/блесне *v.* shine, sparkle, glitter

близнак *m.* twin

близок *adj.* near, close

близу *adv.* near, near by, close

блок *m.* block

блуза *f.* blouse

бљудо *ntr.* dish, course

бог *m.* God

богат *adj.* rich, wealthy

богатство *ntr.* wealth, richness, opulence, affluence, fortune

Богородица *f.* Mother of God, Our Lady, the Virgin

богослов *m.* theologian, seminarist

богослужение *ntr.* (eccles.) worship, service, liturgy

боготвори *v.* deify, worship, *(fig.)* idolize, adore

богохулник *m.* blasphemer

богохулство *ntr.* blasphemy

боен *adj.* fighting, battle, war

боец *m.* warrior, soldier, fighter

божествен *adj.* divine

Божик *m.* Christmas

божур *m.* peony

бои се *v.* fear, be afraid of

бој *m.* 1. fight, battle, struggle; 2. stature, height, growth

боја *f.* color, paint, tincture, dye

бојадиса/бојадисува *v.* color, paint, tincture, dye

бојаџија *m.* 1. painter; 2. *(fig.)* turncoat

боклук *m.* garbage, rubbish

боледува *v.* be ill, be sick, suffer from

болен *adj.* ill, sick, diseased

болест *f.* illness, sickness, disease, disorder

болка *f.* pain, ache, plaint

болница *f.* hospital

бомба *f.* bomb

бомбардира *v.* bombard, shell

бор *m.* pine, pinetree

борба *f.* fight, struggle, contest

борец *m.* fighter

бори се *v.* fight, struggle, strive, combat

борч *m.* debt

бос *adj.* barefoot(ed)

ботаника *f.* botany

ботаничар *m.* botanist

брава *f.* lock

брада *f.* chin, beard

брак *m.* marriage

бракоразвод *m.* divorce

бран *m.* wave

брани *v.* defend, protect

брани се *v.* defend oneself, protect oneself

брат *m.* brother

братство *ntr.* brotherhood, fraternity

братучед, *m.*, **братучедка** *f.* cousin
брашно *ntr.* flour, meal
брбори *v.* babble, chatter
брдо *ntr.* hill, mountain
брег *m.* 1. coast, shore, waterside, strand; 2. hill, mountain
бреза *f.* birch
бреме *ntr.* burden, load, weight
бремена (жена) *adj.* pregnant
брест *m.* ulm tree
брз *adj.* quick, rapid, swift, prompt, brisk
брзина *f.* speed
брзо *adv.* quickly, rapidly, swiftly, fast
бригада *f.* brigade
брилјант *m.* diamond
брич *m.* razor
бричи (се) *v.* shave (oneself)
бришев. wipe, dry, mop, dust
брод *m.* ship, boat
бродар *m.* sailor, seaman
бродење *ntr.* navigation, sea travel
брои *v.* count, number
број *m.* number, figure, numeral
бронза *f.* bronze
брсти *v.* browse, crop
брут *m.* nail, peg
брутален *adj.* brutal
бруто *ntr.* gross
буба *f.* insect, beetle, bug
бубрег *m.* kidney

був *m.* owl
бува *f.* flea
будала *m.* fool
буден *adj.* awake, watchful, vigilant, unsleeping, alert
буди *v.* wake, waken
буди се *v.* wake up, awake
будилник *m.* alarm clock
буен *adj.* luxuriant, lush, voluptuous
буква *f.* letter (of the alphabet)
буквално *adv.* literally
букет *m.* bouquet
булка bride, wife, poppy
буна *f.* rebellion, revolt, uprising, insurrection
бунар *m.* well, pump
бунда *f.* fur coat
буни *v.* excite, agitate, stir up,
буни се *v.* rebel, protest against, be opposed to
бунт *m.* revolt, rebelion, insurrection, riot, rising, uprising, mutiny
бунтовник *m.* rebel, insurrectionist, revolutionary, mutineer
бунтува *v.* instigate a revolt, stir up (the people) to revolt, incite to rebellion
бунтува се *v.* rebel, revolt, rise against, (*mil.*) mutiny
бура *f.* storm, thunderstorm, rainstorm, tempest, gale, squall, snowstorm, blizzard

бургија *f.* drill, borer
буре *ntr.* cask, keg
бурен *adj.* stormy, turbulent
буржоазија *f.* bourgeoisie, middle class

бусија *f.* ambush, ambuscade
бучен *adj.* noisy
бучи *v.* rumble, roar, drone, boom
буџет *m.* budget

В

вага *f.* scales, balance
вагон *m.* car (of a train), coach, carriage
вади *v.* take (pull) out, extract, draw
важен *adj.* important, of importance, crucial
важи *v.* be valid, be in force
ваза *f.* vase
ваја *v.* sculpture, shape
вајар *m.* sculpture
ваканција *f.* holidays, vacation
вакцина *f.* vaccine
валута *f.* currency
валсер, валс *m.* waltz
Вам, вам *pron.* to you, you
вампир *m.* vampire, ghoul
ваму *adv.* here, hither, this way
ваму-таму *adv.* hither and yon
вандализам *m.* vandalism
вапса, вапсува *v.* paint, color, dye, outwit
вар *m. and f.* lime
варварство *ntr.* barbarity, cruelty

варди *v.* look after, keep watch over, guard, watch, be careful
вари *v.* boil, cook
ват *m.* vat
ваш *pron.* your, yours
вгради *v.* build in, wall in, immure, fix into the wall, incorporate
вдахновение *ntr.* inspiration
вдиши, вдишува *v.* breathe in, inhale
вдлаби *v.* dig into, carve into
вдлаби се *v. refl. v.* concentrate, become absorbed in
вдовец *m.* widower; **вдовица** *f.* widow
вегетаријанец *m.* vegetarian
вегетација *f.* vegetation
ведар *adj.* clear, cheerful
ведро (небе) *adj.* cloudless
веднаш *adv.* at once, immediately, on the spot, promptly
ведно *adv.* together
ведро *ntr.* bucket, pail
веѓа *f.* eyelid, eyelash, eyebrow

вее v. blow, wave, flutter

вежба 1. f. exercise, training, practice; 2. v. exercise, train

везден adj. all day long

век m. century, age

велеград m. big city

велелепен adj. magnificent, splendid, superb

вели v. say, tell

Велигден m. Easter

велик adj. great

великан m. giant

великодушен adj. generous. magnanimous

великолепен adj. magnificent, splendid

велича v. praise, glorify

величествен adj. impressive, majestic, imposing

величество ntr. majesty

велосипед m. bicycle, bike

венец m. wreath

венча v. marry, perform the wedding ceremony

вера f. faith, trust, religion, creed

верен adj. true, faithful, loyal

верзија f. version

верига f. chain

веројатен adj. probable, likely

верски adj. religious

верува v. believe, trust, think

весел adj. joyful, gay, merry, cheerful

весник m. newspaper, journal

вест f. news

ветар m. wind, breeze

ветеран m. veteran

ветеринар m. veterinary surgeon

вети, ветува v. promise, give one's word, pledge oneself

веќе adv. already, still

вечен adj. eternal, everlasting

вечер f. evening

вечера 1. f. supper; 2. have supper

вечност f. eternity

вешт adj. skilled, skillful, capable

вештак m. expert, master

вештица f. witch

вживи се refl. v. enter into, live over, to immerse oneself

взаемно adv. mutually, reciprocally, each other

Ви, ви pron. you

вид m. face, look, appearance; eyesight; kind, sort, type; aspect; pretext, excuse

види, видува v. see, look

види се refl. v. see, meet; **видува се** refl. v. see, meet, be seen

виза f. visa

визија f. vision

визита f. visit

вик m. cry, shout, call, yell

вика v. cry, shout, call, yell
вила f. villa, cottage
виљушка f. fork
вина f. guilt
вино ntr. wine
виновен adj. guilty
винт m. screw
виолина f. violin, fiddle
виолончело ntr. violoncello, cello
вир m. puddle, pool
вирее v. grow, thrive
вирус m. virus
виси v. hang, hang down
висок adj. high, tall
вистена f. truth, fact, reality
вит adj. slim, slender
витрина f. shop window
виулица f. snowstorm, blizzard
виц m. funny story, anecdote
виш adj. higher, upper
вишна f. mahaleb cherry; cherry
вклучи v. include, comprise
вклучи се refl. v. join, take part, participate
вклучително adv. including, inclusive
вкорени, вкоренува се v. take root
вкуп adv. together, jointly
вкус m. taste, flavor, sense of taste
вкусно adv. tasty, delicious
влага f. humidity, moisture

влада f. government, reign
владар m. ruler, owner, possessor
владее v. rule, govern, reign
владее се refl. v. keep one's temper, restrain oneself
влажен adj. moist, wet, humid
власт f. power, might
влегува v. enter, come in, get in
влез m. entrance, entry
влезе v. enter, come in, get in, penetrate
влече v. drag, draw, pull, tug
влијае v. influence
влијание ntr. influence
влијателен adj. influential, authoritative
влог m. deposit, stake
вложи v. deposit, invest, stake
вљуби се refl. v. fall in love with
вместо pep. instead of
внатре adv. in, inside, within
внатрешен adj. internal
внесе, внесува v. bring in, carry into, import
внимава v. pay attention
внимание ntr attention, attentiveness; care
внос m. import
внук m. grandson
внука f. granddaughter
во prep. in, at, by, to, into
воведе v. introduce, usher

вода *f.* water

водач *m.* leader, conductor, manager, head

води *v.* lead, conduct, guide

водопад *m.* waterfall

водопровод *m.* water line, water pipe

водород *m.* hydrogen

водоскок *m.* fountain

воедно *adv.* together, at the same time

воен *adj.* military

воз *m.* train

возач *m.* driver

возбуди *v.* excite, move

возбунтува *v.* stir up mutiny, incite revolt

возбунтува се *refl. v.* rise up in arms, revolt against, rebel against

возвишен *adj.* elevated, sublime, superior

возврати *v.* return, restore

воздејствува *v.* influence

воздивнува *v.* sigh

воздишка *f.* sight

воздржан *adj.* restrained, reserved

воздржи се, воздржува се *v.* abstain from, restrain oneself, refrain from

воздух *m.* air

вози *v.* drive, ride

возможен *adj.* possible, likely, feasible, achievable

возмутеност *f.* dissapproval, indignation, resentment, outrage

возникне *v.* begin, originate, establish, arise, result

возрасен *adj.* aged, elderly, old

возраст *f.* age

воин *m.* warrior, fighter

војвода *m.* duke, army commander

војна *f.* war

војник *m.* soldier

војска *f.* army, troops

војува *v.* war, make war, conduct military operations

вокатив *m.* vocative

вол *m.* ox

волја *f.* will

волк *m.* wolf

волт *m.* volt

волшебен *adj.* magical, wonderful, charming, fascinating

вон *adv.* outside, out

вонбрачен *adj.* illegitimate

вонреден *adj.* extraordinary, exceptional, unique, rare

вообразба *f.* imagination

вообрози *v.* imagine

вообшто *adv.* in general, anyway, anyhow, after all

вооружение *ntr.* armament

вооружи *v.* arm

вопросен *adj.* in question,

under consideration

воскресение *ntr.* resurrection

восок *m.* wax

воспаление *ntr.* inflammation

воспита, воспитува *v.* educate

востане *v.* rebel, rise up in arms

востание *ntr.* rising, rebellion, mutiny

востаник *m.* rebel, insurgent

восторг *m.* enthusiasm, rapture, delight

восхити, восхитува *v.* delight, enrapture, admire

вошка *f.* louse

впечаток *m.* impression, effect

впрочем *adv.* anyhow, besides, by the way, indeed, actually

врабец *m.* sparrow

враг *m.* enemy, devil, knave

вран *adj.* black, raven-black

врана *f.* crow, rook

врат *m.* neck

врата *f.* door

врати, врака *v.* return, give back, restore, replace

врба *f.* willow

врви *v.* step, go, walk, move

вред *adv.* by turns, successively

вреден *adj.* diligent, efficient

време *ntr.* time, weather

вретено *ntr.* spindle

врз *prep.* on, upon, over

врие *v.* boil, ferment

врне *v.* (дожд) rain, (снег) snow

врска *f.* connection

врсник *m.* contemporary, person of same age

врти *v.* turn around, spin around, rotate, revolve

врховен *adj.* supreme, highest

врчва *f.* jug, pitcher, jar

вселена *f.* universe

всели *v.* move in(to), colonize

всушност *adv.* actually, in reality, in fact, as a matter of fact

втоне *v.* sink, be sunk

втор(и) *num.* second

вторник *m.* Tuesday

вујко *m.* uncle

вујна *f.* aunt

вулгарен *adj.* vulgar

вулкан *m.* volcano

вчера *adv.* yesterday

Г

гавран *m.* raven

гаден *adj.* disgusting, nauseous,

repulsive, odious

газела *f.* gazelle

гајда *f.* bagpipe
галеб *m.* seagull
галежен *adj.* tender, delicate, gentle
гален *adj.* pet, favorite, darling
гали *v.* caress, hug, fondle
галош *m.* galosh
ганстер *m.* gangster
гаража *f.* garage
гарантира *v.* guarantee, warrant
гарда *f.* guard
гардероба *f.* wardrobe
гарнизон *m.* garrison
гарнитура *f.* garnish, trimming
гас *m.* gas
гаси *v.* exinguish, switch off
гастроном *m.* gastronome, gastronomist
гатка *f.* riddle, conundrum
генерал *m.* general
генератор *m.* generator
генерација *f.* generation
генетика *f.* genetics
гениј *m.* genius
генитив *m.* genitive
географ *m.* geographer
географија *f.* geography
геолог *m.* geologist
геологија *f.* geology
геометрија *f.* geometry
герила *f.* guerilla
гест *m.* gesture
гибел *m.* doom, destruction, ruin, fall
гибелен *adj.* disastrous, fatal, ruinous
гигант *m.* giant, colossus
гимназија *f.* secondary school, high school
гимнастика *f.* gymnastics
гине *v.* die away, perish
гинеколог *m.* gynecologist
гитара *f.* guitar
глава *f.* head, chapter
главатар *m.* leader, chief
главен *adj.* main, capital
главоболие *ntr.* headache
глагол *m.* verb
глад *m.* hunger, starvation
гладен *adj.* hungry, starving, famished
глас *m.* voice, intonation
гласа *v.* vote
глатко *adv.* smooth
гледа *v.* look, see, observe, watch, view
глетка *f.* view
глечер *m.* glacier
глиб *m.* mud, mire, slime, dirt
глина *f.* clay
глоба *f.* fine, penalty
глобален *adj.* total, lump
глоби *v.* fine, penalize
глобус *m.* globe
глотка *f.* bit, particle, speck, grain, crumb
глув *adj.* deaf

глуп, глупав *adj.* foolish, silly, senseless, stupid

гнев *adj.* anger, passion, fury, wrath

гнездо *ntr.* nest

гнет *m.* oppression

гние *v.* rot, putrify

го *pron.* him, it

говори *v.* talk, speak, say, tell

година *f.* year

годишник *m.* annual, almanac

годишнина *f.* anniversary

гол *adj.* naked, nude, bare, stripped, open, uncovered

голем *adj.* big, large, great

гони *v.* chase, hunt, pursue, push

гора *f.* forest, wood

горд *adj.* proud, haughty

горе *adv.* up, above, upstairs

горешт *adj.* hot

горештина *f.* heat, high temperature

гори *v.* burn, flame, glow

гориво *ntr.* fuel

горила *f.* gorilla

горчи *v.* taste bitter

господар *m.* lord, master

господарка *f.* mistress, lady

господин *m.* gentlemen, sir

господствува *v.* dominate, predominate, rule

гости *v.* treat, entertain

гостилница *f.* inn, hostel, tavern, restaurant

гостин *m.* guest, visitor, stranger

гостува *v.* visit, to make a guest appearance

готвач *m.* cook

готви *v.* cook

готов *adj.* ready, finished, complete, prepared, done

граба, граби *v.* grasp at, catch at, grab; rob, plunder

гравура *f.* engraving

град *m.* town, city

градба *f.* building, construction

гради *v.* build, mason

градина *f.* garden

градус *m.* degree

граѓанин *m.* citizen, civilian

грам *m.* gram

грамада *f.* mass, pile

граматика *f.* grammar

граната *f.* shell

грандоманија *m.* megalomania

гранит *m.* granite

граница *f.* boundary, border

гранка *f.* bough, branch, limb

графика *f.* graphics

грација *f.* grace, gracefulness, elegance

грачи *v.* caw, croak

грб *m.* back

грбав *adj.* humpy, hunchbacked

грд *adj.* ugly, plain, nasty

гребен *m.* mountain ridge, crest

грев *m.* sin, fall, fault

греда *f.* beam, rafter
грее *v.* warm, (сонце) shine
грешава, греши *v.* sin, commit sin, do wrong, err, make mistakes
грешка *f.* error, mistake
грива *f.* mane
гривна *f.* bracelet
грижа *f.* care; concern; anxiety
грижи се *v.* care for, take care of, look after, worry
гризне, гризнува *v.* bite in, make a bite
гримаса *f.* grimace
гримира *v.* make up
грип *m.* influenza
грмеж *m.* thunder, thunderstorm
грми, грмува *v.* thunder, boom
грне *ntr.* earthenware pot
грнчар *m.* potter
гроб *m.* grave, tomb
гробишта *pl.* cemetery
гробница *f.* crypt, vault
гроза *f.* horror, terror, shudder, shiver
грозд *m.* bunch of grapes
грозен *adj.* ugly
грозје *ntr.* grapes
гром *m.* thunder
гросист *m.* wholesaler, dealer
гротеска *f.* grotesque
гроф *m.* count
грофица *f.* countess
груб *adj.* rude, brutal, vulgar, rough
група *f.* group
грч *m.* cramp, spasm, convulsion
губи *v.* lose
губи се *refl. v.* get lost
гувернер *m.* governor
гулаб *m.* pigeon, dove
гума *f.* rubber, tire, (~ за џвакање) gum
густ *adj.* thick, dense, close
гушка, гушне, гушнува *v.* embrace, hug
гуштер *m.* lizard

Д

да 1. *part.* yes, well; 2. (prompting) let (Inf.) let's go; may (may) God bless you!; (command, threat) ~ **молчиш** you keep your mouth shut; **дури** ~ although, even if; **како** ~ as if; **место** ~ instead of
даб *m.* oak
дава *v.* give
дага *f.* rainbow
даде *v.* give
дажба *f.* ration, portion
далак *m.* spleen, milt
далеку *adv.* far away, distantly

далечен *adj.* far, distant, remote

далечина *f.* distance

дали *part.* whether

дама *f.* lady

дамка *f.* spot, speck, stain

дамла *f.* stroke, paralysis

данок *m.* tax, taxation, assessment, income tax

дар *m.* gift, donation, present, talent

дарба *f.* gift, talent, endowment

дарител *m.* donor

даровит *adj.* gifted, talented

дарува *v.* give a present

дарчин *m.* cinnamon

даскал *m.* teacher

дата *f.* date

два *num. m.* **две** *num. f.* two

дваж *adv.* twice, two times

дваесет *num.* twenty

дваесетина *num.* about twenty

двајца, двамина *num.* two persons (including a male person)

дванаесет *num.* twelve

дванаесети *num.* twelfth

двапати *adv.* twice

двигател *m.* motor, engine, starter

движење *v.* movement, motion

движи *v.* move, stir, set in motion

двобој *m.* duel

двоен *adj.* double

дволичен *adj.* hypocritical, two-faced

двор *m.* yard, courtyard, court

дворец *m.* castle, palace

дворјанство *ntr.* nobility

двосмислен *adj.* ambiguous, equivocal

двостран *adj.* bilateral, bipartite, two sided

двоуми се *refl. v.* hesitate, doubt

дебел *adj.* fat, thick, corpulent

дебитира *v.* make one's debut

деведесет *num.* ninety

девет *num.* nine

деветнаесет *num.* nineteen

деветстотин *num* nine hundred

девиза *f.* motto; currency

девојка *f.* girl

девствен *adj.* virgin

дедо *m.* grandfather

дежура *v.* be on duty

дезертер *m.* deserter

дезинфицира *v.* disinfect

дејност *f.* activity, activities

дејствува *v.* work, do, act, perform, practice

дека *conj.* that, where

декан *m.* dean

декември *m.* December

декламира *v.* declaim, recite

декларира *v.* declare, state

декор *m.* decor, stage set

декоративен *adj.* decorative

декрет *m.* decree, edict

дел *m.* part, share

делегација *f.* delegation, deputation

дели *v.* divide, part, separate

деликатен *adj.* delicate

делник *m.* weekday

дело *ntr.* work, job, affair, business, act, deed

делта *f.* delta

делфин *m.* dolphin

демагог *m.* demagogue

демне *v.* stalk, watch for, look out for

демократија *f.* democracy

демон *m.* demon, devil

демонстрација *f.* demonstration

ден *m.* day

денес, денеска *adv.* today

деноноќен *adj.* day-and-night; twenty-four-hour

дење *adv.* by day, during the day

депозит *m.* deposit

депонира *v.* deposit, set down

депортација *f.* deportation, transportation

депресија *f.* depression, dejection, despondency

депримира *v.* depress, flatten, discourage

депутат *m.* representative, legislative deputy

дервент *m.* defile, pass

дере *v.* skin, flay; tear, rend, rip; scratch

дере се *refl. v.* bawl, yell, cry

десант *m. (mil.)* landing

десен *adj.* right, right-hand

десерт *m.* dessert

десет *num.* ten

десница *f.* right hand, right arm, (polit.) right wing

деспот *m.* despot, absolute ruler, autocrat, tyrant

деталь *m.* detail

дете *ntr.* child, infant, baby

детектив *m.* detective

детелина *f.* clover

детинство *ntr.* childhood

дефект *m.* defect, blemish, fault, flaw, shortcoming

дефинира *v.* define, determine

дефиниција *f.* definition

див *adj.* wild, savage

диван *m.* couch, divan

диверзан *m.* saboteur

дивеч *m.* game, deer

дивизија *f.* division

дига *v.* lift, elevate, raise

диета *f.* diet

дијагноза *f.* diagnosis

дијагонала *f.* diagonal

дијалект *m.* dialect

дијалог *m.* dialogue

дијамант *m.* diamond

дијаметар *m.* diameter

дијафрагма *f.* diaphragm
диктатор *m.* dictator
диктатура *f.* dictatorship
диктира *v.* dictate
дилема *f.* dilemma
дим *m.* smoke, fume
дими *v.* smoke, fume
динамит *m.* dynamite
динамичен *adj.* dynamic
динар *m.* dinar
династија *f.* dynasty
дињa *f.* melon, cantaloupe
диплома *f.* diploma
дипломат *m.* diplomat
дипломација *f.* diplomacy
директен *adj.* direct
директор *m.* director
дирекција *f.* board, managment
диригент *m.* conductor
диригира *v.* conduct
дисертација *f.* dissertation
дисидент *m.* dissident
диск *m.* disc, discus
дискретен *adj.* discreet
дискриминација *f.* discrimination
дискусија *f.* discussion, debate
диспут *m.* dispoute, debate
дистанција *f.* distance
дисциплина *f.* discipline
диференција *f.* difference
дише, дишне *v.* breath
длабина *f.* depth
длабнатина *f.* pit, hole

длабок *adj.* deep, profound
длабочина *f.* depth
дланка *f.* palm
длето *ntr.* chisel
дневен *adj.* daily, everyday; ~ ред agenda
до *prep.* till, until; од... до *prep.* from - to
доба *f.* time
добар *adj.* добива *v.* get, obtain
добив *m.* gain, profit, winnings
добиток *m.* livestock, cattle
добиче *ntr.* domestic animal
доблест *f.* valor, gallantry
доближи, доближува *v.* approach, come near, get near
добро *ntr.* good, welfare, well being, benefit, benefaction
доброволец *m.* voluntary
доброволец *m.* volunteer
добродетел *f.* virtue
добродушен *adj.* good-hearted
доведе *v.* bring (along, home)
довек *adv.* for ever
довери *v.* confide, entrust
довери се *refl. v.* trust
довечера *adv.* tonight, this evening
довод *m.* argument, reason
доволен *adj.* pleased, satisfied, gratified, contented
догма *f.* dogma, doctrine

договара, договори *v.* negotiate, arrange, agree upon

договора се, договори се *refl. v.* come to an agreement/understanding/contract, make an appointment, arrange a date, arrange to meet sb.

догони *v.* catch up with, run/hunt down

додее *v.* bore, weary

додека *conj.* until, till, as long as, while

дожд *m.* rain

доживее *v.* live to see, experience

доза *f.* dose

дозвола *f.* permission, permit

дои *v.* milk, suckle, nurse

доиспие *v.* drink up, drink all

дојаде *v.* finish eating

дојде *v.* come, arrive; ~ **ми на ум** it occured to me

докаже *v.* prove, indicate, show

доказ *m.* proof, evidence

докрај *adv.* to the end, completely, fully, throughout

доктор *m.* doctor, physician

доктрина *f.* doctrine

документ *m.* document

долап *m.* cupboard

долг *m.* debt

должи *v.* owe, be indebted, be in debt

долина *f.* valley

долу *adv.* down, below, beneath

дом *m.* home, house

домат *m.* tomato

домакин *m.* host;

домакинка *f.* hostess

домакинство *ntr.* household, family

домашен *adj.* domestic, home

донесе *v.* bring

допаѓа се, допадне се *v.* like, to the liking of, suit

допир *m.* touch, contact

допирна (точка) *adj. f.* point of tangency, common ground

дописка *f.* correspondence, report

дополнение *ntr.* complement, supplement, addition

дополни, дополнува *v.* complement, supplement, add

допре (се) *v.* touch, come in contact

допушта *v.* allow, let, tolerate, admit

досада *f.* boredom, annoyance, tedium

досега *v.* reach, touch

досели (се) *v.* move, immigrate

досети се *v.* remember, recall

доскоро *adv.* until recently, until a little while ago

доследен *adj.* consequent, consistent

дословен *adj.* literal, verbal, word for word

доста *adv.* enough, sufficiently

достави *v.* deliver, hand over

достап *m.* access, admission, admittance

достига *v.* catch up, reach

достоен *adj.* worthy, dignified, deserving, merited

дотаму *adv.* this far, up to there, up to the point

дотегне, дотегнува *v.* bore, bother, annoy

дотогај, дотогаш *adv.* until then, until that time

доход *m.* income, return, earnings

доцна *adv.* late, tardy

дочуе *v.* learn, hear, come to know

драг *adj.* dear, beloved

дрвар *m.* lumberjack, woodcutter

дрвен *adj.* wooden, wood

дрво *ntr.* tree

дрводелец *m.* woodworker, carpenter

древен *adj.* ancient, antique

дреме *v.* doze, nap

дресира *v.* train, drill

држва *f.* state

државјанин *m.* citizen

државник *m.* politician

држалка *f.* holder, handle, grip

држање *ntr.* behavior, bearing

држи *v.* hold, keep

дрзок *adj.* impudent, insolent, impertinent, bold

дрипа *f.* rag, tatter

дроб *m.* liver

дрога *f.* drug

дрпав *adj.* tattered, ragged

дрт *adj.* old, aged

друг *adj.* second, next, different

другиден *adv.* the day after tomorrow

дружба *f.* society, friendship

дружељубив *adj.* friendly

друштво *ntr.* society, association

дува, дуе *v.* blow, puff

дуел *m.* duel

дует *m.* duet

дузина *f.* dozen

думан *m.* fog, smoke

дразни *v.* stimulate, excite, irritate, annoy

драка *f.* weed

драма *f.* drama, play

драсне *v.* scratch, claw

дури *part.* even

дух *m.* spirit

душа *f.* soul

душек *m.* mattress

душен *adj.* muffled, suffocating

душман(ин) *m.* enemy

Ѓ

ѓавол *m.* devil, satan, knave
ѓеврек *m.* pretzel
ѓердан *m.* well

ѓон *m.* sole
ѓуле *ntr.* bullet, cannonball
ѓурултија *m.* row

Е

евангелие *ntr.* gospel
евангелиски *adj.* evangelical
еве *interj.* here is, here are
евентуален *adj.* possible
евентуално *adv.* possibly, perhaps
еволуција *f.* evolution
евтин *adj.* cheap, inexpensive
егзалтација *f.* exaltation
егзекутивен *adj.* executive
егзекутира *v.* execute
егзекуција *f.* execution
егземплар *m.* copy
егзистира *v.* exist
егзотичен *adj.* exotic
егоизам *m.* egoism, selfishness
егумен *m.* abbot, prior
еден *num.* one
едикт *m.* decree, order
единаесет *num.* eleven
единствен *adj.* only, unique, sole
единство *ntr.* unity, union (*fig.*) harmony
еднаквост *f.* equality, conformity, sameness
еднаков *adj.* equal, like, alike, similar
еднаш *adv.* once, one day, one time, once upon a time
еднина *f.* singular
еднобоштво *ntr.* monotheism
едновремено *adv.* simultaneously, at the same time
едногласно, еднодушно *adv.* unanimous
едноженство *ntr.* monogamy
еднократен *adj.* single, one time
еднообразен *adj.* uniform, monotonous
еднороден *adj.* homogenous
едноставен *adj.* simple, elementary, plain, modest, primitive, natural
едностојно *adv.* continually, constantly, permanently
едностран *adj.* one-sided, exclusive, unilateral, partial, narrow-minded
едночудо *adv.* plenty, a great many
езеро *ntr.* lake
ек *m.* echo, resonance

екватор *m.* equator
екипа *f.* team
екипаж *m.* crew, equipage
економ *m.* economist, manager
екран *m.* screen
ексеценција *f.* excellency
екскурзија *f.* excursion
екскурзист *m.* tourist
експедира *v.* dispatch, forward, send off, expedite, mail
експеримент *m.* experiment
експерт *m.* expert
експлоатација *f.* exploitation
експлодира *v.* explode
експлозија *f.* explosion
експорт *m.* export
експрес *m.* express
екстаз *m.*, **екстаза** *f.* ecstasy, trance
екстравагантен *adj.* extravagant
екстракт *m.* extract
екстремен *adj.* extreme
ексцентричен *adj.* eccentric
ексцес *m.* excess
ела *f.* spruce
еластичен *adj.* elastic
елеватор *m.* elevator
елегантен *adj.* elegant
електрика *f.* electricity
електрон 1. *m.* electron; 2. *adj.* electronic
електроскоп *m.* electroscope
електротехника *f.* electrotech-nics

елемент *m.* element
елементарен *adj.* elementary, rudimentary
елен *m.* deer, stag, hart
елипса *f.* ellipse
елита *f.* elite
емајл *m.* enamel
еманципација *f.* emancipation
ембрион *m.* embryo
емигрант *m.* emigrant
емиграција *f.* emigration
емисија *f.* emission, broadcast
емоционален *adj.* emotional
енергија *f.* energy, power
ентузијазам *m.* enthusiasm
ентузијаст *m.* enthusiast
енциклопедија *f.* encyclopedia
епидемија *f.* outbreak, epidemic
епизод *m.* **епизода** *f.* episode
епилепсија *f.* epilepsy
епископ *m.* bishop
епопеја *f.* epic poem
епос *m.* epic, epos
епоха *f.* epoch, period, era
ерген *m.* unmarried man, bachelor
ерес *f.* heresy
еретик *m.* heretic
ермик *m.* semolina
ерозија *f.* erosion
еротика *f.* erotic
есеј *m.* essay

есен *f.* autumn, fall
есенција *f.* essence
естествен *adj.* natural
естетика *f.* aesthetics
етажерка *f.* shelves
етапа *f.* stage
етер *m.* ether
етика *f.* ethics
етикета *f.* etiquette
етимологија *f.* etymology

етнички *adj.* ethnic
етнограф *m.* ethnographer
етнографија *f.* ethnography
етнолог *m.* ethnologist
етнологија *f.* ethnology
ефект *m.* effect, result
ех *interj.* Oh! Ah!
ехо *ntr.* echo
ечи *v.* resound
ешта *f.* appetite

Ж

жаба *f.* frog, toad
жабурка *v.* gargle
жал *f.* sorrow, grief, sadness,
pity; ~ ми е be sorry
жалба *f.* complaint, grievance
жален *adj.* sad, sorrowful
жали *v.* mourn, gieve, sorrow
жалост *f.* pity, compassion,
sympathy; sorrow, grief, sadness
жалостив *adj.* compassionate,
pitiful, merciful, gracious
жанр *m.* genre
жар *m.* glow
жаргон *m.* slang, jargon
жари *v.* heat
ждребец *m.* stallion
жега *f.* (broiling) heat, swelter
жед *f.* thirst
жеден *adj.* thirsty
желад *m.* acorn

желателен *adj.* desirable, ad-
visable
желба *f.* wish, desire
железен *adj.* iron
железница *f.* railway, railroad
железо *ntr.* iron
желудник *m.* stomach
жена *f.* woman, wife
женет *adj.* married
жени (се) *v.* marry, get married
женидба *f.* marriage
женственост *f.* feminity, femini-
nity, womanhood
жерав *m.* crane
жесток *adj.* violent, cruel, brutal, merciless
жетва *f.* harvest
жив *adj.* living, alive
живина *f.* live stock, poultry
живинарство *ntr.* veterinary

живопис *m.* painting
живот *m.* life, existence, being
животина *f.* animal, beast
животопис (*lit.*) *m.* biography
жила *f.* vein, artery, streak
жилав *adj.* resilient, tough, stringy
жилиште *ntr.* apartment, flat, house, home
жило *ntr.* sting
жирафа *f.* giraffe
жител *m.* inhabitant, dweller
жито *ntr.* grain, cereal
жица *f.* wire, chord, string

жлезда *f.* gland
жолт *adj.* yellow
жолчка *f.* gall, gallbladder
жолчност *f.* (*fig.*) gall, bitterness
жонглер *m.* juggler
жртва *f.* sacrifice, victim, offering
жртвува *v.* sacrifice; ~ се *refl.* *v.* sacrifice oneself
жугне *v.* spring up, shoot up
жули *v.* pinch, rub
жупник *m.* priest, vicar,
журналист *m.* journalist

3

за *prep.* for (за него for him), by (за рака by the hand), of/about (мисли за thinks of/about)
заб *m.* tooth
забава *f.* party, entertainment
забавен *adj.* pleasing, delightful, amusing, entertaining, funny
забави *v.* delay, retard, hold up, slow up, slow down
забар *m.* dentist
забележи *v.* note, notice, perceive, become aware, remark
забелешка *f.* remark, note
забива *v.* hammer/knock in, fix
заблуда *f.* delusion, error, fallacy, aberration, mistaken opinion, false belief
забобол *m.* toothache
заболекар *m.* dentist
заболи *v.* hurt, cause pain, ache
заборавен *adj.* forgotten, out of mind
заборави *v.* forget
забрана *f.* prohibition, interdiction, suppression
забранет *adj.* prohibited, forbidden
забрани, забранува *v.* forbid, interdict, prohibit, suppress, disallow
забремени *v.* become pregnant, concieve

забрза (се) v. speed up, hurry up

забрка v. stir up, mix, confuse

забркан adj. mixed up, bewildered, confused, puzzeled, chaotic

забуна f. embarrassment, confusion, trouble

забуни v. embarrass, confuse, bewilder

завали v. set fire, light, make a fire

завари v. find, surprise, find, catch; weld

заведе v. mislead, misguide, seduce

завера f. conspiracy, plot

аверник m. conspirator, plotter

завери v. certify, verify, notarize, legalize, attest

завеса f. curtain, drapery

завет m. vow, ledge, oath

завешта v. leave a will/testament, bequeath, devise

завештание ntr. will, testament

завива v. wrap, turn; howl, whine (dog)

завиден adj. enviable, notable, distinctive

завиди, завидува v. envy, be jealous

зависен adj. dependent, subordinate

зависи v. be dependent on, be

subordinate to

завислив adj. jealous, envious

завист f. envy, jealousy

завладее v. conquer, take possession, seize, capture

завод m. factory, mill, works

завој m. curve, serpentine, turn

завојува v. conquer, capture; fight out, win, gain

заврти v. turn, reverse, twist, screw; ~ се turn round

заврши v. finish, complete, end; ~ се, завршува се refl. v. end, be over

завчас adv. at once, immediately, on the spot, straight away

завчера adv. the day before yesterday

загаден adj. infected, contaminated

загадочен adj. mysterious, puzzling, enigmatic

загази v. get into trouble

загаси v. extinguish (a fire), blow out (a candle), switch/turn off (a light), turn out; ~ се refl. v. die down, go out

загатка f. puzzle, enigma, mystery, crossword

загине v. fall a victim to, get killed, die, perish

заглавје, ntr. title, name, headline

загледа се refl. v. look. gaze

заглуши v. deafen, deaden, muffle

загнезди се refl. v. nest, settle, wedge; grip, obsess

загнои v. suppurate

заговор m. conspiracy

заговорник m. conspirator

заграби v. grab, grasp, seize, take hold, usurp

заграда f. parenthesis, bracket, fence

загрева v. warm (up), heat (up)

загрижен adj. concerned, worried, anxious

загуба f. loss, waste, deficit

загуби v. lose, miss

зад prep. behind, beyond

задави v. suffocate, choke

зададе v. give, set, assign, (a task), ask, cause; ~ **се** refl. v. appear, emerge

задача f. task, duty, quiz

задграничен adj. foreign, alien, from abroad

задева v. tease, chaff

заден adj. last, final, ultimate, back

задлабочен adj. profound, deep/absorbed in thought

задоволи v. satisfy, gratify, please

задолжение ntr. obligation, duty, responsibility, engagement, bond, liability, debt

задолжителен adj. obligatory, compulsory

задреме v. fall asleep, doze, drop off

задржи v. hold back, retain, stop, delay

задума v. memorize, remember

задушен adj. choked, suffocated, stifled, muffled

задуши v. suffocate, choke, strangle, stifle, muffle, suppress

заедница f. community, union

заеднички adj. common, mutual, joint, general

заем m. loan

заздрави v. strengthen, reinforce, retrieve

заземa v. occupy, capture

заземји v. ground, earth

зазнае v. realize, become aware of

зазор m. shame, disgrace

зазори се refl. v. the day dawns/breaks

заина(е)ти се refl. v. turn stubborn/obstinate

заинтересираност f. interest, partiality

зајадлив adj. nagging, fault finding, sarcastic

зајак m. rabbit, hare

зајаче ntr. bunny

зајде v. set down (sun), go astray

зајми v. lend, borrow

закален adj. tried, hardy

закаленост f. fitness

закана f. threat

закани се refl. v. threaten

закачи, закачува v. hang, stick up, hitch, hook, attach

заклан adj. slain, slaughtered, butchered

заклет adj. sworn, cursed, damned

заклетва f. oath, vow, swear

заклопи v. shut, close, cover

заклучи v. lock up, conclude

заклучно adv. inclusive, including

закове v. nail, weld; (car) brake to a standstill; rivet

заколнува се v. swear, vow, take oath

закон m. law, statute, act

законодавство ntr. legislation, legislature

закономерен adj. regular, natural, normal

законски adj. legal, lawful, legitimate

закоп m. funeral, burial

закопча v. button (up)

закрепи v. hold, fix, strengthen, consolidate

закрила f. protection

закуп m. lease, tenancy

закуси v. have breakfast, have a snack

закуска f. beakfast, snack

залак m. bite

заледи се refl. v. freeze up

залез m. sunset, (fig.) decline

залепи v. glue (to, on), stick in

залив m. bay, gulf

залог m. pledge, mortgage, deposit

замае v. exalt, make dizzy

замена f. exchange, substitute, substitution, replacement

заљуби v. fall in love, like, be fond of

замени v. exchange, substitute, replace

замине v. leave, depart, go away

замисли v. plan, plot; ~ се ponder (over)

замор m. fatigue, exhaustion, tiredness

заморен adj. tired, exhausted

замрзнат adj. frozen, iced

замрсен adj. contaminated, polluted, dirty

занает m. craft, handcraft, trade

занемарен adj. neglected, untended, unkempt

занес m. enthusiasm, rapture, ecstasy, exaltation

занима, занимава v. occupy, interest, entertain

занимава се refl. v. be employed, be engaged in, occupy oneself with

заобиколи v. go round, surround, encircle; evade, pass over, disregard

заоблен adj. round, rounded

заод m. sunset, end (живот)

заоѓа v. set, set down

заостанатост f. backwardness

заострен adj. sharpened

запад m. Occident, west, the West

западне v. decay, decline, fail

запазен adj. preserved, retained, (храна) unspoiled, reserved, kept; outstanding

запали v. set fire, light, ignite

апалка f. lighter

запечати, запечатува v. seal (up), stamp; (fig.) imprint, impress, engrave

запира v. stop, hold up

запирка f. comma

записка f. note

запише v. take/write/put note down

заплаши v. frighten, scare

заплени, запленува v. confiscate, capture, seize

заплоди v. fructify, fertilize, (fish) milt

заповед f. order, command, direction, commandment

заповеда v. order, command

запознае v. introduce; ~ ce refl. v. meet, get to know

запомни v. memorize, remember

започне v. begin, start, originate

запре v. stop, hold up, halt, staunch

запрега v. yoke, team

запурнина f. sultriness, closeness

запурничав adj. sultry, close, stuffy

запусти, запустува v. abandon, neglect, desert, become desolate

запушти v. neglect

заради prep. because of, for the sake of

зарадува v. please, delight,

зараза f. infection, epidemic, contagion, contamination

зарасне v. heal (over, up)

зарача v. order, place an order

зарзават m. vegetables, greens

заробеник m. captive, prisoner (of war)

заробување ntr. enslavement, enthrallment

зарови v. bury, earth up

зароди ce refl. v. originate, rise, arise

засади v. plant

засебен adj. separate, apart

засева *v.* sow

засега 1. *adv.* for now, for the time being, for the present 2. *v.* concern, affect

заседа *f.* ambush

засее *v.* sow

засекогаш *adv.* for ever

засели *v.* colonize, settle

засили *v.* reinforce, strengthen, intensify

засипе *v.* fill up, bury beneath, cover up

заситен *adj.* saturated

заслаби *v.* weaken, lose weight

заслепен *adj.* blinded, dazzled

заслуга *f.* merit, desert, service, worth, credit, reward

заснова *v.* plan, scheme, contrive, conceive, found

засолне *v.* hide, conceal, keep secret, shade

засолниште *ntr.* shelter, shield, covert

засоли *v.* salt, season with salt

заспан *adj.* dozing, sleeping, sleepy, asleep; (*fig.*) apathetic, indolent, inactive

заспива *v.* fall asleep

засрами *v.* bring shame, make ashamed; ~ се *refl.* *v.* be ashamed

застане, застанува *v.* halt, stand, stop dead, hold up

застапи, застапува *v.* repre-sent, defend; ~ се *refl.* *v.* act on behalf of a person

застари, застарува *v.* become obsolete/antiquated

застој *m.* standstill, stagnation, deadlock

застраши, застрашува *v.* menace, scare, threaten

застрела *v.* shoot, kill by shooting

застуди *v.* become cold

затвор *m.* prison, jail, arrest, imprisonment, confinement

затвореник *m.* prisoner, convict

затвори *v.* close, shut, lock, arrest, imprison

затега *v.* tighten, stretch, pull tight

затемни *v.* darken, dim, eclipse

затне *v.* put a cork, dam up, stuff

затоа *adv.* therefore, consequently

затопли *v.* warm, heat, warm up

заточение *ntr.* banishment

затрудни *v.* become pregnant, conceive

затруе *v.* poison

закори се *refl.* *v.* become blind, (*fig.*) become deluded/deceived

зауми *v.* memorize, remember

заушки; заушници *pl.* mumps

зафатен *adj.* occupied, busy

зачас *adv.* at once, immediately, in a moment

зачисли *v.* enter, put on the list

зачлени (се) *v.* become a member

зачне *v.* conceive, become pregnant, *(fig.)* arise

зачува *v.* keep, preserve, save

зачуден *adj.* amazed, astonished, surprised

зашеметен *adj.* stunned, dazed, dizzy

зашива *v.* sew up

заштеди,заштедува *v.* save, spare, put aside

заштита *f.* defense, protection, shelter

заштити, заштитува *v.* defend, protect, shelter

зашто *conj.* because, for

збере *v.* gather, collect, assemble

збива се *refl. v.* happen, occur, take place

збидне се *refl. v.* be fulfilled, be realized, come true

збие се *refl. v.* happen, occur, take place

збир *m.* sum

зближи *v.* bring together/closer; ~ се become closer/intimate

збогати се, збогатува се *refl. v.* become rich

збогувасе *refl. v.* say good-bye, bid farewell

збогум *adv.* good-bye, farewell

збор *m.* word

зборува *v.* talk, say, tell

збрка *v.* make a mistake, confuse, mix up

збрчи *v.* wrinkle, fold, knit one's brow

збуди *v.* wake up, awake

збунет *adj.* confused, puzzled

звание *ntr.* title, rank

звателен *adj.* vocative

звук *m.* sound

звучи *v.* sound, ring

згази *v.* crush down, trample down

згасне *v.* extinguish, fade, go out, nearing one's end

загине *v.* perish, vanish, disappear, get/be killed (die) in an accident/in a war

зглавје (зглавница) *ntr.* *(f.)* pillow, cushion

зглавка *f.,* **зглоб** *m.* joint, ankle, knuckle

зглоби *v.* joint, join, put together

згние *v.* rot off

зговор *m.* harmony, unity, agreement, settlement

зговори *v.* persuade, reconcile, agree

згода *f.* convenience, advantage

згон *m.* chase, persecution

згора *adv.* from above, besides, moreover, yet, still

згорешти *v.* warm; ~ се *refl. v.* get warm

зготви, зготвува *v.* cook

зграби *v.* grasp, grab, catch, seize

зграда *f.* building

згрева, згрее *v.* warm up

згреши *v.* err, sin, make a mistake

здание *ntr.* building

здив *m.* breath, smell, sniff

здобива се, здоби се *refl. v.* acquire, obtain, get

здола *adv.* from below, underneath, beneath

здолен *adj.* under-, bottom-

здрав *adj.* healthy, well, strong, wholesome

здрави *v.* toast one, greet, salute, bid welcome; ~ се *refl. v.* shake hands

здравица *f.* toast, pledge

здравје *ntr.* health

здрач *m.* twilight, dusk

здравува *v.* toast one, greet, salute, bid welcome

здружение *ntr.* association, union

зебра *f.* zebra

зев *m.* gap

зелен *adj.* green

зеленчук *m.* vegetables, greens

зелје *ntr.* cabbage

земе *v.* take, get

земен *adj.* earthly, terrestrial

земја *f.* earth, globe, land, soil, world, state

земјовладение *ntr.* estate

земјоделие, земјоделство *ntr.* agriculture, farming, agronomy

земјотрес *m.* earthquake

зеница *f.* pupil

зет *m.* son-in-law

зима *f.* winter

злато *ntr.* gold

зло *ntr.* evil, misfortune

злоба *f.* nastiness, spite, malice, malignancy, viciousness

злокобен *adj.* ominous

злонамерен *adj.* spiteful, hostile

злорад *adj.* gloating, full of malicious joy

злосторник *m.* criminal, evildoer

злоупотреба *f.* misusage, abuse

знае *v.* know, be aware of, realize, be informed

знаен *adj.* known, famous, well-known

знаење *ntr.* knowledge, scholarship, erudition

знак *m.* sign, mark, symbol

знаме *ntr.* flag, banner

значаен *adj.* significant, important

значење *ntr.* meaning, significance, sense

значи *v.* mean, matter, indicate, be of importance

значка *f.* badge

зове *v. (lit.)* call, cry for, appeal

зограф *m.* icon painter

зол *adj.* evil, wicked, vicious, bad

зона *f.* zone

зоолог *m.* zoologist

зоологија *f.* zoology

зора *f.* daybeak, sunrise

зорница *f.* morning star

зрел *adj.* ripe, mature

зрно *ntr.* grain, corn, (fruit) berry, (coffee) bean

зошто *adv.* why

зрак *m.* ray, beam

зрачи *v.* radiate, shine, glow, glimmer

зрее *v.* grow ripe, mature

зумбул *m.* hyacinth

S

ѕвезда *f.* star

ѕвек *m.* sound, clink, clank

ѕвер *m.* beast, wild animal

ѕверство *ntr.* brutality

ѕвон *m.* bell-ringing

ѕвонец *m.* bell

ѕвони *v.* ring

ѕенѕа *v.* shake, tremble

ѕид *m.* wall

ѕида *v.* mason, build, construct

и *conj.* and, also, too, likewise, as well, in addition

иако *conj.* although, even though

ива *f.* willow, osier

игла *f.* needle, pin

иго *ntr.* yoke, *(fig.)* rule

игра *f.* play, game

иде *v.* come

идеал *m.* ideal

идеја *f.* idea

иден *adj.* future, coming, next

идиом *m.* idiom

идиот *m.* idiot

идол *m.* idol

избави *v.* rescue, save, deliver

избега *v.* run away, flee, escape

избере, избира *v.* choose, select, pick out, elect

изблик *m.* outburst

избор *m.* choice, selection

избрза, избрзува *v.* rush ahead, make a premature decision, jump to conclusions

избрише *v.* wipe out, rub out, dry, erase

изброи *v.* count (up), list, enumerate

извади *v.* take out, pull out, extract, derive

изваја *v.* sculpture, carve

изведе *v.* bring out, carry out, deduce, execute, accomplish

извесен *adj.* known, familiar, well-known, famous, certain

извести, известува *v.* report, inform, let know

извива *v.* twist, bend, curve

извиди *v.* investigate, inquire into, gather information

извика, извикне *v..* exclaim, cry, shout

извини *v.* excuse, pardon; ~ се *refl. v.* apologize

извир *m.* well, spring, source

извира *v.* well, take rise, spring

извод *m.* conclusion, deduction, inference

извојува *v.* fight out, win

извонреден *adj.* irregular, special, unusual, uncommon, extraordinary, remarkable, outstanding

извор *m.* well, spring, source

изврати *v.* pervert, corrupt

извршен *adj.* fulfilled, execut-ed, done

изврши, извршува *v.* execute, perform, carry out, realize, commit, accomplish

изгаси, изгасне *v.* extinguish, put out a fire

изгладне, изгладнува *v.* famish, starve

изглед *m.* view, sight, perspective, prospect

изгние *v.* rot

изговор *m.* pronunciation, articulation

изгони, изгонува *v.* banish

згради, изградува *v.* build, construct, erect

изгрев *m.* sunrise

издава, издаде *v.* publish, edit, issue; disclose, betray

издив *m.* breath

издига, издигне, издигнува *v.* raise, elevate, lift up

издржи *v.* stand, bear, endure

издршка *f.* maintenance, support

изживее *v.* experience, live through

изискува *v.* require, demand

изјава *f.* statement, declaration

изјасни, изјаснува *v.* explain, clear up

излага *v.* expose, exhibit, display

излади *v.* cool, chill, refrigerate

излаже *v.* lie, cheat, trick; ~ ce *refl. v.* make a mistake, be disappointed

излее *v.* pour out, spill, empty; cast, mold, found

излез *m.* exit, door, way out

излет *m.* picnic, trip, excursion

излечи (ce) *v.* cure, heal, recover

излив *m.* sink, drain, outflow

излишен *adj.* superfluous, needless, unnecessary

изложба *f.* exposition, exhibition, show, display

изложи *v.* exhibit, display, expose

измама *f.* illusion, delusion, deceit

измами, измамува *v.* delude, deceive, mislead

измачи *v.* torture, torment

измени, изменува *v.* change, alter, transform

измери *v.* measure, size

измести *v.* displace, remove, move

измива, измие *v.* wash

измине *v.* pass away, go by, expire

измисли, измислува *v.* invent, devise, contrive, think out, figure out

измори *v.* tire, fatigue, weary

измрзне *v.* freeze, frozen to death

измрси *v.* dirty

изнасили *v.* rape, violate, force

изневера *f.* infidelity, unfaithfulness, faithlessness, disloyalty, betrayal

изневерува, изневери *v.* betray, be disloyal/false

изненада *f.* surprise

изненадува, изненади *v.* surprise, astonish

изнесе *v.* bring out, take out, disclose, bring to light

износ *m.* amount, sum, sum total

изнудува, изнуди *v.* blackmail

изобилен *adj.* abundant, plentiful, ample

изобличи, изобличува *v.* expose, unmask, convict

изолатор *m.* insulator

изолација *f.* insulation, isolation

изостава, изоставува *v.* omit, leave out;

изостане *v.* stay away, fail to come

изработи, изработува *v.* work out, compose, elaborate, make, manufacture, carry out

израз *m.* expression

изрази, изразува *v.* express, utter

израмни, израмнува *v.* even, level, equalize

израсне, израснува *v.* grow up, spring up, sprout

изрод *m.* monster, freak

изум *m.* invention, discovery, device

изутрина *f.* morning

икона *f.* icon, sacred image

иконопис *m.* iconography, icon painting

или *conj.* or; **или ... или** either ... or

илјада *num.* thousand

илузија *f.* illusion

им *pron.* them

има *v.* have, possess, hold, own

име *ntr.* name

имено *adv.* namely

имигрант *m.* immigrant

имот *m.* property

императив *m.* imperative

император *m.* emperor

импонира *v.* impress

импулс *m.* impulse

имунитет *m.* immunity

инаков *adj.* different, another kind

инвалид *m.* disabled person, invalid

инвестира *v.* invest

инвестиција *f.* investment

индустрија *f.* industry

инженер *m.* engineer

иницијатива *f.* initiative

инјекција *f.* injection

инквизиција *f.* inquisition

инкубатор *m.* incubator

инспирира *v.* inspire

инсталира *v.* install, fix

инстинкт *m.* instinct

институт *m.* institute

институција *f.* institution

инструмент *m.* instrument, apparatus, tool

интелект *m.* intellect, mind

интервју *ntr.* interview

интерес *m.* interest

интернат *m.* boarding school
интернист *m.* specialist in internal diseases
интимен *adj.* intimate, private, personal
интрига *f.* intrigue
интуиција *f.* intuition
инфекција *f.* infection
инфинитив *m.* infinitive
инфлација *f.* inflation
информација *f.* information
инцидент *m.* incident, accident
ироничен *adj.* ironical
иселник *m.* emigrant
исипе *v.* pour out
искаже *v.* state, say, express
искине *v.* tear, rend, rag
искити *v.* dress up, decorate
исклучено *adv.* impossible
исклучи *v.* exclude, eliminate, expell
исклучителен *adj.* unusual, exceptional
исклучува *v. s.* исклучи
ископа, ископува *v.* dig out, hollow out, burrow
искорени *v.* unroot, uproot, root out
искра *f.* spark
искрен *adj.* sincere, frank, honest
искриви *v.* twist, bend, crook, misrepresent
искупи *v.* buy off; redeem

искушава, искуси *v.* temptation, probation, testing
иследува, иследи *v.* search, examine, investigate
испарение *ntr.* evaporation, exhalation
испари се, испарува се *refl. v.* evaporate, steam, emit
испече *v.* bake, toast, fry, broil, burn
испит *m.* **испита, испитува** *v.* examine, test
исплакне *v.* rinse
исплата *f.* payment, disbursement
исплаши *v.* frighten, scare, intimidate
исповед *f.* confession
исполин *m.* giant
исползува *v.* use, utilize
исполни, исполнува *v.* fill out, fill up, stuff, fulfill
испоти *v.* sweat
исправа *v.* correct; ~ се *refl. v.* rise, stand up
исправен *adj.* accurate, exact, correct
исправи *v. s.* исправа
испразни, испразнива *v.* empty, vacate
испрати, испраќа *v.* send, dispatch, mail; accompany, convoy
испустен *adj.* devastated

испушта, испушти *v.* drop, omit, leave out

ист *pron.* the same, equal, equivalent

истапи, истапува *v.* resign, withdraw; step out

истега, истегне *v.* stretch, extend, pull out

истек *m.* expiration

истече *v.* flow out, leak out, pass away, go by

истине *v.* cool, catch a cold

историја *f.* history

источен *adj.* eastern, oriental

источник *m.* source

истреби *v.* exterminate

истрел *m.* shot

истрпне *v.* (*fig.*) freeze, be paralyzed/petrified, grow numb

исуши *v.* dry, season, dehydrate

исфрли *v.* throw out, cast out

исход *m.* exit, result, outcome

исхрани, исхранува *v.* feed up; ~ се *refl.* *v.* maintain oneself, make a living

исцели, исцелува *v.* heal

исцело *adv.* completely, fully, entirely

исцрпе, исцрпува *v.* exhaust, use up, spend, pump up

исчезне *v.* disappear

исчисти *v.* clean, cleanse, (sky) clear up

исчуди се *refl.* *v.* wonder, be surprised

ита *v.* rush, hurry

итен *adj.* urgent, pressing

ич *adv.* not at all

исто *adv.* the same, also, likewise

исток *m.* east, the Orient

истолкува *v.* explain, interpret

Ј

ја 1. *pron.* her; 2. *interj.* well!

јболкница *f.* apple tree

јаболко *ntr.* apple

јава *v.* ride (horse)

јавен *adj.* public, open

јави, јавува *v.* let know, inform, report

јаглен *m.* coal, briquette

јаглерод *m.* carbon

јагне *ntr.* lamb

јагода *f.* strawberry

јад *m.* sorrow, grief; gall, poison

јадар *adj.* big, large, corpulent

јаде *v.* eat

јадење *ntr.* meal, dish, eating

јадовито *adv.* angrily

јадовен *adj.* sad, sorrowful

јадоса, јадосува *v.* make angry, annoy; ~ **ce** *refl. v.* be angry/embittered

јадро *ntr.* core, nucleus, heart, kernel, pith

јазди *v.* ride

јазик *m.* tongue, language

јазол *m.* knot, tie, hitch

јајце *ntr.* egg

јак *adj.* strong, robust, firm

јака *f.* collar

јалов *adj.* barren, sterile, fruitless

јама *f.* hole, hollow, mine

јануари *m.* January

јарост *f.* anger, passion, fury

јас *pron.* I

јасен 1. *adj.* clear, obvious, evident; 2. ash tree

јасли *pl.* crib

јастреб *m.* hawk

јато *ntr.* swarm, (fish) shoal

јорган *m.* blanket, quilt

јубилеј *m.* anniversary

југ *m.* South

јужен *adj.* south, southern

јули *m.* July

јунак *m.* hero, young brave man

јуни *m.* June

јурист *m.* jurist, lawyer

јурне *v.* rush, dash

К

кабел *m.* cable

кабина *f.* cabin

кавалер *m.* gentleman, cavalier

кавга *f.* argument, fight, quarrel

када *f.* bath tub

каде *adv.* where, which way

кадра, кадрица *f.* lock, curl

каже *v.* say, tell

казна *f.* punishment

кајмак *m.* cream

кајсија *f.* apricot

како *adv.* how, in what manner

каков *adv.* what, what kind, what sort

кал *m.* dirt, mud, slime

календар *m.* calendar

кали *v.* steel, harden

калкулатор *m.* calculator

калорија *f.* calorie

калпав *adj.* bad, false

калугер *m.* monk

кама *f.* dagger

камбана *f.* bell

камен *m.* stone, rock

камила *f.* camel

камин *m.* fireplace

камион *m.* truck, lorry, camion

камо *adv.* where, which way

кампања *f.* campaign

канал *m.* channel, canal

кандидат *m.* candidate, applicant, competitor, rival
кани *v.* invite
канонада *f.* gunfire, cannon fire
канта *f.* can (milk/water)
кантар *m.* scales
канцеларија *f.* office, bureau
капак *m.* cover, shutter
капан *m.* trap
капе (се) *v.* bathe, wash
капе *v.* leak, drops, ooze
капетан *m.* captain
капитал *m.* capital, funds
капитализам *m.* capitalism
капка *f.* drop
капне *v.* become tired/exhausted
капут *m.* coat, jacket
карактер *m.* character, nature, temperament
карамфил *m.* clove, carnation
каре *ntr.* square
кариера *f.* career
карикатура *f.* cartoon, caricature
карневал *m.* carnival
каросерија *f.* car body
карпа *f.* rock, cliff
карта *f.* card, map, chart
картичка *f.* card, postcard
картографија *f.* cartography
карфиол *m.* cauliflower
каса *f.* cash register, box office, cashbox, safe

касап *m.* butcher
касиер *m.* cashier, teller
каска *f.* helmet
каскет *m.* cap
касмет *m.* fortune, luck
кастел *m.* castle, citadel
кат *m.* floor, story
ката- *pref.* every (катаден)
катадешен *adj.* daily, trivial, everyday
катализатор *m.* catalyzer
каталог *m.* catalog(ue)
катанец *m.* lock, clasplock
катастрофа *f.* catastrophe, accident, disaster
категоризира *v.* classify, categorize
категорија *f.* category
категоричен *adj.* categorical
катедра *f.* desk, chair, professorship
катедрала *f.* cathedral
католик *m.* Catholic
католицизам *m.* Catholicism
католички *adj.* catholic
катран *m.* tar
кауција *f.* guarantee, warranty
кауч *m.* couch, divan
кафе *ntr.* coffee
кафез *m.* cage
качество *ntr.* quality
качи, качува *v.* take up, bring up, put up ~ **се** *refl. v.* rise, go up, climb

каша *f.* pap, mash, mess, gruel
кашла *v.* cough
квадрат *m.* square
квалификација *f.* qualification
квалификува *v.* qualify, train
квартал *m.* quarter, district, city area
квартира *f.* apartment, habitation, lodging
кварц *m.* quartz
квас *m.* yeast
квитанција *f.* receipt
кеј *m.* quay, pier
кекс *m.* cake
келнер *m.* waiter
кенгур *m.* kangaroo
кибрит *m.* match
килер *m.* storage room
килим *m.* carpet, rug
кима *v.* nod
Кина *f.* China
Кинез *m.* Chinese
кинески *adj.* Chinese
киниса, кинисува *v.* depart, go
кино *ntr.* movies, cinema
киоск *m.* kiosk, newsstand
кирија *f.* rent
кирилица *f.* cyrillic alphabet
кисел *adj.* sour
киселина *f.* acid
кислород *m.* oxygen
кити *v.* decorate, adorn
кифла *f.* roll, bun

клавир *m.* piano
клавирист *m.* pianist
кладенец *m.* well, spring
кланица *f.* butchery, slaughterhouse
клас *m.* class, grade
класа *f.* class
класира *v.* classify
класицизам *m.* classicism
класичен *adj.* classical
клати *v.* shake, sway, rock, waddle
клаузула *f.* clause, stipulation
клевета *f.* slander, libel, calumny
клен *m.* maple
клепач *m.* eyelid
клепка *f.* eyelash
клет *adj.* miserable
клетва *f.* oath, vow, curse
клетка *f.* cage
клечка *f.* stick, splinter
клешта *f.* tongs, pincers, forceps, pliers
клиент *m.* client
клима *f.* климат *m.* climate
клисура *f.* clift, crag, gorge
клозет *m.* water closet, toilet, lavatory
клон *m.* branch, department, section
клопка *f.* trap, snare
клуб *m.* club
клун *m.* bill, beak

клуч *m.* key

кмет *m.* mayor

книга *f.* book

книжар *m.* bookseller

книжевен *adj.* literary

книжница *f.* library

коба *f.* fate, destiny

кобен *adj.* fatal, ominous, tragic

кобила *f.* mare

кова *v.* hammer, coin

коварен *adj.* perfidious, insidious

ковчег *m.* coffin, chest, trunk

кога *adv.* when

кого *prep.* whom

кожа *f.* skin, leather

кожув *m.* fur coat

коза *f.* goat

козина *f.* fur, pelt, coat

кој *prep.* who, which

кокиче *ntr.* snowdrop

кокошка *f.* hen

кол *m.* pole, stick, prop

кола *f.* cart, car, wagon

колан *m.* belt

колбас *m.* sausage

колве *v.* peck

коле *v.* slaughter, massacre

колебање, *ntr.* колебливост *f.* hesitation, vacillation

колега *m.* colleague, fellow

колекција *f.* collection

колленица *f.* knee, knee joint

коленичи *v.* kneel

колено *ntr.* knee, knee joint

колиба *f.* cottage, hut, cabin

количество *ntr.* quantity

колку *adv.* how much, how many

коло *ntr.* wheel, circle, cycle

колона *f.* column, pillar, post

колонизира *v.* colonize

команда *f.* command

комар *m.* gambling, game of chance/hazard

комбајн *m.* combine, harvester

комедија *f.* comedy, farce

комета *f.* comet

комисија *f.* commission, board, committee

комотен *adj.* comfortable, cozy, suitable

комоција *f.* convenience, comfort

компанија *f.* company, party

компаратив *m.* comparative

компас *m.* compass

компир *m.* potato

комплицира *v.* complicate

композитор *m.* composer

компромис *m.* compromise

кому *prep.* to whom, whom

комуна *f.* commune

комунизам *m.* communism

комуникација *f.* communication

комуникационен *adj.* communication

комшија *m.* neighbor
кон *prep.* to, toward(s); against
конверзација *f.* conversation
конвој *m.* convoy, escort
конгрес *m.* congress
кондуктер *m.* conductor, ticket collector
конец *m.* yarn, fiber, thread
конзерва *f.* can, tin
конзервира *v.* preserve
конзул *m.* consul
конкретен *adj.* concrete
конкурент *m.* competitor, rival
конкуренција *f.* competition
конспирација *f.* conspiracy
констатира *v.* find out, figure out, ascertain
конституција *f.* constitution
конструкција *f.* construction
консултира *v.* consult
контакт *m.* contact
конто *ntr.* account
контра *adv.* against, in oposition
контролира *v.* control
конференција *f.* conference
конфесија *f.* confession
конфликт *m.* conflict
конфузен *adj.* confusing, embarrassing
концентрира *v.* concentrate
концепција *f.* conception
концерт *m.* concert
коњ *m.* horse, steed

коњица *f.* cavalry
кооператива *f.* cooperative
кооперира *v.* cooperate
координира *f.* coordinate
копа *v.* dig, delve, hoe
копира *v.* copy, imitate
копје *ntr.* spear, lance
копнеж *m.* desire, craving, longing
копнен *adj.* continental, land
копно *ntr.* land, mainland
копче *ntr.* button
кора *f.* bark, rind
корав *adj.* hard, stiff
коректен *adj.* correct, proper
корен *m.* root
кореспондент *m.* correspondent
кореспондира *v.* correspond
кори *v.* blame, criticize
коригира *v.* correct, rectify
корисен *adj.* useful, profitable, lucrative, beneficial
корист *f.* benefit, gain, self-interest
корица *f.* rind, crust; book cover
корумпира *v.* corrupt
коса *f.* hair
коса *f.* scythe
коси *v.* mow, reap
космос *m.* cosmos
котва *f.* anchor
котка *f.* s. мачка
котлина *f.* valley, basin

кочина f. pigsty, pigpen
кошмар m. nightmare
крава f. cow
краде v. steal
крадец m. thief
краен adj. outright, outermost, extreme, final
крај m. end, termination, finish
крајбрежен adj. coastal
крак m. leg
крал m. king
кралски adj. royal
кралство ntr. kingdom
красен adj. beautiful, handsome pretty, nice
краси v. decorate, adorn
красота f. beauty, splendor, magnificence
краставица f. cucumber
кратер m. crater
краток adj. short, brief, concise, laconic
крв f. blood
кревет m. bed
креда f. chalk
кредит m. credit
крепи v. hold up, support
крепок adj. robust, strong, hearty
крепост f. fortress
креч m. cramp, convulsion
крив adj. bent, crooked; wrong, faulty, guilty, mistaken
криви v. bend, limp; accuse, blame
криза f. crisis
крие v. hide, cover
крило ntr. wing
криминален adj. criminal
кристал m. crystal, quartz
критика f. critique, criticism
критикува v. criticize, review
кришен adj. secret, hidden
крма f. fodder, forage
кров m. roof
крокодил m. crocodile
кромид m. onion
кроток adj. gentle, tame
крпа f. towel, rag, patch
крст m. cross, crucifix
крсти v. baptize, name
крсти се refl. v. cross oneself
крстоносен adj. cross;
~ поход crusade
крстоса v. cross, set across
круг m. circle, cycle, company, society
круна f. crown
круниса v. crown
крупен adj. large, big, massive, corpulent; important
крут adj. hard, firm
круша f. pear
крчма f. tavern
куб m. cube
кубатура f. volume
кубе ntr. dome, cupola
кубик m. cubic meter

кујна *f.* kitchen
кука 1. *f.* hook; 2. *v.* cuckoo call
кукавица *f.* cuckoo
кукурига *v.* crow
кула *f.* tower
култ *m.* worship
култура *f.* culture
кумир *m.* idol
куп *m.* pile, heap, mass, a lot
купи, купува *v.* buy, purchase
кураж *m.* courage

курс *m.* course
куршум *m.* bullet
кус *adj.* short, brief
кусоглед *adj.* shortsighted, (*fig.*) narrow-minded
кутија *f.* box, chest, case
куќа *f.* house
куфер *m.* suitcase
куц *adj.* lame, limping
куче *ntr.* dog
кучка *f.* bitch

Л

лабав *adj.* weak, loose, shaky
лабораторија *f.* laboratory
лава *f.* lava
лавиринт *m.* labyrinth
лага *f.* lie, untruth, falsehood
лагер *m.* camp
лад *m.* coolness
ладен *adj.* cool, fresh, cold; (*fig.*) unsensible
лади *v.* make cool, refrigerate; ~ се *refl. v.* become cold, cool down
ладилник *m.* cooler, refrigerater
лага *f.* boat, ship, barge
лае *v.* bark
лаже *v.* lie
лажен *adj.* false, untrue, fake
лажовен *adj.* false, deceptive

лазур *m.* azure, sky blue
лак *m.* varnish, lacquer
лаком *adj.* greedy, avaricious
лале *ntr.* tulip
ламарина *f.* tin
ламба *f.* lamp
лани *adv.* last year
лапа, лапне *v.* devour, swallow up, gobble, bolt
лапа 1. *f.* paw
ласица *f.* weasel
ластовица *f.* swallow
лач *m.* ray, sunbeam
леа *f.* garden bed
леан *adj.* cast, founded
леб *m.* bread, loaf
лебед *m.* swan
лево *adv.* (on/to the) left
легален *adj.* legal, lawful,

legitimate
легенда f. legend
легло ntr. bed
леден adj. icy, ice-cold
лее v. pour; ~ се refl. v. flow, pour
лежи v. lie
лек 1. adj. light; 2. m. remedy, cure
лекар m. physician, doctor
лекарски adj. medical
лекарство ntr. medicine, medicament, drug
лековит adj. curative, healing
лекомислен adj. reckless, thoughtless
лексика f. vocabulary
лексички adj. lexical
лектор m. lecturer
лекува v. heal, cure, treat
лента f. band, tape
леопард m. leopard
лепи v. glue, lime, stick, paste
лепило ntr. glue, lime, gum
лесен adj. easy
лета v. fly
летач m. flier
лето ntr. summer
летопис f. chronic
либерален adj. liberal
ливада f. meadow
лигнит m. lignite
лиже, лизне v. lick
лик m. face, figure, form, shape,

image
ликвидира v. liquidate
ликер m. liqueur
ликува v. jubilate, exult, rejoice
лилав adj. purple, violet, lilac
лимон m. lemon
лимфа f. lymph
лингвистика f. linguistics
линија f. line
линчува v. lynch
липа f. linden, lime tree
лира f. lyre
лирика f. lyrics, lyric poetry
лиса f., **лисец** m., **лисица** f. fox, vixen
лисици pl. handcuffs
лист m. leaf, sheet of paper
литература f. literature
литургија f. liturgy, service
лихва f. (banking) interest
лице ntr. face, physiognomy
лицемерен adj. hypocritical, dissembling
лицемерство ntr. hypocrisy
личен adj. personal, private
личи v. resemble, be alike
личност f. person, personality
лиши v. deprive, take away; ~ се refl. v. renounce
лов m. hunt, chase
логика f. logic
лоза f. vine
лови v. hunt, chase
лозје ntr. vineyard

локал *m.* nightclub
локален *adj.* local
локва *f.* puddle
локомотива *f.* locomotive
ломи *v.* break, split
лопата *f.* spade, shovel
лош *adj.* bad, evil, miserable

лубеница *f.* watermelon
луд *adj.* mad, insane, crazy
лук *m.* garlic
луле *f.* pipe
лулка *f.* swing set, cradle
луна *f.* moon
лут *adj.* sharp, spicy, hot; angry

Љ

љуба *f.* sweetheart, love
љубезен *adj.* kind, friendly
љуби *v.* love, be fond of, like
љубов *f.* love
љубовник *m.* lover

љубовница *f.* mistress
љубоморен *adj.* jealous
љубопитен *adj.* curious
љубопитство *ntr.* curiosity
љубува се *refl. v.* admire, enjoy

М

магазин (магацин) *m.* warehouse, store, shop
магаре *ntr.* donkey
магдонос *m.* parsley
магија (маѓиа) *f.* magic
магистер *m.* master
магистрала *f.* highway, road
магла *f.* fog
магнет *m.* magnet
маж *m.* man, husband
мажи *v.* marry
мај *m.* May
маја *f.* yeast, ferment
мајка *f.* mother

мајмун *m.* monkey
мајор *m.* major
мајстор *m.* skilled worker, master
мајтап *m.* fun, joke
мак *m.* poppy
мака *f.* effort, pain, torture
макар *adv.* at least, although, even though
Македонец *m.* Macedonian
Македонија *f.* Macedonia
мал *adj.* small, little, tiny
малина *f.* raspberry
малку *adv.* a little bit, some-

маловажен

мени (се), менува

what

маловажен *adj.* insignificant, unimportant

малодушен *adj.* timid

малолетен *adj.* underage, minor

малоумен *adj.* stupid, dull

малцинство *ntr* minority

мами *v.* attract, tempt, lure; deceive; ~ се *refl. v.* be mistaken, be wrong

мана *f.* fault, shortcoming, deficiency

манастир *m.* monastery

мандат *m.* mandate

маневрира *v.* maneuver

манија *f.* mania

манипулира *v.* manipulate

манир *m.* manner, way, style

мантил *m.* coat, overcoat

манџа *f.* food, dish

мапа *f.* map

марка *f.* (postage) stamp

маркира *v.* mark, stamp

марлив *adj.* hard working, diligent, industrious

март *m.* March

марш *m.* march

маса *f.* table; mass

масив *m.* massif

масивен *adj.* massive, solid, compact

маска *f.* mask

маскира *v.* mask, disguise, camouflage

масовен *adj.* mass, popular, massive scale

математика *f.* mathematics

матен *adj.* muddy, unclear

материал *m.* materials, substance, stuff

мачен *adj.* hard, difficult

машина *f.* machine

ме *pron.* me

мебел *m.* piece of furniture

мебелира *v.* furnish

мев *m.* stomach, belly, abdomen

мед *m.* honey

медал *m.* medal

медицина *f.* medicine

меѓа *f.* boundary, border, frontier

меѓу *prep.* among, between

меѓувремено *adv.* meanwhile, in the mean time

меѓународен *adj.* international

меѓусебен *adj.* mutual, reciprocal

мек *adj.* soft, tender

мекушав *adj.* weak, feeble, flabby

мелница *f.* (flour-) mill, grinder

мелодија *f.* melody

меморандум *m.* memorandum

мемоари *pl.* memoirs

меморија *f.* memory

мене *pron.* me, myself

мени (се), менува *v.* change, modify, exchange, vary

мера *f.* measure, size, proportion, scale; common pasture/land
мери *v.* measure, weight
мерка *s.* мера
мермер *m.* marble
меродавен *adj.* reliable, trustworthy, authentic, authoritative
месар *m.* butcher
месец *m.* month
месност *f.* region, place, countryside
месо *ntr.* meat
местен *adj.* local
мести (се) *v.* move, settle, put
место *ntr.* place, spot, space, site
метал *m.* metal
металургија *f.* metalurgy
мете *v.* sweep, broom
метеж *m.* revolt, uprising
метла *f.* broom
метропола *f.* metropolis, capital
меќава *f.* blizzard, snowstorm
механизам *m.* mechanism
меч *m.* sword
мечта *f.* dream, reverie
мечтае *v.* dream, imagine
меша *v.* mix, blend, stir
ми *pron.* me
мивка *f.* sink, washbasin
миг *m.* moment, instant, flash
мие *v.* wash
мизерен *adj.* miserable

мизерија *f.* misery, poverty
мијалник *m.* **мијалница** *f.* sink, washbasin
микроб *m.* microbe
микроскоп *m.* microscope
мил *adj.* dear, beloved
милно *adv.* gently
мило *adv.* nicely, sweetly
милост *f.* mercy, grace, pardon, favor
милостина *f.* alms, charity
мимолетен *adj.* passing, transient, ephemeral, evanescent
мина *f.* mine
мине *v.* go, walk (past, by, through), pass
минерал *m.* mineral
минимален *adj.* minimal
минира *v.* undermine
министер *m.* minister
министерство *ntr.* ministry
миноносец *m.* torpedo boat, drifter
минута *f.* minute
мир *m.* peace, concord, rest
миризба *f.* (**мирис** *m.*) smell, fragrance, aroma
мирисне *v.* smell
мирно *adv.* quietly, calmly, peacefully
мировен *adj.* peace
мирољубив *adj.* peaceful, peace loving, pacific
мисија *f.* mission

мисла *f.* thought, idea, mind
мислен *adj.* mental, imaginary
мисли *v.* think, imagine, consider, mean, intend, presume, suppose
мислим *adj.* conceivable, thinkable
мислител *m.* thinker, philosopher
мистерија *f.* mystery
мистика *f.* mysticism
мит *m.* myth, legend
митница *f.* customs
митологија *f.* mythology
мишка *f.* armpit
млад *adj.* young, youthful, adolescent, juvenile, new
младеж *f.* youth
младоженец *m.* (bride) groom
младоженка *f.* bride
младост *f.* adolescence, youth
млака *f.* swamp, marsh, moor
млеко *ntr.* milk
млечен *adj.* milk, dairy, lacteal
мливо *ntr.* flour, meal
мнение *ntr.* opinion, idea, judgment, view
многу *adv.* many, much, plenty of, a lot, a great deal of
многуброен *adj.* numerous
многукратен *adj.* multiple, repeated
множество *ntr.* multitude, plenty, crowd, a great many

множи *v.* multiply, grow, increase, reproduce
мноштво *s.* множество
могила *f.* hill, hillock, knoll
мода *f.* fashion, fashion wear, custom
модел *m.* model
може *v.* can, be able
може би *adv.* perhaps
можност *f.* possibility, chance, opportunity
мозок *m.* brain, medulla, (малиот мозок) cerebellum
мозол *m.* blister
мој, моја, мое, мои *pron.* mine
мокри *v.* wet
молба *f.* request, entreaty; appeal, application, petition, plea
молекул *m.* molecule
моли *v.* ask, request, beg, appeal, entreat, plead; ~ се *refl. v.* pray
молив *m.* pencil
молитва *f.* prayer
молна, молња *f.* lightning
молчи *v.* be silent, keep silent/still
мома *f.* girl, maid, virgin
момент *m.* moment, instant
момче *ntr.* boy
монархија *f.* monarchy
монах *m.* monk

монета *f.* coin
монопол *m.* monopoly
монотеизам *m.* monotheism
монтира *v.* install, fix, assemble, fit, mount
мор *m.* pest, plague
мора 1. *f.* nightmare; 2. *v.* must, have to, ought to
морал *m.* morality, morals
море *ntr.* sea
морков *m.* carrot
мост *m.* bridge
мотика *f.* hoe
мотор *m.* motor, engine
моќ *f.* power, might
мува *f.* fly
мудар *adj.* wise, prudent
музеј *m.* museum

музика *f.* music
музикант *m.* musician
мускул *m.* muscle
муслиман *m.* Moslem
мустак *m.* moustache
мрава *f.* ant
мраз *m.* ice
мрак *m.* darkness, night, gloom, dusk
мрда, мрдне *v.* move
мрежа *f.* net
мрзлив *adj.* lazy, idle, indolent
мрзне *v.* freeze
мрмори *v.* mutter, mumble, murmur
мртов *adj.* dead, lifeless, inanimate
мршав *adj.* skinny, thin, slender

Н

на *prep.* on, upon, to, at, in, by
набави *v.* acquire, obtain, supply, provide
набеди *v.* falsely accuse, slander
набере *v.* pick, gather, collect
набие *v.* beat up, punch, slap, smack; impale
наблизу *adv.* nearby, close by
набљудува *v.* observe, watch
набожен *adj.* godly, religious
набргу *adv.* in a hurry, hastily,

superficial
наброи *v.* count, number
набрчка *v.* fold, wrinkle
навакса *v.* make up, catch up
наваму *adv.* here, hither
наведе *v.* bend (down), incline; ~ се *refl. v.* bow, bend
навек *adv.* ever, always; forever
наверно *adv.* probably, presumably, most likely
навести *v.* make known, let know, foretell, predict

навечер *adv.* in the evening

навидум *adv.* apparently

навик *m.* habit, custom

навикне *v.* get used, get accustomed, grow familiar

нависоко *adv.* high

навистина *adv.* truly, indeed, really

навлезе, навлезува *v.* penetrate, enter

навнатре *adv.* inside, in, into

навод *m.* quotation

наводни, наводнува *v.* water, irrigate

навредува *v.* offend, insult, hurt

навреме *adv.* on time, in time

наган, нагант *m.* s. револвер

нагласи *v.* arrange, prepare, fix, adjust

нагледен *adj.* clear, vivid, obvious, evident

нагло *adv.* rapidly, hastily

наговара *v.* persuade, instigate

нагоди *v.* adapt, adjust, accomodate

нагон *m.* instinct

нагоре *adv.* upward, up, uphill

награда *f.* reward, prize

над *prep.* above, over; higher, more than

надалеку *adv.* far, far away

надарен *adj.* gifted, talented

надвива *v.* overcome, defeat

надвор *adv.* outdoor, outside

надгледа *v.* supervise, keep a watch on

надгледувач *m.* warder, supervisor guard,

надгробен *adj.* funeral, grave

надева се *refl. v.* hope, cherish, expect, anticipate, look forward

надеж *m.* hope, expectation

надзира *v.* supervise, control

надзор *m.* supervision

надлежен *adj.* authorized, competent, in charge of

надмен *adj.* arrogant

надморски *adj.* above sea level

надмоќ *f.* superiority, predominance

надница *f.* wages

надолниште *ntr.* downhill, downward, descent

надолу *adv.* down, downhill

надроби *v.* crumble

надуе *v.* blow, puff up

наедно *adv.* together, at the same time

наем *m.* rent, lease

наемател *m.* tenant

наеме *v.* rent, lease

наесен *adv.* in the autumn/fall

назад *adv.* back, backwards

наздравица *f.* toast

назив *m.* title, name

назначи, назначува *v.* appoint, designate, hire

назрева *v.* grow ripe, mature
наивен *adj.* naive
наизуст *adv.* heart
нај *pref.* (forming the superlative of adjectives and adverbs - нај голем)
најде *v.* find
најпосле *adv.* at last, finally, after all
накаже *v.* punch
наказ *m.* punishment
накај *prep.* toward, against
накисне *v.* soak, steep
наклевети *v.* slander, defame
наковална *f.* anvil
накратко *adv.* in short, shortly, briefly, in few words
накрст *adv.* crosswise, crossed
накуп *adv.* together, on a pile
налбат *m.* blacksmith, farrier
налево *adv.* left, leftward(s) to/on the left
налее, налива *v.* pour (out), fill (a glass etc.)
наличен *adj.* available
налог *m.* order, tax
налутено *adv.* angrily, grimly
намали *v.* reduce, shorten, drop, decline
намера *f.* intention, aim, purpose
намерен *adj.* intended, intentional, deliberate
намерност *f.* premeditation

намести *v.* place, put, set, fix
намеша се *refl. v.* interfere
намига, намигне *v.* wink, blink
намножи се *refl. v.* multiply, grow, increase, breed
намокри *v.* wet, soak
намршти *v.* wrinkle (one's brow)
наназад *adv.* backwards
наново *adv.* again, repeatedly, once more
наоколу *adv.* around, nearby
наопаку *adv.* conversely, inversely, wrongly
наостри *v.* sharpen
напад *m.* attack, assault, aggression, invasion
нападне, напаѓа *v.* attack, assault, assail, fall/jump on, come down on
напакости *v.* harm, damage
напев *m.* melody, song
наперчен *adj.* arrogant, puffed up
напечати *v.* print, publish
напивка *f.* drink
напис *m.* inscription, epigraph
напише *v.* write, inscribe
наплата *f.* payment, settlement, reimbursement
наплеска *v.* smack, slap
наплуе *v.* speck
напои *v.* water
наполни *v.* fill, stuff

напомни v. remind, warn; resemble

напон m. tension

напор m. pressure; effort

направи v. do, make

направо adv. straight, straight ahead, directly, right on

напразен adj. useless, vain, purposeless

напрега v. strain; ~ ce refl. v. strain, make efforts, struggle

напред adv. forward, ahead, in front

напреден adj. progressive

напреж adv. before, prior to

напрежен adj. former, previous, last, past

напреки, напреку adv. across, crosswise

напротив adv. on the contrary, opposite

напука v. crack

напусто adv. vain, to no purpose/avail, without success

напушта(напушти) v. abandon, leave

нарав m. nature, temper, character

нарасне v. grow, expand, extend, increase

нарача v. order, command

нарачба s. наредба

наред adv. one after another, successively, by turns; all right,

under control, OK

наредба f. order, command, rule, regulation, decree, ordinance

нареден adj. following, subsequent, next

нареди v. order, command, regulate

нареже v. cut, slice

нарече v. name, call

наречје ntr. dialect

наркотик m. drug, narcotic

народ m. people, folk, nation

народност f. nationality

нарочно adv. purposely, intentionally, deliberately, on purpose

наруши v. violate, break, disturb

насади v. plant

насамо adv. in private, alone face to face

население ntr. population

насели v. settle, colonize

насила adv. by force, through violence, forcibly

насити v. saturate, sate; satisfy ones hunger; (market) glut; ~ ce be full; have enough of

наскоро adv. soon, shortly

наслада f. delight, pleasure, enjoyment

наследство ntr. inheritance, heritage

насмене, насменува v. mention

насока *f.* direction, trend, tendency

насоли *v.* salt

наспрема *prep.* in accordance with

наспроти, наспротив *adv.* across from, opposite

насред *prep.* in the middle of

настава *f.* classes, instruction

наставник *m.* instructor, tutor, teacher, mentor

настинка *f.* cold

настине *v.* catch a cold

настојчив *adj.* persistent, stubborn

настрана *adv.* aside, to one side, in the background

настроение *ntr.* mood

натажен *adj.* sad, distressed

натаму *adv.* in that direction

натиска *v.* press, force

натопи *v.* water, put under water, wet

натпис *m.* inscription

натпревари *v.* outstrip, get ahead of, leave behind, beat;

натпреварува се *refl.* *v.* compete, rival, contest

натрапи (се) *v.* impose, force

натрапник *m.* intruder

натрупа *v.* accumulate, store

натура *f.* nature

наугоре *adv.* up, uphill, up-

wards

наудолу *adv.* down, downhill, downwards

наука *f.* science

научен *adj.* scientific

нахрани *v.* feed

нацизам *m.* Nazism

нација *f.* nation

началник *m.* head, chief

начас *adv.* at once, immediately

начесто *adv.* frequently, often

начин *m.* way, method, manner

наш *pron.* our, ours

не 1. *part.* no, not; 2. *pron.* us

неа *pron.* her

неблагодарност *f.* ingratitude

небрагопријатен *adj.* disadvantageous, unfavorable

небо *ntr.* sky, heaven, paradise

небрежност *f.* negligence

невалиден *adj.* invalid, void, null and void

невен *m.* marigold

неверен *adj.* unfaithful, disloyal

неверник *m.* unbeliever, godless

неверојатен *adj.* unbelievable, incredible, inconceivable

невеста *f.* bride

невин *adj.* innocent, guiltless

невнимателен *adj.* careless, inattentive, inadvertent, thoughtless

невозможно *adv.* impossible

неволен *adj.* spontaneously, involuntarily

невоспитан *adj.* ill-mannered

негар *m.* black man, negro

негатив *m.* negative

негде *adv.* somewhere

него *pron.* him

негоден *adj.* useless

недалеку *adv.* not far, not far way

недвижен *adj.* immovable; ~ имот real estate

недела *f.* Sunday

недоверба *f.* mistrust, distrust

недоверлив *adj.* suspicious, mistrustful, distrustful

недоволен *adj.* dissatisfied, discontent

недовршен *adj.* incomplete, unfinished

недоразвиен *adj.* underdeveloped, rudimentary

недостаток *m.* defect, disadvantage, fault, shortage, imperfection

недоумева *v.* be puzzled, be bewildered

недуг *m.* disability, defect, infirmity

нежен *adj.* tender, delicate, loving

незабавно *adv.* immediately, promptly

независен *adj.* independent

независност *f.* independence

незаконски *adj.* illegal, unlawful

незгода *f.* accident, misadventure, trouble

неземен *adj.* heavenly

незнаен *adj.* unknown

незначителен *adj.* insignificant, unimportant, inconsiderable

неизбежен *adj.* unavoidable, certain, inevitable

неизлечлив *adj.* incurable

неизмерен *adj.* immense

нека *part.* let, may

некадарност *f.* incapability, incompetence

некаде *adv.* somewhere

некаков *pron.* certain, any, some

некогаш *adv.* once

некој, некоја, некое, некои *pron.* one, some, any

неколку *adv.* a few, some, several

нелегален *adj.* illegal

нели *part.* isn't it so

нем *adj.* numb, mute

нема *v.* not have, be without, be deprived

немарен *adj.* negligent, indolent, careless

неможен *adj.* impossible

немоќ *f.* weakness

ненадеен *adj.* unexpected, sudden

ненаситен *adj.* greedy, insatiable

ненормален *adj.* abnormal, insane, crazy

ненужен *adj.* unnecessary

неограничен *adj.* unlimited, boundless, limitless

неоженет *adj.* single man

неомажена *adj.* single woman

неопитен *adj.* inexperienced

неопходен *adj.* necessary

неоснован *adj.* groundless, unfounded

неоспорен *adj.* unquestionable, indisputable

неотстапен *adj.* steady, constant

неофицијален *adj.* informal, unofficial

неплатен *adj.* unpaid

неповратен *adj.* irrevocable

непогоден *adj.* inconvenient

непогодица *f.* trouble, difficulty, inconvenience

неподвижен *adj.* immovable

непозволен *adj.* forbidden, prohibited

непознат *adj.* unknown

непоколеблив *adj.* firm, unshakeable, unshaken, staunch

непокорен *adj.* disobedient, rebellious, disorderly, unruly

неполезен *adj.* unprofitable, useless

непопуларен *adj.* unpopular

непорочен *adj.* innocent, pure, virginal, taintless

непосилен *adj.* too hard, murderous

непослушен *adj.* disobedient, unruly

непостојан *adj.* inconstant, unstable

непотребен *adj.* needless, unnecessary

неправда *f.* injustice, wrong

неправилен *adj.* irregular, abnormal, wrong, incorrect

непредвиден *adj.* unexpected, unforeseen

непрекинат *adj.* continual, continuous, successive

непрестаен *adj.* continual, constant, incessant

неприемлив *adj.* unacceptable, inadmissable

непријател *m.* enemy, foe

непријатен *adj.* unpleasant

неприличен *adj.* indecent, improper, nasty

непристапен *adj.* inaccessible

непростим *adj.* unforgivable

неразделен *adj.* inseparable

неразумен *adj.* unwise, unreasonable

нерв *m.* nerve

нервен *adj.* neural,, nervous

нерентабилен *adj.* unprofitable

несвест *f.* unconsciousness

несигурен *adj.* insecure, uncertain, unsafe

несомнен *adj.* doubtless, undoubted, obvious

неспогодба *f.* misunderstanding, disagreement

несправедлив *adj.* unfair, unjust

нетактичен *adj.* tactless

неуверен *adj.* uncertain

неудобен *adj.* inconvenient

неук *adj.* unlettered

неуспех *m.* failure, ill-success

неутрален *adj.* neutral

неучтив *adj.* impolite, uncivil

нефт *m.* oil, petroleum, naphtha

нечист *adj.* unclean, dirty

нечовечен *adj.* inhuman

нешто *adv.* something, anything

ни 1. not a, no; 2. ни... ни *conj.* neither, nor 3. *pron.* us, to us

нива *f.* field, cornfield

нивни *pron.* their, theirs

ниво *ntr.* level

ние *pron.* we, ourselves

ниеден *adv.* no, no one, none

ничиј *pron.* nobody's

ништо *adv.* nothing, not anything

нов *adj.* new

новина *f.* news

новинар *m.* journalist, reporter

новост *f.* new, novelty

нога *f.* leg

ноември *m.* November

нож *m.* knife

ножица *f.* (ножици *pl.*) scissors

нокот *m.* nail

номер *m.* number

норма *f.* norm, standard, rate

нормален *adj.* normal

нос *m.* nose

носи *v.* carry, wear, bear

нота *f.* note

ноќ *f.* night

нужда *f.* need, necessity

низок *adj.* low

никаде *adv.* nowhere

никако *adv.* no way

никаков *pron.* none, no

никогаш *adv.* never

никој *pron.* nobody, no one

ниско *adv.* low

О

О! *interj.* o, oh, O!

оаза *f.* oasis (pl. oases)

обвинение *ntr.* accusation, charge

обвинет *m.* defendant, accused

обвинува *v.* accuse

обврзува, обврзе v. bind, oblige, make liable

обедини, обединува v. unite, incorporate, consolidate

обезбеди, обезбедува v. insure, safeguard

обезглавува, обезглави v. be-head, decapitate

обележи, обележува v. mark, signpost

обем m. volume, size, bulk; (fig.) amount, extent

оберува, обере v. pick, gather, rob

обеси, обесува v. hang, hang up, hook

обескуражи, обескуражува v. discourage

обесчести, обесчестува v. rape, dishonor, disgrace, violate

обзема, обземе v. overcome, overwhelm

обид m. experiment, try, test

обичај m. custom, habit

објава f. announcement, advertisement

објаснение ntr. explanation, interpretation

облак m. cloud

област f. region, district, area

облегне се, облегнува се refl. v. lean, rely

облекува, облече (се) v. dress, clothe

облик m. appearance, face, form

облог m. pledge, bet

обмисли, обмислува v. consider, think over

обожава v. adore, worship, idolize

обработи, обработува v. work (on), process, cultivate (land), treat

образец m. model, example, form

образование ntr. education

обратен adj. reverse, opposite, contrary

обратно adv. on the contrary

обред m. ritual, ceremony

обрне, обрнува v. turn, reverse; ~ се refl. v. turn around

обува, обуе v. put on shoes

обучава, обучи v. teach, instruct, train

овде, овдека adv. here

овдешен adv. local

овери, оверува v. attest, verify, certify

овластен adj. authorized, entitled, empowered

овошје ntr. fruit

овца f. sheep

оган (огин, pl. **огнови)** m. fire

огладнет adj. hungry

оглед m. test, experiment, inspection

огледа се, огледува се *v.* look at oneself in a mirror, look round, be reflected

огледало *ntr.* mirror

огниште *ntr.* fireplace

огноотпорен *adj.* fireproof

огорчен *adj.* grieved, hurt, distressed

ограда *f.* fence, wall

ограничен *adj.* limited, bounded, restricted

огрева, огрее *v.* shine, rise (sun), light (up), illuminate

огромен *adj.* huge, immense, enormous, tremendous, gigantic

од *prep.* from, of, by, (time) since, (comparative) than

одавде, одавдека *adv.* hence, from here, then

одамна *adv.* long ago

оданде, одандека *adv.* hence, from there

одбележи, одбележува *v.* mark, make a sign, emphasize, point out

одбива, одбие *v.* reject, refuse

одбере, одбира *v.* choose, select, pick out

одбор *m.* committee, council

одбрана *f.* defense, protection

одвод *m.* conduction pipe, conduit

одвратен *adj.* disgusting

одвреме *adv.* forever, always

одгатне, отгатнува *v.* guess

одглас *m.* response, echo

одговара *v.* answer, reply, respond

одговорен *adj.* responsible, in charge

одговорност *f.* responsibility, liability

одѕив *m.* response, comment, report, review

оди *v.* step, go, walk, move,

одлага *v.* postpone, delay, put off

одлево *adv.* on/from the left

одличен *adj.* excellent

одлука *f.* decision, resolution

одмазда *f.* revenge

одмери *v.* measure, weigh

одмор *m.* rest, relaxation

одназад *adv.* backward(s)

однапред *adv.* from before, in advance

одненадеж *adv.* unexpectedly

однесе, однесува *v.* take, carry; take out/away, carry out/away; refer, relate, assign; однесува се *refl. v.* with reference to, concern

одново *adv.* again anew, once more

однос *m.* relation, connection, respect, reference

одобрение *ntr.* approval

одрази, одразува *v.* express

reflect
одрасне *v.* grow up
одреден *adj.* determined, destined, intended
одржи, одржува *v.* keep up, hold
одушевен *adj.* inspired, enthusiastic
ожеднет *adj.* thirsty
оженет *adj.* married
оженува *v.* marry
ожнива, ожние *v.* harvest
озакони *v.* legalize
озари *v.* light up, illuminate
озгора *adv.* from above
одоздола *adv.* from below, beneath, underneath
оздрави, оздравува *v.* recover, convalesce
означи, означува *v.* mark, check off, indicate, characterize
озон *m.* ozone
океан *m.* ocean
око *ntr. (pl.* очи) eye
оков *m.* chains, shackles, fetters, irons
околија *f.* district, province
околност *f.* circumstance, condition
околу *adv.* around, about
окоп *m.* trench
окоси, окосува *v.* mow,
округ *m.* district, region, province, county

октомври *m.* October
окупатор *m.* invader, occupier
окупација *f.* occupation
окуражи, окуражава *v.* encourage
олесни, олеснува *v.* lighten, make easier, relieve
олово *ntr.* lead
олтар *m.* altar
омажи, омажува *v.* marry
омраза *f.* hate, hatred
омрзне, омрзнува *v.* bore, tire, become boring
онади, онадува make, do, complete
онака *adv.* that way, like that
онаков, онаква, онакво, онакви *pron.* such
онаму *adv.* there, over there
онде, ондека *adv.* there, over there, check off, indicate, characterize
онеми (онеме), онемува *v.* become mute/speechless
оној, онаа, онор онаа.оние *pron.* that
онолку *adv.* as/so much, as/so many
опаку *adv.* inside out, the reverse/wrong side of
опасен *adj.* dangerous, risky, critical
опасност *f.* danger, risk, hazard
опашка *f.* tail

операција *f.* surgery, operation, transaction

опира, опре *v.* lean

опис *m.* description, inventory

опит *m.* attempt, try

опише, опишува *v.* describe

оплакување *ntr.* complaint, morning

оплоди, оплодува *v.* fertilize, fructify

опозиција *f.* opposition

ополномошти, ополномоштува *v.* authorize

опора *f.* support

оправда, оправдува *v.* justify, discharge

определи, определува *v.* determine, define

опсада *f.* siege, blockade

опсег *m.* extent, sphere

опстоен *adj.* detailed

опустен *adj.* deserted, desolate

општ *adj.* general, common

општествен *adj.* public, social

општество *ntr.* society

општина *f.* parish, community

оре *v.* plow

орган *m.* organ

организира *v.* organize

организам *m.* organism

орден *m.* decoration

орев *m.* walnut

орел *m.* eagle

ориз *m.* rice

оркестар *m.* orchestra

орудие *ntr.* tool, instrument

оружје *ntr.* weapons, arms

осамотен *adj.* isolated, lonely

освен *adv.* except, besides, unless

освети, осветува *v.* revenge; consecrate

осека *f.* ebb tide, low tide

осет *m.* sense, perception, feeling

осетлив *adj.* sensitive, delicate

осети, осетува *v.* sense, feel

осигури, осигурува *v.* insure, secure

осило *ntr.* sting

оска *f.* axis, axle

оскверни, осквернува *v.* desecrate, defile, violate

оскуден *adj.* scanty, scant, scarce, meager

ослабне, ослабнува *v.* weaken, decline

осмели се, осмелува се *refl. v.* dare, take the liberty

основа *f.* foundation, fundamentals, basis, base

особа *f.* person, personality

особеност *f.* peculiarity

особина *f.* peculiarity, individuality

особен *adj.* strange, unusual

оспори, оспорува *v.* dispute,

controvert, deny

остави, остава v. leave (behind), remain, desert, abandon

останки pl. remnants, rest, remainders

остане, останува v. stay, remain

остар adj. sharp, harsh, acute

остаток m. rest, remainder, balance

остров m. island

осуда f. sentence, verdict, judgment

осум num. eight

осумнаесет num. eighteen

осумстотин num. eight hundred

отаде adv. from there, on the other side

отвора, отвори v. open

отекува, отече v. swell

оти 1. adv. why; 2. conj. that, because, for

отиде, отидува v. go to

откаже, откажува v. refuse, decline

откако conj. (ever) since

отклони, отклонува v. divert, draw away, refuse

отклуми, отклучова v. unlock

откога 1. adv. since when; 2. conj. since

открај adv. from the very beginning

открива, открие v. uncover,

discover, disclose

откритие ntr. discovery, invention

откуп m. redemption

отопление ntr. heat, heating

отпадок m. waste, garbage

отпатува v. depart, leave

отпечати, отпечатува v. print, imprint, mark

отплата f. payment, repayment, reward

отпор m. resistance, opposition

отпрво, отпрвин adv. at first

отпуска f. leave of absence, holidays, vacation

отров m. poison

отсега adv. from now (on)

отсек m. department, section

отсечка f. segment

отслужи, отслужува v. (mil.) serve one's time, serve a sentence (sacr.) hold a service

отстапи, отстапува v. step back, retire; yield, give in

отстрана adv. on/from/at the side

отстрани, отстранува v. remove, eliminate

отсуство ntr. absence

оттаму adv. from there

оттогаш, оттогај adv. from that time, since then

оттука adv. from here, this way

отфрлен adj. outcast, rejected

отчет *m.* account, report
окорен *adj.* blind
оферта *f.* offer
официер *m.* officer
оценка *f.* valuation, appraisal
оцет *m.* vinegar
оцрта, оцртува *v.* describe, outline

очајание *ntr.* despair
очара, очарува *v.* charm, fascinate
очевиден *adj.* obvious, evident
очекува *v.* expect, await
очила *pl.* eyeglasses
оштети, оштетува *v.* damage, harm

П

па *conj.* and, but, well
пад *m.* fall
падеж *m.* case
падне, паднува *v.* fall, drop, (airplane) crash
пазар *m.* market, market place
пазари, пазарува *v.* shop, buy
пак *adv.* again
пакет *m.* parcel, package, pack
пакт *m.* pact, agreement
палав *adj.* playful, noisy, lively
палата *f.* palace, court, house
пали *v.* burn, light
палец *m.* thumb, big toe
палјачо *m.* clown
палма *f.* palm
палуба *f.* deck
памет *m.* mind, sense, intellect, reason
паметен *adj.* rational, reasonable, intelligent, wise
паметливост *f.* memory

паметник *m.* monument
памук *m.* cotton
паника *f.* panic
паница *f.* bowl
пансион *m.* boarding house
панталони *pl.* trousers, pants
папа *m.* pope
папагал *m.* parrot
пар *m.* pair, two, couple
пара *f.* steam, fume; coin
параброд *m.* steamship, ship
парада *f.* parade, show
паразит *m.* parasite
парализира *v.* paralyze; ~ се *refl. v.* become paralyzed
параход *s.* параброд
пари *pl.* money, coins
парк *m.* park
парламент *m.* parliament
парница *f.* lawsuit, law case
парничи *v.* sue
партизан *m.* partisan, guerilla

партија *f.* party
партнер *m.* partner
парфем *m.* perfume, scent
парче *ntr.* piece, part, share, portion; article
пасе *v.* graze
пасиште *ntr.* pasture
пасош *m.* passport
пат *m.* road, way; time (one time)
патека *f.* path
патешествие *ntr.* journey
патриарх *m.* patriarch
патрон *m.* patron, protector
патува *v.* travel
пауза *f.* pause, break, rest
паун *m.* peacock
пациент *m.* patient
паштерка *f.* stepdaughter
пеач, певец *m.* singer
педесет *num.* fifty
пее *v.* sing
пејсаж *m.* landscape
пекол *m.* hell
пелена *f.* diaper
пелтечи *v.* stammer, stutter
пена *f.* foam, froth
пензија *f.* pension
пепел *m.* ash, ashes
пеперуга *f.* butterfly
перде *ntr.* curtain
пере *v.* wash, launder
период *m.* period, era; menstruation
периодичен *adj.* periodical, regular
перманентен *adj.* permanent, steady
перо *ntr.* father
перон *m.* platform
перспектива *f.* perspective, prospect
перика *f.* wig
перфектен *adj.* perfect, excellent
песна *f.* song
песок *m.* sand
пет *num.* five
пета *f.* heel
петел *m.* cock
петиција *f.* petition
петок *m.* Friday
петстотин *num.* five hundred
печалба *f.* profit, gain, winning
печат *m.* seal, stamp, print(ing), press
печати *v.* print, publish, stamp
пече *v.* bake, roast
печка *f.* stove, oven
пеш, пеши *adv.* on foot, walking
пештера *f.* cave
пиво *ntr.* beer
пивара *f.* brewery
пие *v.* drink
пиеса *f.* play
пијан *adj.* drunk
пила *f.* file, saw
пиле *ntr.* chicken

пилот *m.* pilot
пипа *v.* touch
пир *m.* feast, banquet
пират *m.* pirate
писател *m.* writer, author
писмен *adj.* written
пита 1. *f.* loaf; 2. *v.* ask, request
питом *adj.* domestic
пише *v.* write, type
пиштол *m.* pistol
пладне *ntr.*, пладнина *f.* noon, midday
плажа *f.* beach
плакне *v.* rinse
пламен *m.* flame
пламне, пламнува *v.* flare up
пламти *v.* flame, flare, burn, glow
план *m.* plan, program, project
планета *f.* planet
планина *f.* mountain
планира *v.* plan
пласт *m.* layer
пластика *f.* plastic
плата *f.* salary, payment
плати *v.* pay
платно *ntr.* linen, cloth
платформа *f.* platform
плаќа *v.* pay
плаче *v.* cry, weep
плаши *v.* frighten, terrify, scare
плевна *f.* barn
пледира *v.* plead
племе *ntr.* tribe, clan,

плен *m.* loot
пленик *m.* captive, prisoner
пленство *ntr.* captivity
плени, пленува *v.* plunder, rob, loot; take prisoner/captive
плеска, плеснува *v.* slap
плешка *f.* shoulder blade
плива *v.* swim
плик *m.* envelope
плиска, плисне *v.* splash
плиток *adj.* shallow; (*fig.*) superficial
плови *v.* navigate, sail
плод *m.* fruit
плоден *adj.* fruitful, fertile
плодотворен *adj.* fruitful, fertile, productive
плоштад *m.* square
плуг *m.* plow
пљачка *f.* loot, plunder, booty
пнеумонија *f.* pneumonia
по *prep.* on, upon, after, through, about, round, by, per, for
поарчи, поарчува *v.* spend
побара, побарува *v.* seek, request, demand
победа *f.* victory
побелен *adj.* white, gray-haired
поболи, поболува *v.* make sick; ~ се *refl. v.* sicken, become ill
побрза, побрзува *v.* hurry, hasten
побрка, побркува *v.* drive crazy; ~ се *refl. v.* go mad,

go out of one's mind

побуда *f.* impulse, stimulation, inspiration

побуна *f.* revolt, rebellion

повев *m.* breeze

повева, повее *v.* blow

поведение *ntr.* behavior

повела (повелба) *f.* command, ordinance, order, document

поверен *adj.* entrusted, confined

поверлив *adj.* confidential

повеќе *adv.* more

повик *m.* call, cry

повиши, повишува *v.* increase, raise

повод *m.* motive, occasion, cause, reason

поврати, повратува *v.* return

повремено *adv.* periodically, occasionally

површен *adj.* superficial

повтори, повторува *v.* repeat

погали, погалува *v.* stroke, caress

поглед *m.* look, glance

поговорка *f.* proverb, saying

погодба *f.* condition, term of agreement

поголем *adj.* bigger, larger, taller, higher

погреб *m.* funeral, burial

погребе, погребува *v.* bury

погрешен *adj.* wrong, mistaken, incorrect

погубва, погуби *v.* kill, execute, destroy, ruin

под 1. *prep.* under, below, beneath; 2. *m.* floor

поданик *m.* citizen

поданство *ntr.* citizenship

подарок *m.* present

подбере, подбира *v.* select, pick out

подвиг *m.* heroic deed, feat

подвижен *adj.* mobile, movable, lively

подводен *adj.* submarine

подготвен *adj.* prepared

поддржи, поддржува *v.* hold up, support, keep up

поддршка *f.* support, maintenance

подели, поделува *v.* divide, share, separate

подзглавје *ntr.* pillow

подземен *adj.* underground

подига, подигне, подигнува *v.* raise, lift

подлец *m.* sneak, skunk, bastard

подлога *f.* base, foundation

подмами, подмамува *v.* entice, lure

подмет *m.* *(gram.)* subject

подмолен *adj.* secret, subversive

поднесе, поднесува *v.* present, submit, (resignation) rend

подновен *adj.* restored, renovated, renewed

подобар *adj.* better

подобрен *adj.* improved

подреди, подредува *v.* set, put in order, subordinate

подреми, подремува *v.* nap, doze

подробен *adj.* detailed

поезија *f.* poetry

поема *f.* poem

поет *m.* poet

пожали, пожалува *v.* regret

пожар *m.* fire

пожелува *v.* wish, desire

позволи, позволува *v.* permit, allow

поздрав *m.* greeting, salute

познава, познае *v.* know, be familiar with

познание *ntr.* knowledge

поим *m.* conception, idea, term

појава *f.* appearance, occurrence, phenomenon

појави, појавува *v.* appear

појадок *m.* breakfast

појасни, појаснува *v.* explain

покаже, покажува *v.* show, indicate

показалец *m.* forefinger

показател *m.* index

покајание *ntr.* reget, repetance, penitence

покана *f.* invitation

поклони се, поклонува се *refl. v.* bow down, pay reverence

покоен *adj.* deceased

поколеба се, поколебува се *refl. v.* hesitate

поколение *ntr.* generation

покорен *adj.* obedient

покрај *prep.* besides, by

покрив *m.* roof

покрие, покрива *v.* cover

покровител *ntr.* patron, protector,

покрсти, покрстува *v.* baptize

пол *m.* gender, sex; pole

полани *adv.* the year before last year

поласка, поласкува *v.* flatter

поле *ntr.* field

полева, полее *v.* water

полезен *adj.* useful

полека *adv.* slowly, gently, easily, softly

полет *m.* flight

полза *f.* use, advantage, benefit

полира *v.* polish

политика *f.* politics

полица *f.* shelf; bill

полиција *f.* police

полк *m.* regiment

полковник *m.* colonel

полни *v.* fill (up)

полноќ *f.* midnight

полномошно *ntr.* mandate,

authorization
половина *f.* half
полу *pref.* semi-, demi-, half-
полумесец *m.* half moon
полумрак *m.* twilight, dusk
полуостров *m.* peninsula
помага *v.* help, assist, aid, give a hand
пометне, пометнува *v.* miscarry, abort
помилува *v.* amnesty, stroke, caress
помни *v.* remember, recall, keep in mind
помогне, помогнува *v.* help, assist, aid, give a hand
помоли, помолува *v.* ask (for)
помош *f.* help, assistance, aid
помпа *f.* pump
понапред *adv.* before, in advance, previously
понатаму *adv.* further, farther on
понеделник *m.* Monday
понекогаш *adv.* sometimes
понуда *f.* offer, bid, proposal
поп *m.* priest
попис *m.* list, schedule, register, index
попосле *adv.* afterward(s), later, later on
поправа, поправи *v.* fix, repair, correct

популарен *adj.* popular
поради *prep.* because (of), for
поразен *adj.* defeated, struck, overwhelmed
порази, поразува *v.* defeat, destroy; strike, overwhelm
порака *f.* massage
порано *adv.* earlier, before
порасне, пораснува *v.* grow (up)
порачка *f.* order
поредба *f.* comparison
поредок *m.* order
пороби, поробува *v.* enslave
порода *f.* breed, race
порок *m.* vice, defect
порочен *adj.* vicious
порта *f.* gate
портокал *m.* orange
портрет *m.* portrait, picture
порцелан *m.* porcelain, china
порција *f.* portion, dish
посвети, посветува *v.* dedicate
посебен *adj.* particular, individual, separate, special, extra
посев *m.* crop
поседок *m.* possession, property, estate
поседи, поседува *v.* possess, own; sit a while, rest a while
поседник *m.* owner, holder
посен *adj.* lenten, meatless
посета *f.* visit, attendance

посини, посинува v. adopt a child

после adv. later, afterwards

последен adj. last, final

последица f. result, consequence, effect

послушен adj. obedient

пословица f. proverb, saying

посмртен adj. posthumous

посока f. direction

посоче, посочува v. show, indicate, point out

посредник m. mediator, dealer

пост m. lent, fasting

постапен adj. gradual, successive, progressive

постапка f. acting, action

постапи, постапува v. act, proceed

постига v. succeed, achieve, realize

постои, постоjува v. exist, live, be, there is/are

постоjан adj. constant, steady

пострада, пострадува v. be affected, suffer

пот m. sweat

потврди, потврдува v. confirm, certify

потекло ntr. origin, descent

поти се refl. v. sweat

потисне, потиснува v. oppress, suppress

потков m. horseshoe

поткрепа f. support

поткуп m. bribe

поткупи, поткупува v. bribe, corrupt

потоа adv. afterwards, then, next

поток m. stream

потомок m. descendant, offspring

потоне, потонува v. drown

потоп m. flood

потпали, потпалува v. set on fire, set fire to

потпис m. signature

потполн adj. complete, total, entire, full, whole

потпомага, потпомогне, потпомогнува v. support, help

потреба f. need, necessity

потребен adj. necessary

потроа adv. a little bit

потруди се, потрудува се refl. v. try, endeavor, bother, trouble

потсети, потсетува v. remind

потфат m. undertaking, business, project

потхрани, потхранува v. feed

поука f. lesson, moral

пофали, пофалува v. praise

поход m. march, excursion, expedition

почва f. soil, earth, ground

почест f. honor
почетен adj. honor, honorable
почива v. rest
почит m. respect, honor, esteem
почне, почнува v, begin, start
почувствува v. feel
пошта f. mail, post, post office
прав 1. m. dust, powder; 2. adj.
right, straight
правда f. justice, fairness
правен adj. legal, law
прави v. make, do
правилен adj. regular, correct
правило ntr. rule, principle
право ntr. right, law, justice,
jurisprudence
правоагален adj. rectangular
правопис m. spelling, orthog-
raphy
православен adj. (Greek) Or-
thodox
правосудство ntr. judicature,
justice
праг m. threshold, doorstep
празен adj. empty, blank
празник m. holiday, feast
празнува v. celebrate
практика f. practice, experience
практичен adj. practical
прасе ntr. pig
прати v. send, expedite
пратка f. shipment, parcel
прашен adj. dusty
прв adj. first

првенство ntr. championship
пребледне, пребледнува v.
become pale
преброи, пребројува v. count
(up)
преведе, преведува v. translate
превнук m., превнучка f.
great-grandson,   great-grand-
daughter
превод m. translation; (money)
remittance
превоз m. transport, shipping,
freight, conveyance, carriage
преврат m. takeover, revolt,
coup d'etat
преврска f. bandage
преглед m. examination, review, revise
прегледа, прегледува v. look
through, examine, review, revise
преговара v. negotiate
преграда f. barrier
пред adv. in front of, before
предава, предаде v. hand
over, turn over; transmit; betray;
~ се refl. v. surrender, give up
предавател m. transmitter
предан adj. devoted, loyal, true
предание ntr. legend
предвиде,   предвидува   v.
foresee
предвреме adv. premature,
early

предговор *m.* preface

предградие *ntr.* suburb

преден *adj.* front, former

предизвика, предизвикува *v.* provoke

предимно *adv.* mainly, mostly

предимство *ntr.* advantage, preference

предлага, предложи, предложува *v.* offer, suggest, propose

предмет *m.* object; subject, topic

предок *m.* ancestor

предрасуда *f.* prejudice

предепреди, предупредува *v.* warn, prevent

преживее, преживува *v.* survive, experience

президент *m.* president

презира *v.* dispise, hold in contempt

прекален *adj.* excessive, exaggerated

прекин *m.* break, interruption, pose

прекрасен *adj.* magnificence, beautiful, wonderful

прукрати, прекратува *v.* stop, quit, cease

преку *prep.* across, through

прелета, прелетува *v.* (bird) migrate, fly by

прелом *m.* sudden change, turning point

премести, преместува *v.* move, remove, shift, transfer

премиер *m.* prime minister

премиера *f.* premiere, first performance

премолчи, премолчува *v.* keep silent

пренебрегне, пренебрегнува *v.* neglect, ignore

преовлада, преовладува *v.* predominate, prevail

преод *m.* transition

препира се *refl. v.* argue, dispute

препис *m.* copy

препорака *f.* recommendation, reference

преродба *f.* rebirth, revival

преса *f.* press

пресели, преселува (се) *v.* move, immigrate, settle

пресен *adj.* fresh

пресмета, пресметува *v.* calculate

преспа *f.* avalanche

престане, престанува *v.* stop, cease

престапник *m.* criminal

престол *m.* throne

престраши се, престрашува се *refl. v.* risk, dare

престрелка *f.* firing, exchange of fire, skirmish

пресуда *f.* sentence, verdict, judgment

претендира *v.* claim, pretend

претпазлив *adj.* cautious, preventive

претплата *f.* advance payment, subscription

претполага *v.* suppose, assume, presume

претпоставка *f.* assumption, premise

председател *m.* chairman, president

претстави, претставува *v.* present, introduce

претчувство *ntr.* presentiment, sense

преувеличи, преувеличува *v.* exaggerate

преуморен *adj.*, overworked, exhausted

прехрана *f.* subsistence, maintenance

преценка *f.* appraisal, estimate

пржи *v.* fry

при *prep.* near, by

приближи, приближува (се) *v.* approach

прибор *m.* utensil, instrument (pl.) silverware, cutlery

прибрежие *ntr.* shore, bank

привикне, привикнува *v.* get used to, get accustomed to

привилегија *f.* privilege

привремен *adv.* temporary, provisional

приговор *m.* objection

приготви, приготвува *v.* prepare, get ready

придобие, придобивува *v.* gain, win, earn

придружи, придружава *v.* accompany

прием *m.* reception

призив *m.* appeal, call

признава, признае *v.* confess,

призрак *m.* ghost, spook

пријател *m.* friend

пријатен *adj.* pleasant

прикрепи, прикрепува *v.* attach, affix

прилага *v.* apply; enclose

прилив *m.* rising/high tide

прилика *f.* likeness, resemblance

прилог *m.* adverb

приложи, приложува *v.* add, annex, apply, enclose

прима, прими *v.* receive, accept, approve

пример *m.* example, instance

примка *f.* trap

принадлежи, принадлежува *v.* belong

принос *m.* contribution

принуда *f.* compulsion

принц *m.* , **принцеза** *f.* prince, princess

принцип *m.* principle

припомни, припомнува *v.* recall, remember

прираст *m.* growth, increase

приредба *f.* performance, concert, show

природен *adj.* natural, genuine

природа *f.* nature

пприслужник *m.* servant

приспособи, приспособува (се) *v.* adapt, adjust

пристаниште *ntr.* port, harbor

пристига, пристигне, пристигува *v.* arrive

присуство *ntr.* presence, attendance

притатко *m.* stepfather

притежава *v.* possess, own

притоа *adv.* at the same time

приход *m.* income

причина *f.* cause, reason, motive

проба *f.* test, rehearsal

пробива, пробие *v.* pierce, bore, drill, make one's way

проблем *m.* problem

провери, проверува *v.* check, make sure

провидение *ntr.* providence

провинција *f.* province

проводник *m.* conductor

проглас *m.* proclamation

прогноза *f.* forecast

прогонство *ntr.* persecution

програма *f.* program

прогрес *m.* progress, advancement

продава, продаде *v.* sell, vend

продажба *f.* sale

продолжи, продолжува *v.* continue, proceed, prolong

продукт *m.* product

продуктивен *adj.* productive

продукција *f.* production

проект *m.* project, design, plan

проза *f.* prose

прозорец *m.* window

просева се *refl. v.* yawn

произведе, произведува *v.* produce

прокламација *f.* proclamation

проклет *adj.* damned, cursed

прокоп *m.* tunnel, channel, canal

пролет *m.* spring

промена *f.* change

промет *m.* traffic, turnover

промисли, промислува *v.* think over, deliberate, consider

пронајдок *m.* invention, discovery

проникне, проникнува *v.* penetrate; come to the bottom

пропаганда *f.* propaganda

пропадне, пропаднува *v.* fail

пропис *m.* regulation, rule, precept

проповед *m.* preaching, ser-

mony, lecture
пропуст *m.* negligence, failure
пророк *m.* prophet
просвета *f.* education
проси *v.* beg
прослави, прославува *v.* celebrate, solemnize; ~ се *refl. v.* become famous
проследи, проследува *v.* follow (up), trace
прост *adj.* simple, uncivil
простор *m.* space, room
пространство *ntr.* room, space
прости, простува *v.* forgive, pardon, excuse
протест *m.* protest
против *prep.* against, counter
противи се *refl. v.* oppose
противвоздушен *adj.* air defense
противник *m.* enemy, opponent, rival
противоречи *v.* contradict
протокол *m.* protocol, record

проучи, проучува *v.* study, research
професија *f.* profession
профилактика *f.* prophylaxis
процвета, процветува *v.* bloom, flourish
процедура *f.* procedure
процент *m.* precentage
процес *m.* process, trail
проштава *v.* forgive, pardon
прска *v.* splash, sprinkle
прст *m.* finger
прстен *m.* ring
психијатрија *f.* psychiatry
психологија *f.* psychology
птица *f.* bird
публика *f.* audience, public
публикува *v.* publish
пункт *m.* point
пура *f.* cigar
пуст *adj.* deserted, desolate
пустина *f.* desert, wilderness
пчела *f.* bee
пченица *f.* wheat

P

раб *m.* edge
работа *f.* work, labor
работник *m.* worker, laborer
радијатор *m.* radiator
радијација *f.* radiation
радикален *adj.* radical

радио *m.* radio
радост *f.* joy, gladness
радува (се) *v.* be glad, look forward
разбере, разбира *v.* understand, comprehend, realize

разбоіник *m.* robber, burglar

разбуди, разбудува *v.* wake up

разбунтува *v.* revolt, stir up, rebel

разведен *adj.* divorced

развева, развее *v.* wave

развесели се, развеселува се *refl. v.* cheer up

развива, развие *v.* develop, advance

развод *m.* divorce

разврат *m.* immorality, sexual offense

разврзе, разврзува *v.* untie, unbind

разврска *f.* outcome, conclusion

разгален *adj.* spoiled, pampered

разгласи, разгласува *v.* announce, make public, spread news

разглоби, разглобува *v.* take apart, disassemble

разговара *v.* talk, discuss

разговор *m.* conversation, talk

раздава, раздаде *v.* distribute, dispense

разделба *f.* separation

раздразни, раздразнува *v.* irritate, annoy

разен *adj.* various, diverse, different

разіасни, разіаснува *v.* explain

разлага *v.* decompose

разлива, разлие (се) *v.* spill, pour out, flood

разлика *f.* difference, distinction

различен *adj.* different, diverse; pretty, beautiful, handsome

размена *f.* change, exchange, trade

размер *m.* size, scale; (*fig.*) degree, extend

размине, разминува *v.* pass each other

размисли, размислува *v.* think over, consider

размножи, размножава *v.* multiply, breed

разногласност *f.* disagreement

разнообразен *adj.* diverse, various

разора, разорува *v.* (*financially*) ruin, destroy

разоружување *ntr.* disarmament

разочаран *adj.* disappointed, disillusioned

разреши, разрешува *v.* permit, solve, settle

разрушава, разруши *v.* ruin, destroy, demolish, wreck

разузнае, разузнува *v.* investigate, find out, inquire

разум *m.* mind, reason, intelli-

gence
разумен *adj.* reasonable
thoughtful, rational
разучи, разучува *v.* research,
study
рај *m.* paradise
рак *m.* crab, cancer
рака *f.* hand, arm
ракав *m.* sleeve, (river) arm
ракета *f.* rocket
раководи *v.* lead, manage
раководство *ntr.* leadership,
guidance, management
ракопис *m.* manuscript, hand-
writing
ракоплеска *v.* applaud, clap
ракува се *refl. v.* shake hands
рамка *f.* frame
рамнодушен *adj.* indifferent
рамномерно *adv.* even, steady
рамноправен *adj.* equal (in
rights)
рамо *ntr.* shoulder
рана *f.* wound
рано *adv.* early
рапорт *m.* report
раса *f.* race
раскаже, раскажува *v.* tell,
tell a story, narrate
расказ *m.* story, tale
раскол *m.* split, schism
раскошен *adj.* luxurious, magnificent, splendid
распадне се, распаднува

се, **распаѓа се** *v.* fall apart/to
pieces, break up
распис *m.* circular
расписка *f.* receipt
распне, распнува *v.* crucify
распознава, распознае *v.*
recognize, tell apart, distinguish
располага *v.* have something at
one's disposal
расположение *ntr.* mood, position, location, situation
расправа се *v.* debate, quarrel, argue
распуст *m.* holiday, school
break
распушта, распушти *v.* dismiss, dissolve
расрди, расрдува *v.* make
angry; ~ се *ref. v.* get/be-
come/grow angry
раст *m.* stature, growth
раствор *m.* solution
**раствора, раствори, рас-
твори** *v.* dissolve
растеж *m.* growth, increase,
rising
растение *ntr.* plant
растовари, растоварува *v.*
unload, discharge
растојание *ntr.* distance
растрел *m.* shooting, execution
расход *m.* expense
расцвет *m.* s. **расцут**
расцут *m.* bloom, flourishing

рата f. payment, installment
ратифицира v. ratify
рафинерија f. refinery
рафт m. shelf
рационален adj. rational
реагира v. react
реален adj. real, genuine, material, concrete
реализира v. realize; ~ се refl. v. become true
реалистички adj. realistic
реалност f. reality
ревизија f. revision, inspection
револвер m. revolver
револуција f. revolution
регистар m. file, register
регулира v. regulate
ред m. order
редактира v. edit
реди v. arrange, put in order; ~ се refl. v. line up
редица f. row, line
редовен adj. regular, ordinary
редок adj. spare, rare
реже v. cut
режим m. regime
резервира v. reserve, book
резиме ntr. resume, summary
резолуција f. resolution
резултат m. result
река f. river
реклама f. advertisement
рекламација f. claim
ректор m. rector, president

религија f. religion
ремонт m. repair, remodeling
реноме ntr. reputation
рента f. rent
рентген m. X-ray (apparatus)
рентгенолог m. radiologist
репортажа f. report, reporting
репродуцира v. reproduce
република f. republic
репутација f. reputation
респект m. respect
ресторан m. restaurant
ретко adv. seldom, rarely
реферат m. paper, essay, presentation
референдум m. referendum
рефлекс m. reflex, reflection
реформа f. reform
реформација f. reformation
рецензира v. review, criticize
рецепта f. prescription, recipe
реч f. word, speech
речник m. dictionary
решава, реши v. decide, make up one's mind, solve
решителен adj. resolute, determined
риба f. fish
ризик m. risk, hazard, danger
ритуал m. ritual
рицар m. knight
роб m. slave, captive
ров m. trench, ditch, dike
рог m. horn

род *m.* family, origin, gender, sex, kin
роди *v.* bear, give birth; ~ се *refl. v.* be born
родител *m.* parent
роднина *f.* relative
родство *ntr.* relationship
роза *f.* rose
рој *m.* swarm

ролја *f.* role, part, acting
роман *m.* novel
роса *f.* dew
роси *v.* bedew, drizzle
руда *f.* ore
рудник *m.* mine
рус *adj.* blond
рутина *f.* routine
рбет *m.* back, spine

С

сабја *f.* saber
сабота *f.* Saturday
сади *v.* plant
саем *m.* fair, market
сака *v.* want, desire
саксија *f.* flowerpot, plant pot
сал *m.* raft
салама *f.* sausage, salami
салата *f.* salad
салдо *ntr.* balance
салон *m.* hall
салфетка *f.* napkin
сам *adj.* alone, single, by oneself
само *adv.* only
самодржавие *ntr.* autocracy
саможив *adj.* unsociable, reserved
самољубив *adj.* selfish
самоодбрана *f.* self-defense
самостоен *adj.* independent, autonomous

самотен *adj.* solitary, lonely
самоубие се, самоубива се *refl. v.* commit suicide
самоуверен *adj.* self-confident
самоуправа *f.* self-management
сандак *m.* chest, box
санкција *f.* sanction
сапун *m.* soap
сатана *m.* Satan
сателит *m.* satellite
свадба *f.* wedding
свари, сварува *v.* cook, boil
сведение *ntr.* information, report
сведок *m.* witness, eyewitness
свеж *adj.* fresh
свест *f.* consciousness
свет *m.* world
свети *v.* bless, sanctify; light, shine

светлина *f.* light

светец, светија *m.* saint, holy man

световен *adj.* world

свеќа *f.* candle

свештеник *m.* priest, minister

свидетел *m.* witness, eyewitness

свикне, свикнува *v.* get used to/accustomed

свиња *f.* pig, swine

свод *m.* arch, arcade

своеволен *adj.* self-willed, willful, arbitrary

своевремено *adv.* in time

свој *pron.* my, your etc.; own

својствен *adj.* characteristic, typical

свврдел *m.* drill, screw

сврзан *adj.* bound, tied

сврзе, сврзува *v.* bind, tie together, connect, join, fasten

свршува, сврши *v.* finish, complete, end

се *refl. pron.* me, you, him, her etc.

се *pron.* all, everything

себичен *adj.* selfish, egoistic

север *m.* north

сега *adv.* now

сегашен *adj.* present, current

седи *v.* sit

седло *ntr.* saddle

седеф *m.* mother-of-pearl

сее *v.* sow

седне, седнува *v.* sit down

сезона *f.* season

секаде *adv.* everywhere

секаков *adj.* any, various, of all kinds/sorts

секогаш *adv.* always

секој *pron.* every, each

секојдневен *adj.* daily, everyday

секретар *m.* secretary

секретно *adv.* secret

секс *m.* sex

секта *f.* cult, sect

секунда *f.* second

селанец *m.* (селанка *f.*) *m.* peasant, villager

село *ntr.* village

семе *ntr.* seed

семестар *m.* term, semester

сенат *m.* senate

сензација *f.* sensation

сено *ntr.* hay

сепак *adv.* however, still, yet, even though

септември *m.* September

сервира *v.* serve

сериозен *adj.* serious

сесија *f.* session

сестра *f.* sister, nurse

сети се *refl. v.* remember

сетне *adv.* afterwards, later

се уште *adv.* still

сив *adj.* gray (grey)

сигнал

сигнал *m.* signal
сигурен *adj.* sure, certain, positive, reliable, secure
сила *f.* strength, power, force
симбол *m.* symbol
симпатичен *adj.* nice, likeable
син 1. *m.* son; 2. *adj.* blue
сирак *m.* orphan
сирење *ntr.* cheese
систем *m.* system
ситуација *f.* situation
скака *v.* jump, hop
скакулец *m.* grasshopper
скала *f.* scale, stairs
скандал *m.* scandal
скапоцен *adj.* precious
скара *f.* grill
скелет *m.* skeleton
скија *f.* ski
скија се *refl. v.* ski
скине, скинува *v.* tear
скита *v.* wander, roam
скица *f.* sketch, draft
склад *m.* warehouse. storage
склучи, склучува *v.* conclude
сконцентрира *v.* concentrate
скоро *adv.* soon
скратеница *f.* abbreviation
скрива, скрие, скријува *v.* hide
скришен *adj.* secret, hidden
скромен *adj.* modest, simple
скулптура *f.* sculpture
скут *m.* lap

слаб *adj.* weak, thin
слава *f.* glory
славеј *m.* nightingale
слага *v.* put, lay, place, set
сладок *adj.* sweet
сладолед *m.* ice cream
слама *f.* straw
слатко *ntr.* jam
следен *adj.* next, coming, following
следи *v.* follow, watch, spy
слеп *adj.* blind, sightless
слива 1. *f.* plum; 2. *v.* fuse, combine, unite
слика *f.* photograph, picture, painting
слободен *adj.* free
сложен *adj.* complicated
слон *m.* elephant
слуга *f.* servant
служба *f.* service, employment, job, occupation
слух *m.* hearing
случаен *adj.* accidental
случај *m.* chance, case, occasion, opportunity
случајност *f.* chance, coincidence
случка *f.* event, occurrence, incident
случва се, случи се *refl. v.* happen
слуша *v.* listen, hear
смее се *refl. v.* laugh, mock

смел *adj.* courageous

смее *v.* dare

смени, сменува *v.* change, replace

смета *v.* calculate; think, consider

смешен *adj.* funny

смеша, смешува *v.* mix, mix up, confuse

смисла *f.* sense, meaning

смрди *v.* stink

смрт *m.* death

снаа *f.* daughter-in-law

снабди, снабдува *v.* supply, provide

снег *m.* snow

сношти *adv.* last night

со *prep.* with, by

собере, собира *v.* gather, collect

соблазни, соблазнува *v.* tempt, seduce

собрание *ntr.* assembly, meeting, conference

собуе, собува (се) *v.* pull off one's shoes

совест *m.* conscience

совет *m.* advice

советува *v.* advise

современ *adj.* contemporary

согласи се *refl. v.* agree

согради, соградува *v.* build, erect

сограѓанин *m.* fellow citizen

содејство *ntr.* collaboration, cooperation

содржи *v.* contain, hold

соединет *adj.* united

сожали, сожалува *v.* regret, be sorry

создава, создаде *v.* create, originate, found

сознава, сознае *v.* realize, know

сознание *ntr.* consciousness

созвездие *ntr.* constellation

соја *f.* soya, soybean

сојуз *m.* union, alliance, league, federation, confederation

сок *m.* juice

сол *m.* salt

солза *f.* tear

солиден *adj.* firm, stable

сомнева се *refl. v.* doubt, suspect

сон *m.* dream, sleep

сонда *f.* drill

сонце *m.* sun

соображение *ntr.* consideration, motive

сообразност *f.* accordance, compliance, conformity

соодветен *adj.* respective, corresponding

соопштение *ntr.* announcement, message, report

сопира, сопре *v.* stop, hold up

сопруг *m.* husband, spouse

сопственик *m.* owner, proprietor

сорта *f.* sort, kind

сосед *m.* neighbor

состав *m.* composition, structure

состои се *refl. v.* consist

соученик *m.* school friend/mate, classmate

социјален *adj.* social

социалист *пл* ядйсювсяш

сочувство *ntr.* compassion, condolence

спална *f.* bedroom

спаси, спасува *v.* save, rescue

спрема *v.* prepare, get ready

специален *adj.* special

спие *v.* sleep

списание *ntr.* magazine

список *m.* list, register

спогодба *f.* agreement

спокоен *adj.* calm, quiet

спомага *v.* contribute

спомен *m.* memory, remembrance, recollection

спор *m.* argument, dispute

според *prep.* according to

спорт *m.* sport(s)

способен *adj.* able, capable, skillful

справедливост *f.* justice

справка *f.* reference

спрема *prep.* according to

спроти *prep.* opposite, against, on the other side of

сразмерност *f.* proportion

срам *m.* shame

срами *v.* disgrace

срдечен *adj.* hearty, cordial, affectionate

сребро *ntr.* silver

сред *prep.* among

среда *f.* Wednesday

среден *adj.* middle

средоземен *adj.* Mediterranean

средство *ntr.* instrument, means

среќен *adj.* lucky, fortunate

срна *f.* deer, roe

срок *m.* term, deadline

срце *ntr.* heart

стабилен *adj.* stable

става, стави *v.* put, place, set

стадион *m.* stadium

стадиум *m.* stage, phase

стадо *ntr.* herd

стаја *f.* room, chamber

стакло *ntr.* glass

станица *f.* station, stop

становиште *ntr.* viewpoint

стане, станува *v.* stand up, get up, rise

стапало *ntr.* foot, step

стапка *f.* step

стапи, стапува *v.* step

стар *adj.* old, ancient

старец *m.* old man

старина *f.* antiquity

статиа *f.* article

статистика *f.* statistics
статуа *f.* statue
стварен *adj.* real, actual
степен *f.* degree, grade, extend
стерилен *adj.* sterile
стигне, стигнува *v.* arrive, reach, come
стил *m.* style, manner
стипендија *f.* scholarship, fellowship, grant
стих *m.* verse
сто *num.* hundred
стока *f.* goods, wares, merchandise
стол *m.* chair
столица *f.* capital
стомак *m.* stomach
стопи, стопува *v.* melt
страда *v.* suffer
стража *f.* guard
страна *f.* side
странец *m.* foreigner, alien
страница *f.* page
страст *f.* passion, lust
стратегија *f.* strategy
страшен *adj.* terrible, horrible
стрела *f.* arrow
стреми се *ref.* *v.* seek, aspire, strive, endeavor
строг *adj.* strict, severe
строеж *m.* structure, construction, texture
струка *f.* profession, occupation, branch

структура *f.* structure
струна *f.* string
стручен *adj.* skilled, professional
студен *adj.* cold
студент *m.* student
студија *f.* study
субјект *m.* subject
субјективен *adj.* subjective
сув *adj.* dry
суд *m.* court of law
судја *m.* judge
судбина *f.* fate, destiny, fortune
субоносен *adj.* fatal
суеверје *ntr.* superstition
суета *f.* vanity
сум *v.* be
сума *f.* sum, amount
справа, справи *v.* clean up, put in order
супа *f.* soup
суредба *f.* order
суров *adj.* raw, crude, harsh, brutal
сутурен *m.* basement
суши (се) *v.* dry (up)
сушт *adj.* same, very
сушност *f.* essence, substance
суштество *ntr.* creature, being
суштествува *v.* exist
сфаќа, сфати *v.* comprehend
сфера *f.* sphere
сцена *f.* scene
сценарист *m.* scriptwriter

та *conj.* and, even, so (that), well, then

таа *pron.* she

табла *f.* board

таблица *f.* table

табло *ntr.* headboard, board

таван *m.* ceiling, attic

тага *f.* sorrow, grief, mourn

таен *adj.* secret

таинствен *adj.* mysterious

така *adv.* so, thus, like this/that, in such a way

таков, таква, такво, такви *pron.* such

такса *f.* fee, tax, rate

тактика *f.* tactics, strategy

тактичен *adj.* tactful

таму *adv.* there

танец *m.* dance

танок (тенок) *adj.* thin, slim, slender

тап *adj.* stupid

тапа *f.* cork

тапан *m.* drum

татко (тате) *m.* father, daddy, dad, pop

твој, твоја, твое, твои *pron.* your

творба *f.* artwork, (literary) work

творец *m.* creator, artist, poet, writer, composer

твори *v.* create, work

тврд *adj.* hard, solid, firm

театар *m.* theater

тебе *pron.* you

тежи *v.* weigh

тежок *adj.* heavy, difficult

текст *m.* text

текстил *m.* textile

текушт *adj.* current

тел *m.* wire

теле *ntr.* calf

телевизија *f.* television

телевизор *m.* television set

телеграма *f.* telegram, cable

телесен *adj.* physical, bodily

телефон *m.* telephone

телефонира *v.* phone, ring up, call

тело *ntr.* body, corpse

тема *f.* topic, theme, subject

темен *adj.* dark

температура *f.* temperature

тенденција *f.* tendency, trend

тенџере *ntr.* pot, saucepan

теологија *f.* theology

теорија *f.* theory

терминологија *f.* terminology

термометар *m.* thermometer

терор *m.* terror

терорист *m.* terrorist

тесен *adj.* tight, narrow

тест *m.* test

тестамент *m.* testament, will

тетрадка *f.* notebook

техника *f.* technique
тече *v.* flow, stream
ти *pron.* you
тиган *m.* pan
тигар *m.* tiger
тиква *f.* pumpkin
тим *m.* team
тип *m.* type
тираж *m.* press run, circulation
тиранизира *v.* tyrannize
тире *ntr.* dash, hyphen
тих *m.* quiet, still
тишина *f.* silence
тоа *pron.* that
тоалет *m.* lavatory, restroom, watercloset
товар *m.* load, cargo, fright
тогај, тогаш *adv.* then
тој, таа, тоа, тие *pron.* he, she, it, they; this one
токму *adv.* just
толпа *f.* crowd, people
том *m.* (book) volume
топка *f.* ball, football
топли *v.* wram, warm up
топографија *f.* topography
торба *f.* beg, sack
торпедо *ntr.* torpedo
торта *f.* cake
точка *f.* period, full stop, point
точен *adj.* exact, precise
трагедија *f.* tragedy
традиција *f.* tradition
трае *v.* last

траен *adj.* lasting, stable
трактор *m.* tractor
трамвај *m.* tram
транспорт *m.* transport, transportation
трансформатор *m.* transformer, converter
траска *v.* slam
траур *m.* mourning
трафика *f.* traffic
треба *v.* need, is necessary
трева *f.* grass
тревога *f.* alarm, anxiety, alert
тревожи (се) *v.* worry
тренинг *m.* training
трепери *v.* tremble, shudder
тресе (се) *v.* shake; rock
три *num.* three
триаголен *adj.* triangular
трибуна *f.* tribune
трие *v.* rub
триесет *num.* thirty
трпелив *adj.* patient
трпение *ntr.* patience
труба *f.* pipe, trumpet
труд *m.* effort, labor, work
трудов *adj.* labor, working
труп *m.* (dead) body
туберкулоза *f.* tuberculosis
тужба *f.* complaint, claim
тука *adv.* here
тринаесет *num.* thirteen
триста *num.* three hundred
триумф *m.* triumph

трн *m.* thorn
трогне, трогнува *v.* touch, affect, move
тропа *v.* knock
тротоар *m.* sidewalk
тумор *m.* tumor
тунел *m.* tunnel

тура, тури *v.* put, place
туризам *m.* tourism
турист *m.* tourist
тутун *m.* tobacco
туш *m.* shower
тушира се *refl. v.* take a shower

Ќ

ќе *part.* will, shall
ќелеш *m.* scabby/mangy fellow
ќерка *f.* daughter
ќилим *m.* carpet, rug

ќор *adj.* blind in one eye
ќофте *ntr.* meatball
ќоше *ntr.* corner
ќумур *m.* charcoal

У

убав *adj.* beautiful, pretty, handsome
убеди, убедува *v.* convince
убива, убие *v.* kill, murder
убост *f.* beauty
уважение *ntr.* respect, esteem
увеличи, увеличува *v.* increase, extend
убост *f.* beauty
уверен *adj.* sure, certain
увери, уверува *v.* assure, convince
уво *ntr.* ear
увод *m.* introduction, preface
увоз *m.* import

угасне, угаснува *v.* extinguish, blow out
угоден *adj.* pleasant, convenient
удави, удавува (се) *v.* drown
удар *m.* hit, kick, stroke
удобен *adj.* comfortable, convenient
удостои, удостојува *v.* honor
ужас *m.* terror, horror
узреан *adj.* ripe, mature
ука *f.* custom, habit
указ *m.* decree, order
укине, укинува *v.* cancel, revoke
укори, укорува *v.* blame

украси, украсува v. decorate
улица f. street, avenue, alley
ум m. mind
умен adj. smart, intelligent, bright, clever
умее v. be able, can
уметник m. artist
умира, умре v. die, pass away
умножи, умножува v. multiply
уморен adj. tired, exhausted
умори (се), уморува (се) v. get tired
умствен adj. mental, intellectual
унер m. wonder, miracle
универзитет m. university
унижи, унижува v. humiliate
уништи, уништува v. destroy, exterminate
упати, упатува v. direct
уплаши, уплашува v. frighten, scare
употреба f. use, usage
управа f. management, administration, board
управник m. manager
ураган m. tornado
уран m. uranium
уредба f. order, organization
урок m. lesson
усет m. sense, feeling, perception
усје ntr. mouth of a river
услов m. condition, term

усложни, усложува v. complicate
услужи, услужува v. do a favor
усна f. lip
успева, успее v. succeed, prosper
успех m. success
успокои, успокојува v. calm, relieve
уста f. mouth
установи, установува v. establish, found
устен adj. oral, verbal
устројство ntr. organization, establishment, system, structure
утеха f. comfort, consolation
утеши, утешува v. comfort
утре adv. tomorrow
утро ntr. morning
ухо n. (pl. уши) ear
учебен adj. school-, educational
учебник m. textbook
ученик m. student, pupil
учен m. scholar
учесник m. participant
учествува v. participate
учи v. learn, study
училиште ntr. school
учител m. teacher
учтив adj. polite, kind
учуден adj. amazed, astonished, surprised
уште adv. still, yet, more

Ф

фабрика *f.* factory, mill
фабрикант *m.* manufacturer
фабрикат *m.* product
фабула *f.* fable, story, plot
фаза *f.* stage, period, phase
факел *m.* torch
факт *m.* fact
фактички *adj.* in fact, actually, as a matter of fact
фактура *f.* invoice, bill
факултет *m.* department, faculty
фалира *v.* go bankrupt
фалсификат *m.* fake, falsification, imitation
фамилија *f.* family
фанатизам *m.* fanaticism
фантазија *f.* fantasy, imagination
фар *m.* lighthouse
фараон *m.* pharaoh
фарма *f.* farm
фасада *f.* facade, frontside
фатален *adj.* fatal
фашизам *m.* fascism
февруари *m.* February
федерален *adj.* federal
федеративен *adj.* federal, federative

феномен *m.* phenomenon
ферментација *f.* fermentation
фигура *f.* figure
физика *f.* physics
физиологија *f.* physiology
филијала *f.* branch
филм *m.* film
филозофија *f.* philosophy
филологија *f.* philology
филтер *m.* filter
фин *adj.* fine, delicate
фирма *f.* firm, company
фоаје *ntr.* lobby, foyer
фокус *m.* focus
фонд *m.* fund
форма *f.* form, shape
формалност *f.* formality
формула *f.* formula
фотелја *f.* armchair
фотографија *f.* photography
фраза *f.* phrase, idiom
фризер *m.* hairdresser
фрла, фрли *v.* throw
фронт *m.* front
фудбал *m.* football, soccer
функција *f.* function
фураж *m.* forage, fodder, provender
фурнир *m.* veneer

X

хајка *f.* hunt, chase, persecution
хангар *m.* shed, hanger
хартија *f.* paper
хегемонија *f.* hegemony
хеј! *interj.* hello, hullo, hey
хеликоптер *m.* helicopter
хемија *f.* chemistry
херој *m.* hero
херцег *m.* duke
хигиена *f.* hygiene
хидрауличен *adj.* hydraulic
хиена *f.* hyena
химна *f.* hymn
хипноза *f.* hypnosis
хирург *m.* surgeon

хлор *m.* chlorine
хмел *m.* hop
ходник *m.* corridor, gallery
хол *m.* lounge, living room
хонорар *m.* fee
хор *m.* choir, chorus
хоризонт *m.* horizon
хотел *m.* hotel
храбар *adj.* brave, courageous
храм *m.* temple
храна *f.* food, forage
храни *v.* feed, nourish
христијанство *ntr.* Christianity
хроника *f.* chronicle
хумор *m.* humor, fun

Ц

цака *f.* trick
цар *m.* tsar
царство *ntr.* kingdom
цвет *m.* color
цвеќе *ntr.* flower
цел 1. *f.* purpose, aim; 2. *adj.*
whole, entire
целокупен *adj.* whole, complete
целосен *adj.* total, integral,
entire
целива *v.* kiss, smack
целулоза *f.* cellulose
цена *f.* price, cost

цени *v.* value
центар *m.* center
церемонија *f.* ceremony
цивил *m.* civilian
цивилизација *f.* civilization,
culture
циганин *m.* gypsy
цигара *f.* cigarette
цигла *f.* brick
циклус *m.* cycle
циничен *adj.* cynical
циркулација *f.* circulation
циркус *m.* circus
цистерна *f.* tank, cistern

цитат
чушка

цитат *m.* quotation
цифра *f.* figure, number, cipher
црвен *adj.* red
црвило *ntr.* lipstick
црвец *m.* worm

цреша (црешна) *f.* cherry
црква *f.* church
црн *adj.* black, dark
црта 1. *f.* line, stripe; 2. *v.* draw
цут *m.* blossom

Ч

чадор *m.* umbrella
чај *m.* tea
чакија *f.* penknife
чалма *f.* turban
чанта *f.* handbag, bag, purse
чар *m.* charm, fascination
час *m.* hour
часовник *m.* clock, watch
чаша *f.* glass, cup
чек *m.* check
чека *v.* wait
чекмеже *ntr.* drawer
чело *ntr.* violincello, cello
ченгел *m.* hook
черга *f.* rug, carpet
череп *m.* skull
чесен *adj.* honest, fair
чест *m.* honor
чести *v.* celebrate
често *adv.* often, frequently
четврток *m.* Thursday
четири *num.* four
четка *f.* brush
четник *m.* rebel, brigand
чешел *m.* comb

чешма *f.* tap, fountain
чиј, чија, чие, чии *pron.* whose
чин *m.* desk
чинија *f.* plate, dish
чиновник *m.* clerk
чист *adj.* clean, pure
чита *v.* read
чифт *m.* pair
чичо *m.* uncle
член *m.* member, fellow; article
човек *m.* man, person
човешки (човечки) *adj.* human, humane
човештво *ntr.* humanity, mankind, human race
чоколада *f.* chocolate
чорап *m.* sock, stock
чува *v.* keep, protect
чувство *ntr.* feeling, sense
чудо *ntr.* miracle, wonder
чудовиште *ntr.* monster
чуе *v.* hear, learn
чума *f.* plague
чучулига *f.* lark
чушка *f.* pepper

Џ

џагор *m.* noise, rumor
џаде *ntr.* road, street
џам *m.* glass, window
џамија *f.* mosque
џвака *v.* chew
џеб *m.* pocket

џез *m.* jazz
џентламен *m.* gentleman
џепане *ntr.* ammunition
џинс *m.* race, breed
џумбуш *m.* noisy celebration
џуџе *ntr.* dwarf

Ш

шаблон *m.* pattern, stencil, cliché
шадраван *m.* fountain
шал *m.* scarf
шамар *m.* slap
шампанско *ntr.* champagne
шампион *m.* champion
шанса *f.* chance, opportunity
шапка *f.* hat, cap
шарен *adj.* bright, colorful
шарлатан *m.* charlatan, crook
шах *m.* chess
шахта *f.* shaft
шега *f.* joke, fun
шема *f.* scheme
шепа *f.* handful
шепне, шепнува *v.* whisper
шест *num.* six
шеќер *m.* sugar
шеф *m.* chief, boss
шивач *m.* tailor
шие *v.* sew, stich
шија *f.* neck
шимпанзо *ntr.* chimpanzee

шина *f.* rail, splint, braces
широк *adj.* wide, broad
шифра *f.* code
шише *ntr.* bottle
шкаф *m.* cupboard
шкембе *ntr.* belly
школа *f.* school, school building
шлем *m.* helmet
шнур *m.* cord, cable
шовинист *m.* chauvinist
шокира *v.* shock
шофер *m.* driver, chauffeur
шпекулира *v.* speculate
шпион *m.* spy
шрифт *m.* style, font
штаб *m.* headquarters
штека *f.* ski pole
штембил *m.* stamp, seal
штета *f.* damage, loss
штит *m.* shield
што *conj. and prep.* what, which
шум *m.* noise, tumult
шумка *f.* ham
шушне, шушнува *v.* whisper

ENGLISH - MACEDONIAN
АНГЛИСКО - МАКЕДОНСКИ

a, an /ei, ∂n/ *art.* еден, некој

aback /∂bæk/ *adv.* назад

abandon /∂'bænd∂n/ *v.* напуща, остава,одрекува од

abandonment/∂bænd∂nm∂nt/ *n.* напуштање, одрекување,

abase /∂'beis/ *v.* понижува, снижува

abbey /'æbi/ *n.* опатија

abbot /'æb∂t/ *n.* опат

abbreviate /∂'bri:vieit/ *v.* скратува

abdicate /'æbdikeit/ *v.* абдицира

abdomen /'æbd∂men/ *n.* стомак

abduct /æbdʌkt/ *v.* отвлекува, отведува

abide /∂'baid/ *v.*˙ трпи; престојува

ability /∂'biliti/ *n.* способност

able /'eibl/ *adj.* способен, кадарен; be ~ (to) е во состојба, може

abolish /∂'boliʃ/ *v.* укинува, понищува

abound /∂'baund/ *v.* изобилува (in/with)

about /∂'baut/ *adv.* околу, наоколу; приближно

above /∂'bʌv/ 1. *adv.* горе; 2. *prep.* над; преку

abridge /∂'bridʒ/ *v.* скратува

abroad /∂'bro:d/ *adv.* во странство, надвор

abrupt /∂'brʌpt/ *adj.* ненадеен, отсечен

absence /'æbsns/ *n.* отсутност, недостиг

absent /'æbsnt/ *adj.* отсутен

absolve /∂b'zolv/ *v.* ослободува(од обвинение/одговорност)

absorb /∂b'zo:b/ *v.* апсорбира, впива, всмуква; опфаќа

abstain /∂b'stein/ *v.* се воздржува (from/од)

absurd/∂b's3:d/ *adj.* бесмислен, глуп, апсурден

abuse /∂'bju:s/ 1. *n.* злоупотреба, навреда

abyss /∂'bis/ *n.* бездна, понор

acacia /∂'keiʃ∂/ *n.* багрем, акација

academic /æk∂'demik/ *adj.* академски, научен

academy /∂'kæd∂mi/ *n.* академија

accept /∂k'sept/ *v.* прима, признава, се согласува

access /'ækses/ *n.* достап, пристап, приод

accident /'æksid∂nt/ *n.* случајност, несреќен случај, незгода

acclaim /əˈkleim/ v. поздрабу-
ва, одобрува

acclamation /ˌækləˈmeiSən/ n.
скандирање, акламирање

accommodate /əˈkamədeit/ v. се
приспособува, прима на
преноќување

accommodation n. /əˈkamədeiSn/
n. приспособување, удоб-
ност, засолниште

accomplish /əˈkʌmpliS/ v. извршува, исполнува, постигнува

accord /əˈkɔːd/ 1. v. се
согласува, се сложува се

accordance /əˈkɔːdəns/ n. согласност; (in ~ with) во
согласност с

accordingly /əˈkɔːdingli/ adv.
согласно, според тоа

account /əˈkaunt/ n. сметка

accumulation /əˈkjuːmjuleiSn/ n.
натрупување, акумулација

accumulator /əˈkjumjuleitor/ n.
акумулатор

accuracy /ˈækjərəsi/ n. точност,
правилност

accurate /ˈækjərət/ adj. точен,
правилен

accusative /əˈkjuzətiv/ n. акузатив

accuse /əˈkjuːz/ v. обвинува

accustom /əˈkʌstəm/ v. привикнува

ache /eik/ 1. n. бол; 2. v. боли

achieve /əˈtSiːv/ v. постигнува

achievement /əˈtSiːvmənt/ n. успех

acknowledge /əkˈnɔlidʒ/ v. признава, потврдува

acquaint /əkweint/ v. запознава

acquire /əkwaiə/ v. стекнува,
набавува, се здобива со

acquisition /ˌækwiˈziSn/ n. доби-
вање; набавка

acrobat /ˈækrəbæt/ n. акробат

across /əkrɔs/ 1. adv. напреку,
наспроти; 2. prep. преку,
спроти

act /ækt/ 1. n. постапка, дело,
закон, чин документ; 2. v.
прави, постапува, се однe-
сува, глуми, игра

active /ˈæktiv/ adj. активен,
вреден, работлив, енергичен

actual /ˈæktSjuəl/ adj. вистински, суштествен, сегашен

acute /əˈkjuːt/ adj. акутен

adapt /əˈdæpt/ v. приспособува, прилагодува

add /æd/ v. додава, собира

address /ˈædres/ 1. n. адреса;
/əˈdres/ 2. v. адресира, се
обраќа (до некого)

adjective /ˈædʒiktiv/ n. при-
давка

adjust /∂dʒʌst/ v. прилагодува, приспособува, наместува

administration /∂dmini'streiSn/ n. управа, влада, администрација

administrative /∂dministr∂tiv/ adj. управен, административен

admire /∂dmai∂/ v. се восхитува, цени

admission /∂dmiSn/ n. достап, пристап, примање

admit /∂d'mit/ v. допушта, признава

admonish /∂d'moniS/ v. опоменува, предупредува

adolescence /æ'dol∂sns/ n. младост

adopt /∂'dapt/ v. посвојува, посинува, прифаќа, усвојува

adorable /∂'do:r∂bl/ adj. почитуван, обожуван

adore /∂'do:/ v. обожава

adorn /∂do:n/ v. украсува

adult /'∂dʌlt/ 1. adj. n. возрастен, полнолетен човек

advance /∂d'va:ns/ 1. v. напредува; 2. n. напредок; 3. adv. in ~ однапред

advantage /∂d'va:ntid3/ 1. n. предимство, надмоќ

adventure /∂d'ventS∂/ 1. n. авантура, доживување

adverb /'ædv∂:b/ n. (грам.) прилог

advertise /ædv∂taiz/ v. рекламира, огласува

advise /∂d'vaiz/ v. советува, посоветува

advocate /ædv∂k∂t/ n. застапник, адвокат

affair /∂'fe∂ / n. работа,зделка, вопрос, афера

affect /∂'fekt/ v. влијае, воздејствува

affection /∂fekSn/ n. љубов, наклоност, приврзаност

affirm /∂f3:m/ v. тврди, потврдува

affix /∂'fiks/ v. придодава, прилепува

afford /∂'ford/ v. (can ~) си дозволува, (е во состојба), има средства за

afraid /∂'freid/ 1. adj. уплашен; 2. be ~ of се плаши од

after /a:ft∂/ 1. adv. потоа, после; 2. prep. после, по, зад

afternoon /'a:ft∂nu:n/ n. попладне

again /∂'gein/ adv. пак, повторно

against /∂'genst/ prep. против, наспроти

age /eid3/ n. ера, возраст

agenda /∂'d3end∂/ n. дневен

ред

agent /ˈeidʒnt/ *n.* агент

aggregate /ˈægrəgeit/ 1. *n.* агрегат

aggresive /əˈgresiv/ *adj.* агресивен

ago /əˈgəu/ *adv.* пред

agony /ˈægəni/ *n.* агонија

agree /əˈgri:/ *v.* се согласува, се договара

agriculture /ˈægriˈcʌltʃə/ *n.* земј оделство, аграрство

ahead /əˈhed/ *adv.* напред, начело, однапред

aim /eim/ *n.* цел, намера

air /eə/ *n.* воздух

airport /ˈeəpo:t/ *n.* аеродром

alarm /əˈla:m/ *n.* тревога

album /ˈælbəm/ *n.* албум

alcohol /ˈælkəhol/ *n.* алкохол

alert /əˈlərt/ *adj.* буден, подготвен

alien /ˈeiliən/ 1. *adj.* стран, странски; 2. *n.* стран државјанин, тугинец

alike /əˈlaik/ 1. *adj.* сличен; 2. *adv.* еднакво

alive /əˈlaiv/ *adj.* жив

all /o:l/ *adj.* цел(иот), сиот, секој

alley /ˈæli/ *n.* патека, сокак

alligator /ˈæligeitə/ *n.* алигатор

allow /əˈlou/ *v.* позволува

alliance /əˈlaiəns/ *n.* сојуз

ally /əˈlai/ *v.* соединува, здружува

almost /ˈo:lməust/ *adv.* за малку, речиси

alms /a:mz/ *n.* милостина

alone /əˈləun/ *adj.* /adv.* сам, единствен

along /əˈloʒ/ *adv.* понатака, со себе

aloud /əˈloud/ *adv.* гласно, на глас

alphabet /ˈælfəbet/ *n.* азбука

already /o:lˈredi/ *adv.* веќе

alright /o:lˈrait/ *adv.* добро

also /ˈo:lsəu/ *adv.* исто (така), како и, освен тоа

altar /ˈo:ltə/ *n.* олтар

alternative /o:lˈtə:nətiv/ 1. *n.* алтернатива, избор; 2. *adj.* алтернативен, друг

although /o:lˈðəu/ *conj.* иако, макар што

altitude /ˈæltitju:d/ *n.* висина

always /ˈo:lweiz/ *adv.* секогаш

amaze /əˈmeiz/ *v.* зачудува

ambition /æmˈbiʃn/ *n.* амбиција

ambulance /ˈæmbjuləns/ *n.* болничка кола

ammunition /æmjuˈniʃn/ *n.* муниција, оружје

among(st) /əˈmʌʒ(st)/ *prep.* меѓу, помеѓу

amount /ə'mount/ n. сума

amusement /ə'mju:zmənt/ n. забава

ancestor /'ænsəstə/ n. прадедо

anchor /ænkə/ n. котва

ancient /'einSnt/ adj. древен, прастар, старински

and /ænd/ conj. и, а, па

anew /ə'nju:/ adv. одново, пак

angel /'eind3l/ n. ангел

anger /'æħgə/ n. гнев

angle /æŋgl/ n. агол, гледиште

animal /'æniml/ n. животно

ankle /ænkl/ n. зглоб (на нога)

annex /ə'neks/ v. анексира, присвојува

anniversary /æni'v3rsəri/ n. годишница

announce /ə'nauns/ v. објавува, огласува, известува

anouncement n. објава

annoy /ə'noi/ v. досадува, нервира

annual /'ænjuəl/ adj. годишен

another /ə'nʌðə/ pron. друк, инаков, уште (еден/два)

answer /'ænsə/ n. одговор, решение

ant /ænt/ n. мрава, мравка

anticipate /æn'tisipeit/ v. очекува, претчуствува

antique /ænti:k/ adj. старински, антички

any /'eni/ pron. кој било, каков било; ~body /'enibody/ pron. некој, кој било; ~ how /'enihou/ adv. како било; ~thing /'eniθiŋ/ pron. нешто, што било; ~way /'eniwei/ adv. како било, сепак; ~where /'eniweð/ adv. негде, насекаде, каде било

apartment /ə'partmənt/ n. апартман

apologize /ə'polədʒaiz/ v. се извинува

apparent /ə'perənt/ adj. привиден, на изглед, јасен

apparently /ə'perəntli/ adv. се чини, изгледа

appeal /ə'pi:l/ n. жалба, тужба

appear /ə'piə/ v. се покажува, се појавува

applaud /ə'plo:d/ v. плеска, аплаудира

apple /æpl/ n. јаболка

apply /ə'plai/ v. се употребува, се става; дава молба

appoint /ə'point/ v. наредува, одредува, договара

appointment /ə'pointmənt/ n. состанок, служба

appreciate /ə'pri:Sieit/ v. цени, оценува, благодарен е за

approach /ə'prəutS/ 1. v. пристапува, приближува; 2. n. пристап, пристапување appropriate /∂'pr∂upri∂t/ adj. погоден

approve /∂pru:v/ v. одобрува, признава

approximately /∂'praksim∂tli/ adv. приближно, околу

apricot /'æpricat/ n. кајсија

arbitrate /'arbitreit/ v. пресудува

arch /artS/ n. свод

archaic /ar'keik/ adj. архаичен, древен

archipelago /arkipel∂g∂u/ n. архипелаг

architect /'arkitekt/ n. архитект

archives /'arkaivz/ n. архива, архивски материал

area /'eri∂/ n. област, сфера, крај

argent /'a:d3∂nt/ n. сребро

argue /'argju/ v. се расправа, се кара

argument /'argjument/ n. аргумент, причина, карање

arise /∂'raiz/ v. се појавува, се покажува

arithmetic /∂'riθm∂tik/ n. аритметика

ark /ark/ n. сандак, ковчег

arm /arm/ 1. n. рака, ракав; 2. v. (се вооружува)

army /'armi/ n. армија

around /∂'raund/ adv. околу, наоколу

arrange /∂'reind3/ v. аранжира, (се) договара, (се) средува

arrest /∂'rest/ v. задржува

arrive /∂'raiv/ v. пристига, стигнува, доаѓа

arrogant /'ær∂g∂nt/ adj. дрзок, арогантен

arrow /'ær∂u/ n. стрела, стрел-ка

art /art/ n. уметност, умешност; pl. хуманитарни науки

artery /'art∂ri/ n. артерија

article /'artikl/ n. артикал, член, точка, параграф, статија

articulate /ar'tikj∂leit/ v. изго-ворува

artillery /ar'tilri/ n. артилерија

artist /'artist/ n. уметник, ар-тист, глумец

as /æz/ adv. исто така, исто толку, како (на пример)

ash /æS/ n. јасен, пепел, посмртни останки

ashamed /∂'Seimd/ adj. по-срамен

aside /∂'said/ adv. на страна, отпат

ask /æsk/ v. прашува, моли, повикува, поканува

asleep /∂sli:p/ adj. заспан

aspect   **automatic**

aspect /'æspekt/ *n.* гледиште, аспект

assassin /∂'sesin/ *n.* (потплатен) убиец, атентатор

assault /∂'so:lt/ *n.* напад

assembly /∂'sembli/ *n.* собрание, собир, совет

assign /∂'sain/ *v.* определува, избира, припишува

assist /∂'sist/ *v.* (пот)помага

associate /∂'s∂uSieit/ *n.* здружува, поврзува

association /∂'s∂uSieiS∂n/ *n.* друштво, здружение, асоцијација

assume /∂'su:m/ *v.* претполага, смета, си мисли

assure /∂'Su∂/ *v.* уверува, убедува, осигурува

astonish /∂s'tonish/ *v.* изненадува, зачудува

astronaut /'æstr∂no:t/ *n.* астронаут

astronomy /∂stron∂mi/ *n.* астрономија

at /æt/ *prep.* на, во, до, по, при

athlete /'æθli:t/ *n.* атлетичар

atlas /'ætl∂s/ *n.* атлас

atmosphere /'ætm∂sfi∂/ *n.* атмосфера

attach /∂'tætS/ *v.* (се) додава, (се) прикопчува, (се) прилепува, (се) придава

attack /∂'tæk/ 1. *n.* напад, атак; 2. *v.* напаѓа, навалува

attempt /∂'tempt/ 1. *v.* се обидува (да стори); 2. *n.* обид, потфат

attendance /∂'tend∂ns/ *n.* присуство, посета, публика

attention /∂'tenSn/ *n.* внимание, почит

attest /∂'test/ *v.* потврдува, докажува

attitude /'ætitu:d/ *n.* однос, сто јалиште

attorney /∂'tз:ni/ *n.* адвокат

attract /∂'trækt/ *v.* привлекува

attribute /'ætribju:t/ *n.* својство, особина, атрибут

auction /'o:kSn/ *n.* лицитација

audience /'o:di∂ns/ *n.* публика, слушатели, аудиенција

aunt /'ænt/ *n.* тетка, вујна, стрина

authentic /o:θentik/ *adj.* автентичен

author /o:θ∂/ *n.* автор, писател, составувач

authority /∂θoriti/ *n.* авторитет

authorization /o:θ∂rizeiSn/ *n.* ополномоштување

autobiography /o:t∂baiagr∂fi/ *n.* автобиографија

automatic /o:t∂mætik/ *adj.* автоматски

automobile /o:tɔmɑbil/ *n.* аутомобил, ауто

autonomy /o:tonɔmi/ *n.* автономија, самостојност

autumn /o:tɔm/ *n.* есен

average /'ævrid3/ *n.* средна вредност, просек

aviation /eivieiSn/ *n.* авијација

avoid /ɔ'void/ *v.* одбегнува, избегнува

await /ɔ'weit/ *v.* чека, очекува

awake /ɔ'weik/ *adj.* буден

award /ɔ'word/ *n.* награда

aware /ɔ'weɑl/ *adj.* свесен (of за)

away /ɔ'wei/ *adv.* далеку, вон

awkward /o:'kwɑd/ *adj.* неснаодлив, незгоден, непри јатен

ax /æks/ *n.* секира

B

baby /'beibi/ *n.* бебе, малечко

back /'bæk/ *adv.* назад, одзади

bacon /beikɑn/ *n.* сланина

bad /bæd/ *adj.* лош, зол

badge /bæd3/ *n.* значка, грб, амблем

bag /bæg/ *n.* торба, чанта

baggage /'bægid3/ *n.* багаж

bake /beik/ *v.* пече

balance /'bælɔns/ *n.* биланс, остаток, салдо

balcony /'bælkɔni/ *n.* балкон

ball /bo:l/ *n.* топка; бал

ballast /'bælɔst/ *n.* баласт

ballet /bælei/ *n.* балет

balloon /bɔ'lu:n/ *n.* балон

banana /bɔ'nænd/ *n.* банана

band /bænd/ *n.* група, чета ,

забавен оркестар; лента

bandage /'bændid3/ *n.* завој

banish /'bæniS/ *v.* прогонува

bank /bænk/ *n.* брег, насип, банка

banner /'bænɑl/ *n.* бајрак, знаме, транспарент

baptize /bæp'taiz/ *v.* покрстува, крштева

barbecue /'barbikju/ *n.* ражен, шиш, забава на отворено

bare /beɑl/ *adj.* гол, бос

bargain /bargin/ *n.* спогодба

bark /bark/ *v.* лае, се дере

barn /barn/ *n.* плевна, амбар

barometer /bɔramitɑr/ *n.* барометар

barracks /'bærɑks/ *n.* барака, касарна

barricade /'bærikeid/ *n.*
барикада
barrier /'bæriд/ *n.* бариера,
запрека
base /beis/ *n.* основа, база, воj
ничка база
basis /'beisis/ *n.* основа
basket /'bæskit/ *n.* кош,
кошница
bastard /'bæstдd/ *n.* копиле
bath /bæθ/ *n.* бања, капење
bathe /beiд/ *v.* (се) капе, (се)
бања
battalion /bдtæliдn/ *n.* баталjон
battery /'bætry/ *n.* батерија,
акумулатор
battle /'bætl/ *n.* битка, боj
bay /bei/ *n.* залив; ловорово
дрво
be /bi/ *v.* е, се наоѓа, престоj
ува
beach /bi:tS/ *n.* плажа, брег
bear /beд/ 1. *n.* мечкам 2. *v.*
носи, трпи
beard /biдd/ *n.* брада
beast /bi:st/ *n.* звер, животно
beat /bi:t/ *n.* удир, такт, ритам
beauty /'bku:ti/ *n.* убавина,
убавица
beautiful *adj.* убав, личен
because /bi'ko:z/ *conj.* зашто,
затоа што
bed /bed/ *n.* кревет, легло

beef /bi:f/ *n.* говедско месо
beer /biд/ *n.* пиво, бира
before /be'for/ *adv.* порано, ве
ќе
beg /beg/ *v.* проси, (се) моли
begin /bi'gin/ *v.* почнува,
започнува
behalf /bi'hæf/ *n.* on ~ of во
името на некого
behave /bi'heiv/ *v.* се држи, се
однесува
behind /bi'haind/ *adv.* одзади,
назад
belief /bi'li:f/ *n.* вера, верба
bell /bel/ *n.* звонче, камбана
belly /'beli/ *n.* стомак
belong /bi'loђ/ *v.* припаѓа,
спаѓа
beloved /bi'lʌvd/ *adj.* омилен
below /bi'lдu/ *adv.* подолу, по
ниско
belt /belt/ *n.* колан
bench /bentS/ *n.* маса за
работа
bend /bend/ *v.* (се) свиткува,
(се) навалува
beneath /bi'ni:θ/ *prep.* под,
подолу од
benefit /'benefit/ *n.* корист,
предност
benzene /'benzi:n/ *n.* бензин
berry /'beri/ *n.* зрнест плод
beside /bi'said/ *prep.* покраj,
краj

bet /bet/ 1. *v.* се обложува; 2. *n.* облог

betray /bi'trei/ *v.* предава, изневерува

between /bi'twi:n/ *prep.* меѓу, помеѓу

beverage /'bevrid3/ *n.* пијалак

beware /bi'weð/ *v.* внимава, варди

beyond /bi'jand/ *prep.* зад, преку, вон, од другата страна

Bible /'baibl/ *n.* библија

bibliography /bibli'ogrðfi/ *n.* библиографија

bicycle /baisikl/ *n.* велосипед

big /big/ *adj.* голем

bile /bail/ *n.* жолчка, жолч

bilingual /bailingwðl/ *adj.* двој азичен

bill /bil/ *n.* сметка

bind /baind/ *v.* врзува, обврзува

biography /bai'ogrðfi/ *n.* биографија

birch /bз:rtS/ *n.* бреза

bird /bз:d/ *n.* птица

bison /'baisn/ *n.* бизон

bit /bit/ *n.* парченце, трошка

bitch /bitS/ *n.* кучка, уличарка, курва

bite /bait/ *v.* каса, апе, гризе

bitter /'bitð/ *adj.* горчлив, огорчен, тежак

black /blæk/ *adj.* црн, тмурен, темен

blame /bleim/ *v.* обвинува, осудува

blank /blæŋk/ *adj.* празен, чист

blanket /blæŋkit/ *n.* прекривка, покривка

blast /blæst/ *n.* удар, јак налет (на ветар), експлозив

bleach /bli:tS/ *v.* 1. *n.* белило; 2. *v.* белее

blend /blend/ *v.* (се) меша, (се) спојува

bless /bles/ *v.* благословува

blind /blaind/ *adj.* слеп, непромислен

blister /'blistð/ *n.* плуска, меур

blizzard /'bliðd/ *n.* снежна ве-јавица

block /blok/ *n.* блок

blockade /blo'keid/ *n.* блокада

blond /blond/ *adj.* рус, русокос

blood /blʌd/ *n.* крв

bloom /blu:m/ *n.* цвет

blossom /'blasm/ *n.* цут, цвет

blouse /blaus/ *n.* блуза

blow /blðu/ *v.* дува, вее, фучи

blue /blu:/ *adj.* син, модар

blurb /blз:b/ *n.* реклама

blush /blʌS/ *v.* се заруменува, се вцрвенува

booth /bu:θ/ *n.* кабина, сергија

border /'bordðr/ *n.* граница,

меѓа
borough /bʌrɒu/ n. општина
borrow /'barɒu/ v. заема на заем
boss /bɒs/ n. управител, шеф
both /bɒuθ/ pron. обата, двата, двајцата
bother /bɒðɒr/ v. додева, досадува
bottle /bɒtl/ n. шише
bottom /bɒtɒm/ n. дно, долен дел
boundary /baundɒri/ n. граница, меѓа
bow /bau/ v. се поклонува
bowl /bɒul/ n. длабока чинија; кегла
box /bɒks/ n. кутија, сандак
boy /bɒi/ n. момче
boycott /bɒikɒt/ v. бојкотира
brain /brein/ n. мозок, ум
brake /breik/ n. сопирачка (во автомобил) board /bɒrd/ n. плоча, табла, комитет, совет
boat /bɒut/ n. кајче, брод
body /'badi/ n. тело, труп
boil /bɒil/ v. (се) вари, (се) врие
bold /bɒuld/ adj. грабар, смел
bomb /bam/ n. бомба
bond /band/ n. обврска, врска
bonus /'bɒunɒs/ n. премија, награда
book /buk/ n. книга, либрето
boot /bu:t/ n. чизма

branch /bræntʃ/ n. гранка, ветка; филијала
brand /brænd/ n. вид, сорта, факел
brave /breiv/ adj. храбар
bread /bred/ n. леб
break /breik/ v. крши, скршува, кине, скинува, разбива
breakfast /brekfɒst/ n. поручек, појадок
breast /brest/ n. града, гради
breath /breθ/ n. здив, дишење
breed /bri:d/ v. (се) размножува, одгледува
brew /bru:/ v. вари, ферментира
bribe /braib/ n. поткуп
brick /brik/ n. тула, цигла
bride /braid/ n. невеста
bridge /bridʒ/ n. мост
brief /bri:f/ adj. кус, краткотраен
bright /brait/ adj. светол, сјаен, паметен
bring /briŋ/ v. донесува, дава, доведува
broad /brɔ:d/ adj. широк, простран
broadcast /brɔ:dcæst/ v. емитува, распрскува
broker /brɒukɒr/ n. посредник
broom /bru:m/ n. метла
brother /brʌðɒr/ n. брат

brow /brau/ *n.* веѓа
brown /braun/ *adj.* кафех
bruise /bru:z/ *n.* синица, модрица
brush / brʌS/ *n.* четка
brutal /'bru:tl/ *adj.* брутален, суров, нечовечен
budget /bʌdʒit/ *n.* буџет
buffalo /'bʌfǝlǝu/ *n.* бивол, бизон
buffet /bǝ'fei/ *n.* бифе, шведска маса, шанк
bug /bʌg/ *n.* дрвеница, стеница
build /bild/ *v.* гради, изградува
bull /bul/ *n.* бик, говедо
bullet /'bulit/ *n.* куршум
bulletin /'bulǝtin/ *n.* билтен
bump /bʌmp/ *v.* (се) чукнува, (се) удира
bunch /bʌntS/ *n.* китка, снопче, множество
bunker /'bʌnkǝ/ *n.* бункер
bunny /'bʌni/ *n.* зајаче
burden /'bɜ:dn/ *n.* бреме, товар
burglar /'bɜ:glǝ/ *n.* разбивач
burn /bɜ:n/ *v.* гори, изгорува
bury /'beri/ *v.* погребува, закопува
bus /bʌs/ *n.* автобус
bush /buS/ *n.* честак, буш
business /'biznis/ *n.* зделка, работа, занает
busy /'bizi/ *adj.* вреден, зафатен
but /bʌt/ 1. *adv.* само; 2. *prep.* освен
butter /bʌtǝ/ *n.* масло
button /bʌtn/ *n.* петлица, копче
buy /bai/ *v.* купува
by /bai/ 1. *adv.* блиску; 2. *prep.* бриску до, до, покрај, кон, со, накај, откај, по

C

cab /kæb/ *n.* такси
cabbage /'kæbidʒ/ *n.* зелка
cabin /'kæbin/ *n.* колиба, бродска кабина
cafeteria /kæfitiriǝ/ *n.* ресторан за самообслужване
cage /'keidʒ/ *n.* кафез
cake /keik/ *n.* торта
calculate /'kælkjǝleit/ *v.* смета, калкулира, претроставува
calendar /kælindǝ/ *n.* календар
calf /ka:f/ *n.* теле
caliber /kælibǝ/ *n.* калибар
call /ko:l/ *v.* вика, извикува, телефонира, нарекува, свикува

calm /kalm/ *adj.* мирен, спокоен, тих

calorie /'kæl∂ri/ *n.* калорија

cam /kæm/ *n.* гребен

camel /'kæml/ *n.* камила

camera /'kæmra/ *n.* камера, фотографски апарат

camp /kæmp/ *n.* камп, табор

campaign /kæm'pein/ *n.* акција, операција, политическа/општествена кампања

campus /'kæmp∂s/ *n.* универзитет/колец(со околните згради)

can /kæn/ 1. *v.* може, умее; 2. *n.* конзерва

canal /k∂'næl/ *n.* канал, прокоп

cancel /'kænsl/ *v.* откажува, сторнира, анулира

cancer /'kæns∂/ *n.* рак, карцином

candidate /'kændideit/ *n.* кандидат

candle /'kændl/ *n.* свеќа

candy /'kændi/ *n.* бонбонче

canoe /k∂nu:/ *n.* кану

canyon /'kænj∂n/ *n.* клисура, кањон

cap /kæp/ *n.* капа, качкет, капак

capable /'keip∂bl/ *adj.* способен, надарен, спремен

capacity /k∂'pæsiti/ *n.* содржина, носивост; состојба

capital /'kæpitl/ 1. *adj.* главен, основен; 2. *n.* главен град, престолнина; капитал; капител

capsule /'kæpsl/ *n.* капсула, чаура

captain /'kæptin/ *n.* капетан

captive /'kæptiv/ *adj.* фютен, заробен

car /car/ *n.* автомобил, вагон

carbon /'karb∂n/ *n.* јагленород

card /kard/ *n.* визит карта, поштенска карта, честитка, карта (за играње)

care /ke∂/ *n.* грижа, внимателност

career /k∂'ri∂/ *n.* кариера, животен пат, професија

caress /k∂'res/ *v.* гали, милува

cargo /ka:g∂u/ *n.* товар

carnation /kar'neiSn/ *n.* каранфил

carol /'kær∂l/ *n.* божиќна/коледарска песна

carpenter /'karpint∂/ *n.* дрводелец

carpet /'karpit/ *n.* килим

carriage /'kærid3/ *n.* кола, вагон, кочија

carrot /'kær∂t/ *n.* морков

carry /'kæri/ *n.* носи, донесува, вози, држи, потпира

cartoon /kar'tu:n/ *n.* карикатура

case /keis/ *n.* случај, кутија

cash /'kæʃ/ *n.* пари

casserole /'kæsərðul/ *n.* тава

cassette /kð'set/ *n.* касета

castle /'kæsl/ *n.* тврдина, дворец

casual /'kæʒuðl/ *adj.* случаен, повремен

cat /'kæt/ *n.* мачка

catalog/catalogue /'kætðlog/ *n.* каталог

catastrophe /kðtæstrðfi/ *n.* катастрофа

catch /kætʃ/ *v.* фаќа, зграпчува

category /kætigri/ *n.* категорија

cathedral /kð'θi:drðl/ *n.* катедрала

cattle /'kætl/ *n.* добиток

cause /ko:z/ *n.* причина, повод

caution /'ko:ʃn/ *n.* внимание

cave /keiv/ *n.* пештера

cease /'si:s/ *v.* престанува, прекинува

ceiling /'si:liŋ/ *n.* таван

celebrate /'selibreit/ *v.* празнува, прославува, слави

cell /sel/ *n.* ќелија, клетка

cemetery /'semiteri/ *n.* гробишта

center /'sentð/ *n.* центар, средина

century /'sentʃðri/ *n.* век, столетие

ceremony /'serimðuni/ *n.* церемонија

certain /'s3:tn/ *adj.* сигурен

certify /'s3:tifai/ *v.* сведочи, издава свидетелство

chain /tʃein/ *n.* верига

chair /tʃeð/ *n.* стол

chalk /tʃo:k/ *n.* креда

challenge /'tʃælind3/ *n.* предизвик

champion /tʃæmpiðn/ *n.* победник, шампион

chance /tʃæns/ *n.* случај, шанса, изглед(и)

change /tʃeind3/ *v.* (се) менува, (се) изменува

channel /'tʃænl/ *n.* канал

chaos /'keias/ *n.* хаос

chapter /'tʃæptð/ *n.* глава, период

character /'kæriktð/ *n.* карактер

charge /tʃard3/ *v.* задолжува, става на сметка

charity /'tʃæriti/ *n.* милосрдие, добротворност

chart /tʃart/ *n.* мапа, графикон

chase /tʃeis/ *v.* гони, тера

chat /tʃæt/ *n.* разговор, ардорење

cheap /tʃi:p/ *adj.* ефтин, низок,

банален
cheat /tSi:t/ *v.* лаже, мами
check / tSek/ 1. *v.* прегледува, контролира; 2. *n.* чек
cheer /tSi∂/ *n.* радост, веселба
cheese /tSi:z/ *n.* сирење
chemistry /'kemistri/ *n.* хемија
cherish /eriS/ *v.* почитува, одгледува
cherry /tSeri/ *n.* черешна
chess /'tSes/ *n.* шах (игра)
chest /'tSest/ *n.* гради, граден кош
chew /tSu:/ *v.* џвака, прежива
chicken /'tSikin/ *n.* пиле
chief /'tSi:f/ *n.* водач, лидер, шеф
child /'tSaild/ (*pl.* children) /'tSildr∂n/ *n.* дете
chimney /'tSimni/ *n.* оџак
chin /'tSin/ *n.* брада
china /'tSain∂/ *n.* порцелан
chocolate /'tSaklit/ *n.* чоколадо
choke /'tS∂uk/ *v.* (се) гуши, (се) дави
choose /'tSu:z/ *v.* одбира, избира, се определува
Christian /'kristS∂n/ *adj.* христијанин
Christmas /'krism∂s/ *n.* Божиќ, Рождество Христово
chronology /kr∂'nal∂d3i/ *n.* хронологија
church /'tS3:tS/ *n.* црква

cigar /si'gar/ *n.* пура
circle /'s3:kl/ *n.* круг, кружна линија
circumstance /'s3:k∂st∂ns/ *n.* околност, факт, случај
circus /'s3:k∂s/ *n.* циркус
citizen /'sitizn/ *n.* граѓанин, жител, државјанин
city /'siti/ *n.* град
civil /'sivl/ *adj.* цивилен, државен
civilization /civlazeiSn/ *n.* цивилизација, култура
claim /kleim/ 1. *v.* присвојува; 2. *n.* барање, рекламација
clan /klæn/ *n.* род, племе, клан
clasp /klæsp/ 1. *n.* прегратка; 2. *v.* прегрнува
class /klæs/ *n.* класа, вид, сорта, клас
clause /klo:z/ *n.* клаузула, точка
claw /klo:/ *n.* шепа, челуст
clay /klei/ *n.* глина
clean /kli:n/ *adj.* чист, уреден
clear /kli∂/ *adj.* чист, светол, ведар
clerk /kl3rk/ *n.* службеник, писар
clever /'klev∂/ *adj.* умен, итар, снаодлив
client /'klai∂nt/ *n.* клиент
cliff /klif/ *n.* гребен, карпа
climb /klaim/ *v.* (се) изкачува,

(се) качува

clock /klak/ *n.* часовник

close /klƏus/ 1. *adj.* близок, интимен, затворен; 2. *v.* затворе, завршува, ликвидира

cloth /kloθ/ *n.* материјал, ткаенина

clothes /klƏuz/ *n. pl.* облека

cloud /klaud/ *n.* облак

clown /klaun/ *n.* кловн

club /klʌb/ *n.* клуб, друштво

coach /kƏutS/ *n.* тренер

coal /kƏul/ *n.* јаглен, камен јаглен

coast /kƏus/ *n.* брег, крајбрежје

coat /kƏut/ *n.* палто, обвивка, слој

cockroach /'kakrƏutS/ *n.* лебарка

cocoa /'kƏukƏu/ *n.* какао

code /kƏud/ *n.* код, шифра

coffee /kofi/ *n.* кафе

coffin /kofin/ *n.* ковчег

coin /koin/ *n.* монета, пара

cold /kƏuld/ *adj.* студен, смрзнат, нељубезен

collar /'kalƏ/ *n.* јака, панделка

colleague /'kali:g/ *n.* колега

collect /kƏlekt/ *v.* собира, прибира, наплатува

college /'kalid3/ *n.* колец,, висока школа

collide /kƏ'laid/ *v.* се судрува

colony /kalƏni/ *n.* колонија

color /'kʌlƏ/ *n.* боја, тон, колорит

column /kalƏm/ *n.* столб, колона

comb /kƏum/ *n.* гребен

combine /kƏm'bain/ *v.* комбинира

come /kʌm/ *v.* доаѓа, стигнува, се доближува

comfort /kʌmfƏrt/ *n.* удобност, комфор

comma /'kamƏ/ *n.* запирка

command /kƏmænd/ *v.* заповеда, наредува

comment /kamƏnt/ *n.* забелешка, коментар

commerce /'kamƏrs/ *n.* трговија

commit /kƏ'mit/ *v.* обврзува, извршува

committee /kƏmitit/ *n.* комитет, комисија

common /'kaƏn/ *adj.* општ, обичен, прост

communicate /kƏ'mjunikeit/ *v.* соопштува

communism /kamjƏnism/ *n.* комунизам

community /kƏmjuniti/ *n.* општина, заедништво

company /'kʌmpƏni/ *n.* компанија, друштво, гости, театарска група

compare /kɔm'peɘ/ *v.* (ce) споредува, (ce) изедначува

compartment /kɔm'partmɘnt/ *n.* оддел, купе

compassion /kɔmpeSn/ *n.* сочуство, сожалување

compatible /kɔm'pætɘbl/ *adj.* соодветен, дозволен

compensate /kompɔnseit/ *v.* (ce) обештетува, (ce) компензира

compete /kɔm'pi:t/ *v.* се натпреварува, се конкурира

competent /'kompitɔnt/ *adj.* компетентен

complain /kɔm'plein/ *v.* се жали, негодува

complete /kɔm'pli:t/ 1. *v.* довршува, дополнува; 2. *adj.* завршен, комплетен

complicate /'kamplikeit/ *v.* усложнува, компликува

compose /kɔmpɔuz/ *v.* составува, твори, сочинува, компонира

comprehend /kampri'hend/ *v.* разбира, сфаќа

compromise /'kamprɔmaiz/ *n.* компромис

comrade /kamræd/ *n.* другар

concentrate /'kansɔntreit/ *v.* се концентрира

concept /'kansept/ *n.* поим, замисла

concern /kɔns3:n/ *n.* грижа, значење, концерн

concert /kansɔrt/ *n.* концерт

conclude /kɔn'klu:d/ *v.* одлучува, (ce) завршува

concrete /katȷ'kri:t/ 1. *adj.* конкретен; 2. *n.* бетон

condense /kɔn'dens/ *v.* (ce) кондензира

condition /kɔndiSn/ *n.* услов, положба, состојба

conduct/condɔkt/ *v.* води, диригира, спроведува

confederation /kɔfedɔreiSɔn/ *f.* конфедерација

confess /kɔn'fes/ *v.* признава, исповеда

confide /kɔn'faid/ *v.* (ce) доверува (in на)

confirm /kɔn'f3:m/ *v.* потврдува

conflict /kanflict/ *n.* конфликт

conform /kɔnform/ *v.* се приспособува

confuse /kɔn'fȷu:z/ *v.* збркува, збунува

congratulate /kɔngrætSɔleit/ *v.* честита

congress /kangris/ *n.* конгрес

connect /kɔnekt/ *v.* поврзува

conquer /kankɔ/ *v.* победува,

покорува, совладува
conscience /'kanSns/ *n.* совест,
свест
consequent /kansikw∂nt/ *adj.*
следен, како последица
consider /k∂nsid∂/ *v.* проценува, смета, размислува,
разгледува, зема во пред-
вид
consist /k∂nsist/ *v.* се содржи,
се состои
consolidate /k∂nsalideit/ *v.* (се)
обединува, консолидира
conspiracy /k∂nspir∂si/ *n.* завера, конспирација
constitution /konsti'tju:Sn/ *n.* конституција
constrain /k∂nstrein/ *v.* ограничува, спречува
construct /k∂nstrʌkt/ *v.* кон-
струира, гради, проектира
consult /k∂nsʌlt/ *v.* обраќа до,
консултира
consume /k∂nsu:m/ *v.* консу-
мира, уништува
contact /'kantækt/ *n.* допир,
врска, контакт
contain *v.* /k∂ntein/ *v.* содржи,
зафаќа
contest /kantest/ *n.* натпревар
context /kantekst/ *n.* контекст
continent /'kantin∂nt/ *n.* конти-
нент

continue /k∂ntinju:/ *v.* продолжува
contract /kantrækt/ *n.* договор,
спогодба
contrary /kantreri/ *adj.* проти-
вречен; on the ~ напротив
contribute /k∂ntribju:t/ *v.* придонесува
control /k∂ntr∂ul/ *n.* контрола,
надзор
convenient /k∂nvi:ni∂nt/ *adj.*
практичен, удобен
conversation /kan'v∂rseiSn/ *n.*
разговор
convict /k∂nvikt/ 1. *v.* прогласува виновен; 2. *n.* осу-деник,
затвореник
convince /k∂nvins/ *v.* уверува,
убедува
cook /kuk/ *v.* (се) готви, (се)
вари
cool /ku:l/ *adj.* студен, рамнодушен, про-мислен, дрзок
cooperate /k∂uap∂reit/ *v.* соработува
coordinate /k∂uordinit/ *v.* координира
copy /kopi/ *n.* копија, препис
cork /kork/ *n.* тапа, затворач
corn /korn/ *n.* зрно, пченка
corner /korn∂r/ *n.* акол, ќоше
corporate /'korp∂rit/ *adj.* кор-
порациски

correct /kɔ̂rekt/ adj. исправен, коректен, без грешка

correspond /karispond/ v. се совпаѓа

corrode /kɔ̂rʊud/ v. кородира

corrupt /kɔ̂rʌpt/ adj. поткупен, подмитен

cosmos /kazmɔ̂s/ n. вселена, космос

cost /kost/ v. чини, резултира

costume /kostju:m/ n. костум, носија

cotton /'katn/ n. памук

couch /kautS/ n. кауч, софа

cough /kaf/ v. кашла

council /kaunsθl/ n. совет, собрание, концил

count /kaunt/ v. брои, смета, важи, се потпира

country /'kʌntri/ n. земја, татковина, околина, село

couple /'kʌpl/ n. пар, два, неколку

courage /'kʌrid3/ n. смелост, храброст

course /kors/ n. курс, насока, развој

court /kort/ n. двор, кралски двор, суд

cousin /'kʌzn/ n. братучед, братучедка

cover /'kʌvθl/ v. покрива, крие, заштитува

cow /kau/ n. крава

crab /kræb/ n. морски рак

crack /kræk/ v. напукнува, (се) расцепува, открива, дознава

cramp n. /kræmp/ n. грч

crane /krein/ n. жерав

crash /kræS/ n. тресок, судар, пад

crawl /kro:l/ v. лази, ползе

crazy /'kreizi/ adj. залуден, занесен

cream /kri:m/ n. шлаг, кајмак

create /kri'eit/ v. создава, креира, твори

creature /'kri:tSθl/ n. суштество

credit /'kredit/ n. кредит, доверба

crew /'kru:/ n. персонал, екипаж, посада

crime /kraim/ n. злосторство, злочин

crisis /kraisis/ n. криза

criticize /'kritisaiz/ v. критикува

crocodile /'krakθdail/ n. крокодил

crop /krap/ n. жетва, принос

cross /kros/ 1. n. крст, страдание; 2. v. прекрстува, прецртува, спречува (планови), преминува преку, попречно лежи, се разминува

D

dad /dæd/ *n.* тате

dagger /'dæg∂/ *n.* кама

dairy /'de∂ri/ *n.* млекара, мле-
карство

dam /dæm/ *n.* насип, брана

damage /'dæmid3/ *n.* штета

damn /dæm/ *v.* проколнува,
осудува

dance /da:ns/ *n.* тан(е)ц, игра

danger /'deing3∂/ *n.* опасност

dare /de∂/ *v.* смее, се
осмелува

dark /dark/ *adj.* темен, мрачен

date /deit/ *n.* дата, рандеву

daughter /'do:t∂/ *n.* ќе,uд

dawn /do:n/ *n.* зора, мугри

day /dei/ *n.* ден

daily /deili/ 1. *adj.* дневен; 2.
adv. (секој)дневном 3. *n.*
дневник (весник)

deaf /def/ *adj.* глув

deal /di:l/ *v.* тргува, се
справува, соработува, дели

dear /di∂/ *adj.* мил, драг

debate /di'beit/ *v.* дискутира,
(се) расправа

debit /'debit/ *n.* долг, задолженост

decade /de'keid/ *n.* десетлетие

deceased /di'si:s/ *adj.* покоен

deceive /di'si:v/ *v.* мами, лаже

decide /di'said/ *v.* решава

deck /dek/ *n.* палуба

declare /di'kle∂/ *v.* објавува,
декларира

decrease /di'kri:s/ *v.* (се) снижува, (се) намалува

decree /di'kri:/ *n.* указ, декрет,
наредба

dedicate /'dedikeit/ *v.* посветува

deep /di:p/ *adj.* длабок

defect /di'fect/ *n.* недостаток,
дефект, грешка

defend /di'fend/ *v.* (се) брани,
заштитува

define /di'fain/ *v.* дефинира,
формулира, определува

defrost /di:'frost/ *v.* (се) одмрз-
нува

degree /digri:/ *n.* степен, науч-
чен степен, титула

delay /di'lei/ *v.* одолжува, одложува, касни

delegate /'deligit/ *n.* пратеник,
делегат

delete /dili:t/ *v.* испушта

deliberate /di'lib∂rit/ *adj.*
намерен, промислен

delicious /di'liS∂s/ *adj.* вкусен

delicate /delikit/ *adj.* фин, нежен, слабикав

delight /di'lait/ *n.* задоволство

deliver /di'liv∂/ *v.* доставува

demand /di:mænd/ *n.* барање,
потреба

democracy /di'mokrəsi/ *n.* демократија

demolish /di'moliS/ *v.* уништува, растура, демолира

demonstrate /'demənstreit/ *v.* покажува, демонстрира

denote /di'nəut/ *v.* означува

denounce /di'nəuns/ *v.* разобличува

deny /di'nay/ *v.* одрекува, негира

depart /di'part/ *v.* заминува, напушта

department /di'partmənt/ *n.* оддел, ресор, министерство

depend /di'pend/ *v.* зависи

deport /di'port/ *v.* депортира

deposit /dipazit/ *v.* вложува

depression /di'preSn/ *n.* притисок, потиштеност, стагнација, криза

describe /di'skraib/ *v.* опишува

desert /'dezət/ 1. *n.* пустина; 2. /di'zз:t/ *v.* дезертира

deserve /di'zз:v/ *v.* заслужава

design /di'zain/ *n.* нацрт, скица, план, модел, конструкција

desire /di'zaiə/ 1. *v.* пожелува, посакува; 2. *n.* желба, копнеж

desk /desk/ *n.* работна маса, шалтер

desperate /'despərit/ *adj.* очаен, безнадежен

despise /di'spaiz/ *v.* презира

despite /di'spait/ *prep.* покрај тоа

dessert /di'zз:t/ *n.* десерт, сладко

destroy /di'stroi/ *v.* уништува, руши, разурнува

detach /di'tætS/ *v.* одделува

detail /di'teil/ *n.* детаљ, поединост

detergent /di'tз:dʒənt/ *n.* детергент, прашок за перење

determine /di'tз:min/ *v.* определува, утврдува

detour /'di:tuə/ *n.* (за)обиколување

devastate /'devəsteit/ *v.* опустошува, разурнува

develop /di'veləp/ *v.* (се) развива

devil /'devl/ *n.* ѓавол

devote /di'vəut/ *v.* посветува, оддава

dew /du:/ *n.* роса

diagnose /'daiəgnəuz/ *v.* дијагностицира

diagonal /dai'ægənl/ *n.* дијагонала

dial /'daiəl/ *v.* (се) бира, врти (број на телефон)

dialect /'daiəlekt/ *n.* наречје, говор

dialogue /daiəlog/ *n.* дијалог, разговор

diamond /ˈdaiɱɒnd/ *n.* дијамант; брилијант
diaper /daipɒ/ *n.* пелена
diary /ˈdairi/ *n.* дневник
dictate /ˈdikteit/ *v.* диктира, заповеда
die /dai/ *v.* умира
death /deθ/ *n.* смрт
diet /ˈdaiɒt/ *n.* диета
differ /ˈdifɒ/ *v.* се разликува
difficult /ˈdifikɒlt/ *adj.* тежок
dig /dig/ *v.* копа, ископува
dignify /ˈdignifai/ *v.* велича
dilemma /diˈlemɒ/ *n.* дилема
diligent /ˈdilidɜnt/ *adj.* работлив
dimension /daiˈmenSn/ *n.* голе-
мина, мерка, димензија
dine /dain/ *v.* обедува, руча
diploma /diˈplɒumɒ/ *n.* диплома, свидетелство
diplomacy /diˈplɒumɒsi/ *n.* ди-
пломатија
direct /dairekt/ 1. *v.* насочува,
раководи, адресира; 2. *adj.*
директен, непосреден
directive /diˈrektiv/ *n.* наредба,
заповед
dirt /dɜːt/ *n.* нечистотија, земја, кал
disability /disˈɒbiliti/ *n.* неспо-
собност, инвалидност
disabled /diseibld/ *adj.* инвалид, сакат

disadvantage /disɒdˈvæntidɜ/ *n.*
недостаток, загуба
disagree /disɒˈgri/ *v.* не се согласува, се разликува
disappear /disɒˈpiɒ/ *v.* исчез-
нува
disappoint /disɒˈpoint/ *v.* разо-
чарува
disapprove /disɒˈruːv/ *v.* не о-
добрува
disarm /disˈarm/ *v.* (се) разо-
ружава
disaster /diˈzæstɒ/ *n.* несреќа,
катастрофа
disciple /diˈsaipl/ *n.* следбеник
disclose /disˈklɒuz/ *v.* (раз)-
открива
disconnect /diskɒnekt/ *v.* прекинува, исклучува
discontinue /diskɒnˈtinjuː/ *v.* (се)
прекратува
discount /ˈdiskaunt/ *n.* попуст
discourage /disˈkʌridɜ/ *n.* обес-
храбрува
discover /disˈkʌvɒ/ *v.* открива
discreet /disˈkriːt/ *adj.* внима-
телен, претпазлив
discuss /diˈskʌs/ *v.* дискутира
disease /diˈziːz/ *n.* болест,
заболување
disguise /disˈgaiz/ *v.* (се) прео-
блекува, (се) престорува, (се)
маскира
disgust /dizˈgʌst/ *v.* се гади

dish /diS/ *n.* чинија, јадене, *pl.* садове

disinfect /disin'fekt/ *v.* дизинфицира

disk /disk/ *n.* диск

dislike /dis'laik/ *v.* не му се допаѓа, не трпи

dismember /dis'memb∂/ *v.* расчленува, раскинува

dismiss /dis'mis/ *v.* распушта

disobey /dis∂'bei/ *v.* не послушува, откажува

disorder / dis'ord∂r/ *n.* безредие, растројство

dispatch /di'spætS/ *v.* (ис)праќа

dispense /di'spens/ *v.* дели

display /di'splei/ *v.* покажува

dispute /si'spju:t/ *v.* (се) спори, (се) расправа

disregard /disri'gard/ *v.* игнорира, не обрнува внимание

disrespect /disri'spekt/ *n.* непочитување

disseminate /di'semineit/ *v.* шири, сее (идеи)

dissolve /di'zalv/ *v.* растворува

distant /'dist∂nt/ *adj.* далечен, воздржан, резервиран

distinction /di'stinkSn/ *n.* разлика, одлика

distract /di'strækt/ *v.* одвлекува, свртува (внимание from од)

distribute /di'stribku:t/ *v.* распределува, расподелува, дистрибуира

district /'distrikt/ *n.* област, округ, околија

disturb /di'st3:b/ *v.* пречи

dive /daiv/ *v.* нурка, се нурнува

diverse /daiv3:s/ *adj.* различен, разнообразен

divide /di'vaid/ *v.* (се) дели, (се) поделува

divine /di'vain/ *adj.* бежествен

divorce /di'vors/ *n.* развод

dizzy /dizi/ *adj.* замајан, зашеметен

do /du:/ *v.* врши, извршува, исполнува, прави

dock /dak/ *n.* док, пристаниште

doctor /dokt∂/ *n.* лекар, доктор

document /dakj∂m∂nt/ *n.* документ

dog /dog/ *n.* пес, куче

doll /dol/ *n.* кукла

dolphin /'dolfin/ *n.* делфин

domain /d∂mein/ *n.* област, територија, домен

domestic /d∂'mestic/ *adj.* домашен, внатрешен

donate /'d∂uneit/ *v.* дарува

donkey /'danki/ *n.* магаре

door /dor/ *n.* врата

dormitory / ˈdormitori/ n. студентски дом, општа спална

dot /dat/ n. точка

double /ˈdʌbl/ adj. двоен, двосмислен

doubt /daut/ n. сомнение, недоверба

down /daun/ adv. (на)долу

doze /dəuz/ v. дреме

dozen /ˈdʌzn/ n. дузина

draft /dræft/ n. нацрт, скица

drag /dræg/ v. влече, трга

drain /drein/ v. (се) цеди, (се) исцедува

drama /ˈdra:mə/ n. драма

draw /dro:/ v. црта, потегнува

dream /dri:m/ n. сон, мечта

dress /dres/ v. (се) облекува

drift /drift/ v. отпловува, (се) навева; ~ apart се отуѓува

drink /drink/ v. пие, испива

drive /draiv/ v. вози, одвезува, дове-дува

drop /drap/ n. капка

drown /draun/ v. (се) дави

drowse /drauz/ v. дреме

drug /drʌg/ n. дрога, лек, наркотик

dry /drai/ adj. сув, исушен

duck /dʌk/ n. патка

due /du:/ adj. должен, исплатив

dune /du:n/ n. дина

duplicate /ˈdu:plikeit/ n. копие, дупликат

dusk /dʌsk/ n. квечерина

dust /dʌst/ n. прав, прашина

duty /du:ti/ n. долг, должност

dynamite /ˈdainðmait/ n. динамит

dynasty /dainðsti/ n. династија

E

each /i:tS/ pron. секој; ~ other меѓусебно

eager /i:gðl/ adj. желен, нестр-пелив, напнат, алчен

ear /iðl/ n. уво

early /ɜ:li/ adj. ран, првобитен, поранешен

earn /ɜ:n/ v. заработува, печели

earth /ɜ:θ/ n. земја, почва

easy /i:zi/ adj. лесен

east /i:st/ n. исток, ориент

Easter /i:stðl/ Велигден

eat /i:t/ v. јаде

ebb /eb/ n. оддлив

echo /ˈekðu/ n. одек

eclipse /iˈklips/ n. затемнување

ecology /iˈkɔlðdʒi/ n. екологија

economy /iˈkɔnðmi/ n. стопанство, економија

edge /edʒ/ *n.* раб, сечило, острина

edit /'edit/ *v.* редигира, уредува

educate /'edʒɵkeit/ *v.* образува, школува, воспитува

education /'edʒɵkeiSn/ *n.* образование

effect /i'fekt/ *n.* последица, резултат, следствие

efficient /i'fiSnt/ *adj.* ефикасен

effort /'efɵt/ *n.* напор, сила, обид

either /'aiðɵ/, /i:'ðɵ/ *pron.* прв или втор (од два), обајцата

eject /i'dʒekt/ *v.* исфрла, отфрла, отстранува

elastic /i'læstik/ *adj.* растеглив, еластичен

elbow /'elbɵu/ *n.* лакот

election /i'lekSn/ *n.* избор, избирање

electric /i'lektrik/ *adj.* електричен

elegant /'eligɵnt/ *adj.* елегантен

element /'elimɵnt/ *n.* елемент

elephant /'elifɵnt/ *n.* слон

elevate /'eliveit/ *v.* подигнува, возвишува

eliminate /i'limineit/ *v.* отстранува, елиминира

elk /elk/ *n.* северен елен, лос

ellipse /i'lips/ *n.* елипса

else /els/ *adv.* друго, оште

emancipation /imænsi'peiSn/ *n.* ослободување, еманципација

embarass /im'bærɵs/ *v.* засрамува, посрамува

embargo /im'bargɵu/ *n.* забрана, ембарго

embassy /'embɵsi/ *n.* амбасада

embrace /im'breis/ *v.* прегнува

emerge /i'mɜ:dʒ/ *v.* испливува, се појавува, се открива

emergency /i'mɜrdʒɵnsi/ *n.* нужда, опасност

emigrate /'emigreit/ *v.* се иселува, емигрира

emotion /i'mɵuSn/ *n.* чувство, емоција

empire /'empaiɵ/ *n.* империја, царство

employ /'imploi/ *v.* прима на работа, вработува

empty /'empti/ *adj.* празен

enable /i'neibl/ *v.* овозможува, овластува

enchain /in'tSein/ *v.* оковува

enclose /in'klɵus/ *v.* вклучува, опкружува

encourage /in'kɜridʒ/ *v.* окуражува

encyclopedia /in'saiklɵ'pi:diɵ/ *n.* енциклопедија

end /end/ *n.* крај, предел,

свршеток

endorse /in'dors/ v. потпишува

enemy /'enəmi/ n. непријател

energy /'enədʒi/ n. енергија

enforce /in'fors/ v. спроведува, налага

engage /in'geidʒ/ v. ангажира, се врзува

engine /'endʒin/ n. мотор

engineer /endʒi'niə/ n. инженер

engrave /in'greiv/ v. гравира

enjoy /in'dʒoi/ v. се радува на, се весели, се насладува на

enlarge /in'lardʒ/ v. увеличува, зголемува

enlighten /in'laitn/ v. просветува, расветлува

enlist /in'list/ v. повикува во војска

enormous /inorməs/ adj. огромен, грамаден

enough /i'nʌf/ adv. достаточно

enrich /in'ritS/ v. обогатува

enroll /in'rəul/ v. (се) запишува

enslave /in'sleiv/ v. заробува

ensure /in'Suə/ v. осигурува

enter /'entə/ v. влегува, се запишува

entertain /entə'tein/ v. забавува

enthusiasm /in'θu:ziæzm/ n. ентузијазам

entire /in'taiə/ adj. цел, севкупен

entrance /'entrəns/ n. влез, пристап

entry /'entri/ n. влез, пријава за учество

envelope /in'veləp/ n. коверт, плико

environment /in'vairənmənt/ n. околина, средина, околност

envy /'envi/ n. завист, завидливост

epicenter /epi'sentə/ n. епицентар

episode /'episəud/ n. епизода

epoch /'epak/ n. епоха

equal /'i:kwəl/ adj. еднаков, ист

equator /i'kweitə/ n. екватор

equipment /i'kwipmənt/ n. опрема, прибор

era /'iərə/ n. ера, епоха

erase /i'reis/ v. избришува

erode /i'rəud/ v. гризе, еродира

erotic /i'ratik/ adj. еротичен

erupt /i'rʌpt/ v. пробива, избива

escalate /'eskəleit/ v. засилува, заострува

escape /i'skeip/ v. побегнува, избегнува

escort /'escort/ n. свита, придружба

especially /i'speSəli/ adv. на-

рочно, посебно
essay /e'sei/ *n.* есеј
essential /i'senSl/ *adj.* важен, неопходен
establish /i'stæbliS/ *v.* формира, оснива, утврдува
estate /i'steit/ *n.* имот
estimate /'estimeit/ *v.* оценува, проценува
eternal /i'tɜ:nl/ *adj.* вечен, бесмртен
ethnic, ethnical /'eθnik/ *adj.* етнички
evacuate /i'vækjueit/ *v.* евакуира
evaluate /i'væljueit/ *v.* оценува, проценува
evaporate /i'væp∂reit/ *v.* испарува
eve /i:v/ *n.* предвечерие
even /'i:v∂n/ 1. *adj.* рамен, плоснат; 2. *adv.* дури, исто така
evening /'i:vniñ/ *n.* вечер
event /i'vent/ *n.* случка, настан
eventual /i'ventSu∂l/ *adj.* конечен, краен
ever /'ev∂/ *adv.* секогаш, кога било
every /'evri/ *adj.* секој
evidence /'evidns/ *n.* доказ
evident /'evidnt/ *adj.* видлив, очигледен
evil /'i:vl/ *adj.* лош, зол
exact /ig'zækt/ *adj.* точен,

егзактен
exaggerate /ig'zæd3∂reit/ *v.* преувеличува
examine /ig'zæmin/ *v.* испитува, проверува
example /ig'zæmpl/ *n.* пример
except /ik'sept/ *prep.* освен, си исклучок
exchange /iks'tSeind3/ *n.* размена, замена, девизен курс, берза
excitement /ik'saitm∂nt/ *n.* возбува, развразненост
exclude /iks'klu:d/ *v.* исклучува
excuse /ik'skju:z/ *v.* извинува
execute /'eksikju:t/ *v.* извршува, спроведува
exercise /'eks∂saiz/ *v.* вежба, примена, вршење
exhaust /ig'zo:st/ *v.* изморува, истоштува
exhibition /eksi'biSn/ *n.* изложба
exist /ig'zist/ *v.* постои, живее, егзистира
expand /ik'spænd/ *v.* (се) шири, (се) распространува
expect /ik'spekt/ *v.* очекува, се надева на
experience /ik'spiri∂ns/ *n.* доживување, искуство
experiment /ik'sperim∂nt/ *n.* опит, проба, експеримент
expire /ik'spai∂/ *v.* истекува, изминува

explain /ik'splein/ v. објаснува,
толкува
explode /ik'spləud/ v. експлодира
explore /ik'splor/ v. проучува
export /ik'sport/ v. експорт
express /ik'spress/ 1. adj. брз,
експресен; 2. v. изразува,
искажува
extend /ik'stend/ v. продолжува, проширува
extensive /ik'stensiv/ adj. опши-
рен, простран
exterminate /ik'stɜ:mineit/ v.
уништува
extinguish /ik'stingwiʃ/ v. изгас-
нува, угасува
extra /'ekstrə/ adj. додатен,
дополнителен
extraordinary /ik'strordneri/ adj.
извонреден, редок
extreme /ik'stri:m/ adj. краен,
екстремен
eye /ai/ n. око

F

fable /'feibl/ n. басна
fabric /'fæbrik/ n. ткиво, материјал
face /feis/ n. лице, образ
fact /fækt/ n. факт, стварност,
вистина
factor /'fæktə/ n. фактор
factory /'fæktri/ n. фабрика
fail /feil/ v. не успева, про-
паѓа
faint /feint/ adj. слаб, немошен
fair /feə/ adj. искрен, чесен,
непристрастен
faith /feiθ/ n. вера, доверба
fake /feik/ v. фалсификува,
мами
fall /fo:l/ v. паѓа, се срушува,
се навалува
false /fo:ls/ adj. лажен, фалси-
фикуван
familiar /fə'miliə/ adj. познат,
обичен
family /'fæmli/ n. семејство,
род
fan /fæn/ n. вентилатор;
обожавател
fantasy /'fæntəsi/ n. фантазија,
измислица
far /far/ adv. далеку
farm /farm/ n. фарма
fascinate /'fæsineit/ v. фасци-
нира
fascism /'fæʃizm/ n. фашизам
fashion /'fæʃn/ n. мода, облик
fast /fæst/ 1. v. пости; 2. adj.
брз

fat /fæt/ *adj.* дебел, згоен, тежок

fatal /'feitl/ *adj.* фатален

fate /feit/ *n.* судба

father /'fa:ðə/ *n.* татко, отец

fault /fo:lt/ *n.* грешка, недостаток

favor /'feivə/ *n.* услуга, помош, љубезност

fear /fiə/ *n.* страв

feather /'feðə/ *n.* перо

federation /fedəreiSn/ *n.* федерација

fee /fi:/ *n.* хонорар, такса

feed /fi:d/ *v.* храни, исхранува, крми

feel /fi:l/ *v.* (се) осеќа, (се) чувствува

fellow /'felou/ *n.* другар, колега

female /'fi:meil/ *adj.* женски

feminine /'feminin/ *adj.* женствен

fence /fens/ *n.* ограда

ferry /'feri/ *n.* траект, превоз; ~boat /feribout/ *n.* траект

fertile /'f3rtl/ *adj.* плоден, плодоносен

fever /'fi:və/ *n.* треска

few /'fju:/ *pron.* малку, неколку

fiction /'fikSn/ *n.* измислица, прикаска, белетристика

fiddle /'fidl/ *n.* виолина, гусла

field /fi:ld/ *n.* поле, нива

fight /fait/ *v.* се бие, спречува, се бори

figure /'figə/ *n.* лик, фигура, карактер

file /fail/ *n.* досие, картотека, регистар

fill /fil/ *v.* (се) полни, (се) наполнува

film /film/ *n.* филм

final /'fainl/ *adj.* краен, финален, заден, завршен

finance /'fainæns/ *n.* финансии, парични средства

find /faind/ *v.* наоѓа, открива

fine /fain/ *adj.* нежен, фин

finger /'fingə/ *n.* прст

finish /'finiS/ *v.* (се) завршува, (се) свршува, престанува

fire /faiə/ *n.* оган, жар, пламен

firm /f3:m/ 1. *adj.* солиден, тврд; 2. *n.* фирма, компанија

first /f3:st/ *pron.* прв

fish /fiS/ *n.* риба

fix /fiks/ *v.* залепува, закачува, пришива, поправа, сместува

flag /flæg/ *n.* знаме, знаменце

flame /fleim/ *n.* пламен, жар, страст

flash /flæS/ *v.* блеснува

flat /flæt/ *adj.* сплескан, (водо)рамен

flatter /'flætə/ *v.* ласка, додворува

flavor /'fleivə/ *n.* вкус, мирис,

арома
flea /fli:/ *n.* болва
flee /fli:/ *v.* бега, побегнува, напушта
flesh /fleS/ *n.* месо, чулност
flirt /flɜ:t/ *v.* кокетира, флертува
flood /flʌd/ *n.* потоп, наплив, поплава
floor /flor/ *n.* под, земја
flour /flauƏ/ *n.* брашно
flow /flƏu/ *v.* тече, дотекува
flower /'flauƏ/ *n.* цвет, цвеќе
fluent /'flu:Ənt/ *adj.* течен (говор)
fluid /'fluid/ *adj.* течен
flute /flu:t/ *n.* флаута
flutter /'flʌtƏ/ *v.* трепери, трепка
fly /flai/ *v.* лета, латнува, спопаѓа
flight /flait/ *n.* летање, лет
foam /fƏum/ *n.* пена
focus /'fƏukƏs/ *n.* фокус, центар
fog /fag/ *n.* магла
folk /fƏuk/ *n.* народ, луѓе, домашни, родители
follow /'falƏu/ *v.* следи, преследува, придружава
fond /fand/ *adj.* вљубен, нежен
food /fu:d/ *n.* храна
fool /fu:l/ *n.* глупак
foot /fut/ *n. pl.* **feet** /fi:t/ нога,

стапало
for /for/ *prep.* за, наместо, поради, доколку што
force /fors/ *n.* сила, енергија
foreign /farin/ *adj.* странски, туѓ
forest /'farist/ *n.* гора, шума
forget /for'get/ *v.* заборава
forgive /fƏ'giv/ *v.* простува
fork /fork/ *n.* вилица, вила
form /form/ *n.* форма, лик
formal /'fo:ml/ *adj.* формален, церемонијален
former /'formƏr/ *adj.* пораншен, бивш, претходен, некогашен
formula /'formjƏlƏ/ *n.* формула
forth /forθ/ *adv.* напред, понатака
fortune /'fortSn/ *n.* среќа, судбина, судба, богатство
forward /'forwƏrd/ *adj.* преден, напреден, напреднат
foster /'fostƏ/ *v.* одгледува, се грижи за; ~ **-child** /'fostƏtSaild/ *n.* посвоче
fountain /'fauntin/ *n.* извор, водоскок
four /for/ *num.* четири
fox /faks/ *n.* лисица
fracture /'fræktSƏ/ *n.* фрактура
frame /'freim/ *n.* рамка
frank /frænk/ *adj.* искрен, отворен
fraud /'fro:d/ *n.* измама

free /fri:/ *adj.* слободен, независен

freedom /fri:dəm/ *n.* слобода

freeze /fri:z/ *v.* (се) замрзнува, (се) заледува

freight /freit/ *n.* товар, превоз

fresh /freS/ *adj.* свеж, студен, чист

friend /frend/ *n.* пријател

frighten /fraitən/ *v.* уплашува, застрашува

frog /frag/ *n.* жаба

from /frəm/ *prep.* од

front /frʌnt/ *n.* чело, предна/ челна страна, фасада

frost /frost/ *n.* мраз, слана

fruit /fru:t/ *n.* овошка, плод

frustrate /frʌstreit/ *v.* фрустрира

fry /frai/ *v.* пржи

fuel /fjuəl/ *n.* гориво

fugitive /fju:d3itiv/ *n.* бегалец

fulfill /ful'fil/ *v.* исполнува, задоволува

full /ful/ *adj.* полн, испомнет, наполнет, сит

fume /fju:m/ *n.* чад, испарување

fun /fʌn/ *n.* шега, забава, задоволство

function /'fʌnkSn/ *n.* функција, служба, должност

fundament /'fʌndəmənt/ *n.* основа, фундамент

funeral /'fju:nrl/ *n.* погреб, закоп

fur /fз:/ *n.* кожув, крзно

furnish /'fз:niS/ *v.* полни со покукнина

furniture /'fз:nitSəl *n.* покукнина

further /'fз:ϑəl *adv.* понатака

future /'fju:tSəl 1. *n.* иднина; 2. *adj.* иден

G

gaff /gæf/ *n.* рибарска кука

gain /gein/ *v.* добива

gall /go:l/ *n.* жолчина

gallery /'gælðri/ *n.* галерија

gallon /'gælðn/ *n.* галон

gamble /'gæmbl/ *v.* игра комар

game /geim/ *n.* игра, шега

gang /gæђ/ *n.* група, банда

gap /gæp/ *n.* пукнатина, процеп, празнина

garage /gðra3/ *n.* гаража

garbage /'ga:bid3/ *n.* смет

garden /'gardn/ *n.* градина

garlic /'garlik/ *n.* лук

gas /gæs/ n. гас

gasp /gæsp/ v. зема воздух

gate /geit/ n. порта, врата

gather /'gæϑəl/ v. (се) собира, бере

gay /gei/ adj. весел, ведар; хомосексуален

gel /dʒel/ n. гел

gene /dʒi:n/ n. ген

general /'dʒenrəl/ 1. adj. општ, главен, основен; 2. major-~ n. генерал-мајор

generate /'dʒnəreit/ v. произведува, создава, причинува

generation /dʒenəreiSn/ n. поколение

generous /'dʒenrəs/ adj. благороден, великодушен

genius /'dʒi:nius/ n. гени

gentle /dʒentl/ adj. нежен, мил, благ

geography /dʒi'agrəfi/ n. географија

geology /dʒi'alədʒi/ n. геологија

geometry /dʒi'amitri/ n. геометрија

germ /dʒ3:m/ n. микроб, бацил

gesture /'dʒestSəl/ n. гест, знак

get /get/ v. добива, прима, купува, зема

ghost /gəust/ n. дух

giant /'dʒaiənt/ n. гигант

gift /dift/ n. дар, подарок

giraffe /dʒ'ræf/ n. жирафа

girl /g3:l/ n. девојка, момиче

give /giv/ v. дава, задава, дозволува

glad /glæd/ adj. задоволен, весел, радосен

glance /glæns/ v. погледнува, фрла поглед

glare /gleəl/ v. свети, блеска

glass /glæs/ n. стакло

glimmer /'gliməl/ n. слабо светка, мижурка

globe /gləub/ n. глобус, земјина топка

glory /'glori/ n. слава, чест

glove /glʌv/ n. ракавица

glow /gləu/ v. се жари

glue /glu:/ n. лепило

go /gəu/ v. оди, си оди, трггнува, трае

goal /gəul/ n. цел, гол

goat /gəut/ n. коза

god /gad/ n. бог, божество

gold /gəuld/ n. злато

golf /galf/ n. голф

good /gud/ adj. добар

goose /gu:s/ n. (pl. geese /gi:s/) гуска

gorgeous /gordʒəs/ adj. прекрасен

gorilla /gə'riləl/ n. горила

govern /'gʌvðn/ v. владее, управува

grab /græb/ v. грабнува, зграпчува

grace /greis/ n. милост, попусливост

grade /greid/ n. степен, клас, оценка

graduate /'grædʒuit/ v. дипломира, завршува (студии)

grain /grein/ n. зрно

grammar /'græmðl/ n. граматика

grand /grænd/ adj. голем, велик

grant /grænt/ v. одобрува, дозволува, доделува

grape /greip/ n. грозје

grasp /græsp/ v. фаќа, зграпчува

grass /græs/ n. трева

grate /greit/ n. решетка

grateful /'greitfl/ adj. благодарен

grave /greiv/ 1. adj. сериозен, тежок; 2. n. гроб

gravity /'græviti/ n. гравитација

great /greit/ adj. голем, значителен, велик

greed /gri:d/ n. юлчност, лакомост

green /gri:n/ adj. зелен, млад, неискусен

grey, gray /grei/ adj. сив, грао, сед

grid /grid/ n. решетка, мрежа

grief /gri:f/ n. жалба, чемер, мака

grill /gril/ n. скара

grim /grim/ adj. мрачен, суров

grind /graind/ v. (се) меле, (се) дроби, (се) трие

grocer /'grðusðl/ n. бакалин

groom /grum/ n. младоженец

ground /graund/ n. земјю, почва, основа

group /gru:p/ n. група

grow /grðu/ v. расте, израстува, одгледува

guarantee /gærðn'ti:/ n. гаранција

guard /gard/ n. стража, чувар

guess /ges/ v. погодува, одгатнува, претпоставува

guest /gest/ n. гостин, гост

guide /gaid/ n. водич, приращник

guillotine /gilð'ti:n/ n. гилотина

guilt /gilt/ n. вина

gulf /gʌlf/ n. залив

gum /gʌm/ n. каучук, гума, мастика, гума за џвакање

gun /gʌn/ n. револвер, пушка, огнено оружје

guy /gai/ n. момче, човек, маж

gymnasium /dӡm'neiziðm/ n. фискултурна сала

gypsy /'dʒipsi/ n. циганин

habit /'hæbit/ *n.* навик, обичај

hair /heðr/ *n.* коса, влакно

half /hæf/ *n.* половина

hallucinate /hð'lu:sineit/ *v.* халуцинира

ham /hæm/ *n.* шунка, бут

hammer /'hæmðr/ *n.* чекан

hand /'hænd/ *n.* рака; ~cuffs /'hændkʌfs/ *n.* лисици; ~writing /'hændraitiŋ/ *n.* ракопис

handle /'hændl/ 1. *n.* рачка, дршка; 2. *v.* постапува, управува се, се занимава со

handsome /'hænsm/ *adj.* убав

hang /hæŋ/ *v.* беси, обесува, закачува

happen /'hæpðn/ *v.* се случва, се одигрува

happy /'hæpi/ *adj.* среќен, радосен

harass /hð'ræs/ *v.* вознемирува, измамува

harbor /'harbðr/ *n.* пристаниште, засолниште

hard /hard/ *adj.* тврд, тежок, строг, неразбирлив, силен

harm /harm/ 1. *n.* штета; 2. *v.* нанесува штета

harmony /'harmðni/ *n.* хармонија, созвучје

harvest /'harvist/ *n.* жетва

hassle /'hæsl/ *n.* расправија, непријатност

haste /heist/ *n.* брзање

hat /hæt/ *n.* шапка

hate /heit/ 1. *v.* мрази; 2. *n.* омраза

have /hæv/ *v.* има, содржи

haven /'heivn/ *n.* пристаниште

hawk /ho:k/ *n.* јастреб, сокол

hay /hei/ *n.* сено

hazard /'hæzðd/ *n.* опасност, ризик, хазардна игра

he /hi/ *pron.* тој

head /hed/ *n.* глава; ~master /hed'ma:stðr/ *n.* директор, управител на училиште; ~quarters /hedkwotðz/ *n.* главен штаб

heal /hi:l/ *v.* лекува, смирува

health /helθ/ *n.* здравје

hear /hiðr/ *v.* слуша, испрашува, сослушува

heart /hart/ *n.* срце

heat /hi:t/ *n.* топлина

heaven /'hevðn/ *n.* небо

heavy /'hevi/ *adj.* тежок

hectic /'hektik/ *adj.* возбудлив

helicopter /'helikaptðr/ *n.* хеликоптер

hell /hel/ *n.* пекол, ад

helmet /'helmit/ *n.* шлем

help /help/ 1. *v.* помага, придонесува; 2. *n.* помош

hen /hen/ *n.* кокошка

hence /hens/ *adv.* отсега, оттука, значи

her /hз:/ *pron.* неа
herb /hз:b/ *n.* трева, билка
herd /hз:d/ *n.* стадо, толпа
here /hiд/ *adv.* овде, на ова место, во овој случај
hero /hirдu/ *n.* херој, јунак
hesitate /ˈheziteit/ *v.* се двоуми, се колеба
hide /ˈhaid/ *v.* (се) сокрива, (се) крие
high /hai/ *adj.* висок, голем
hijack /ˈhaidƷæk/ *v.* грабнува, киднапира
hike /haik/ *v.* пешачи
hill /hil/ *n.* рид, кеп, возвишение
hint /hint/ *n.* знак, алузија
hire /haiд/ *v.* вработува, заема во служба
his /hiz/ *pron.* негов
history /ˈhistri/ *n.* историја
hit /hit/ *v.* удира, треска
hobble /ˈhabl/ *v.* куца, накривува
hobby /ˈhobi/ *n.* хоби
hold /hдuld/ *v.* држи, задржува, придржува
hole /hдul/ *n.* дупка, отвор
holiday /ˈhalidei/ *n.* празник, *pl.* распуст, годишен одмор
holocaust /ˈhalдko:st/ *n.* погром, масово уништување
holy /ˈhдuli/ *adj.* свет
home /hдum/ *n.* дом, стан, куќа

homicide /ˈhamisaid/ *n.* убиство
honest /ˈanist/ *adj.* чесен, искрен
honey /ˈhʌni/ *n.* мед
honor /ˈanдr/ *n.* чест, слава, почитување
hoof /hu:f/ *n.* копито
hook /huk/ *n.* кука, закачалка, замка
hoot /hu:t/ *n.* свирка, сирена
hope /hдup/ *n.* надеж
horizon /hдˈraizдn/ *n.* хоризонт
horn /horn/ *n.* рог
horror /ˈharдr/ *n.* ужас, страотија
horrible /ˈharibl/ *adj.* ужасен
horrify /ˈharifai/ *v.* ужаснува, застрашува
horse /hors/ *n.* коњ
hospital /ˈhaspitl/ *n.* болница
host /hдust/ *n.* домаќин
hostage /ˈhastidƷ/ *n.* заложник
hot /hat/ *adj.* топол, жежок
hotel /hдuˈtel/ *n.* хотел
hour /auд/ *n.* час, саат
house /haus/ *n.* куќа, дом, зграда; ~**hold** /haushдuld/ *n.* домаќинство
how /hau/ *adv.* како, на кој начин
hug /hʌg/ *v.* прегрнува, милува
huge /hju:dƷ/ *adj.* огромен, многу голем

human /'hju:mən/ *adj.* човечки,
човечен; ~ kind /hju:mən kaind/ ,
~ race /hju:mən reis/
човечки род
humid /hju:mid/ *adj.* влажен
humiliate /hju:milieit/ *v.*
понижува
humor *n.* хумор
hunch /hʌntS/ *n.* грба, израсток
hundred /'hʌndrid/ *num.* сто

hunger /'hʌɟgə/ *n.* глад, гладу-
вање
hunt /'hʌnt/ *n.* мов, потера
hurry /hʌri/ *v.* брза, забрзува
hurt /hɜ:t/ *v.* (се) ранува, боли
husband /hʌzband/ *n.* сопруг,
маж
hyphen /'haifn/ *n.* тире
hypothesis /hai'poθisis/ *n.*
хипотеза

I

ice /ais/ *n.* лед, мраз
idea /ai'diə/ *n.* идеја, мислење
identify /ai'dentifai/ *v.* (се)
иден-тификува
identity /ai'dentiti/ *n.* идентитет,
идентичност
ideology /aidi'alədʒi/ *n.*
идеологија
idiot /'idiət/ *n.* идиот
idol /aidl/ *n.* идол
if /if/ *conj.* ако, во случај да
ignition /ig'niSn/ *n.* запалување
ignore /ig'nor/ *v.* игнорира, не
обрнува внимание
ill /il/ *adj.* болен
illegal /i'li:gl/ *adj.* незаконит,
противзаконит
illegitimate /ili'dʒitimit/ *adj.* вонбрачен, незаконит
illiterate /i'litərit/ *adj.*

неписмен, неук
illusion /i'lu:ʒn/ *n.* илузија,
изма-ма
image /'imidʒ/ *n.* слика, прет-
става
imagine /i'mædʒin/ *v.* претставува, мисли, верува
imitate /'imiteit/ *v.* подражава,
имитира
immediate /i'midiət/ *adj.* непосреден, директен
immense /i'mens/ *adj.* огромен
immigrate /'imigreit/ *v.*
имигрира
immortal /i'mortl/ *adj.* бесмртен
immune /i'mju:n/ *adj.* имун, за-
штитен
impact /'impækt/ *n.* (сила) на
удар, влијание
imperative /im'perətiv/ 1. *adj.*

нужен, заповеден; 2. *n.*
императив

imperial /imˈpiriəl/ *adj.* царски,
имперски

implant /imˈplænt/ *v.* всадува,
вдахнува

implicate /ˈimplikeit/ *v.* вовлекува,
вплеткува

imply /imˈplai/ *v.* имплицира,
подразбира

import /imˈport/ *v.* внесува, уво-
зува

important /imˈportnt/ *adj.* важен,
значаен

impose /imˈpouz/ *v.* воведува, (се)
натрапува (на гости)

impossible /imˈpasəbl/ *adj.*
не(воз)можен

impress /imˈpres/ *v.* остава впе-
чаток/отпечаток

impression /imˈpreSn/ *n.* впечаток

imprint /imˈprint/ *v.* печати, отпечатува

imprison /imˈprizn/ *v.* затвора

improper /imˈprapər/ *adj.* неумесен, неприличен

improve /imˈpru:v/ *v.* усомршува,
унапредува, напредува

imprudent /imˈpru:dnt/ *adj.* не-
претпазлив

impulse /ˈimpʌls/ *n.* импулс,
поттик

in /in/ *prep.* в(о), внатре, на, при,
по

inadmissible /inədˈmisəbl/ *adj.*
недопустлев, недозволив

inappropriate /inəˈprəupriət/ *adj.*
несоодветен, неумесен

incarnate /inˈkarnit/ *v.* олице-
творува, претвора во крв и
месо

inch /intS/ *n.* инча

incident /ˈinsidnt/ *n.* случка,
епизода, инцидент

include /inˈklu:d/ *v.* содржи,
вклучува

income /ˈinkʌm/ *n.* доход

incompetent /inˈkampitnt/ *adj.*
неспособен

incomplete /inkəmˈpli:t/ *adj.* недовршен

inconsequent /inˈkansikwənt/ *adj.*
недоследен, нелогичен

inconvenient /inkənˈvi:niənt/ *adj.*
непогоден, незгоден

incorrect /inkəˈrekt/ *adj.* нето-чен

increase /inˈkri:s/ *v.* (се) сголе-
мува

incredible /inˈkredibl/ *adj.* неверој
атен, чудесен

incriminate /inˈkrimineit/ *v.* обвинува

indebted /inˈdetid/ *adj.* задол-
жен, благодарен

indeed /inˈdi:d/ *adv.* навистина,
всушност

indefinite /inˈdefənit/ *adj.* нејасен, неодреден

independent /indi'pendƏnt/ *adj.* независен, самостоен, слободен

indicate /'indikeit/ *v.* сигнализира, укажува на, дава на знаење

indifferent /in'difrƏnt/ *adj.* незаинтересиран, рамнодушен

indirect /indi'rekt/ *adj.* посреден, обиколен

indiscreet /indi'skri:t/ *adj.* непромислен, нетактичен

individual /indi'vidЗuƏl/ *adj.* единичен, одделен, личен, приватен

indoor /'indor/ *adj.* внатрешен, домашен, куќен

industry /'indƏstri/ *n.* индустрија

inert /i'nз:t/ *adj.* тромав, бавен

inevitable /i'nevitƏbl/ *adj.* неизбежен, неминовен

inexpensive /inik'spensiv/ *adj.* ефтин

inexplicable //inik'splikƏbl/ *adj.* необјаснив

infant /'infƏnt/ *n.* бебе, дете

infantry /'infƏntri/ *n.* пешадија

infect /in'fekt/ *v.* заразува, инфицира

infiltrate /'infiltreit/ *v.* се пробива, се вовлекува

infinite /'infinit/ *adj.* бескраен, бесконечен

infirm /in'fз:m/ *adj.* слаб, немоќен

inflame /in'fleim/ *v.* распалува, воспалува

influence /'influƏns/ *n.* влијание

inform /in'form/ *v.* информира, известува, соопштува

informal /in'forml/ *adj.* обичен, неформален

infuse /in'fju:z/ *v.* влева, накиснува

inhabit /in'hæbit/ *v.* населува, живее во

inhale /in'heil/ *v.* вдишува

inherit /in'herit/ *v.* наследува

initiate /i'niSieit/ *v.* иницира, воведува, почнува

injure /'indЗƏ/ *adj.* рани, ранува, навредува

injustice /in'dЗлstis/ *n.* неправедност, неправда

ink /ink/ *n.* мастило, туш

inland /'inlƏnd/ *adj.* сувоземен, домашен, внатрешен

inlaws /'inlo:z/ *n. pl.* сватови

inn /in/ *n.* костилница, ан

inner /'inƏ/ *adj.* внатрешен, скриен

innocent /'inƏsnt/ *adj.* невин, чист, наивен

input /'input/ *n.* влез

inquire /in'kwaiƏ/ *v.* се распрашува, се интересува

insane /in'sein/ *adj.* луд, безумен

insect /'insekt/ *n.* инсект

insecure /insi'kju∂/ *adj.* несигурен

insert /in's3:t/ *v.* става, вметнува

inside /'insaid/ *adv.* внатре

insinuate /in'sinjueit/ *v.* напомнува, нафрлува

insist /in'sist/ *v.* настојува

inspect /in'spekt/ *v.* прегледува, контролира

inspire /in'spai∂/ *v.* вдахнува, инспирира

install /in'sto:l/ *v.* поставува, монтира

instance /inst∂ns/ *n.* случај, пример

instant /inst∂nt/ *adj.* моментен

instead /in'sted/ *adv.* (на)место

instinct /'instinkt/ *n.* инстинкт

institute /'institu:t/ *n.* институт

instruct /in'strʌkt/ *v.* упатува, подучува

instrument /'instr∂m∂nt/ *n.* прибор, инструмент

insulate /'ins∂leit/ *v.* изолира

insult /in'sʌlt/ *n.* навреда

insure /in'Su∂/ *v.* осигурува, обезбедува

integrate /'intigreit/ *v.* обединува, вклопува

intelligent /in'telid3nt/ *adj.* интелигентен

intend /in'tend/ *v.* има намера, планира

interest /'intrist/ *n.* интерес

interfere /int∂'fi∂/ *v.* се меша

internal /in't3:nl/ *adj.* внатрешен

international /int∂'næS∂nl/ *adj.* меѓународен

interpret /in't3:prit/ *v.* толкува, разбира, објаснува

interrupt /int∂'rʌpt/ *v.* прекинува

interview /int∂vju:/ *n.* разговор, интервју

intimate /'intimit/ *adj.* интимен, личен, приватен

intimidation /in'timideiSn/ *n.* закана

into /'intu:/ *prep.* во, внатре

intoxicate /in'taksikeit/ *v.* (се) опива

intrigue /in'tri:g/ 1. *n.* интрига

introduce /intr∂du:s/ *v.* воведува, внесува, втерува

intrude /in'tru:d/ *v.* (се) натрапува

intuition /intu'iSn/ *n.* претчуство, интуиција

invade /in'veid/ *v.* напаѓа, навлегува

invaluable /in'vælj∂bl/ *adj.* непроценлив

invent /in'vent/ *v.* изумува, измислува

invest /in'vest/ *v.* вложува

investigate   joke

investigate /in'vestigeit/ v. испитува, иследува
invisible /in'viz∂bl/ adj. невид-
лив
invite /in'vait/ v. кани, поканува
invoice /'invois/ n. сметка, фактура
involve /in'valv/ v. вклучува,
подразбира
iron /ai∂rn/ n. железо, пегла
irregular /i'regj∂l∂l/ adj. нере-
довен, неправилен
irrelevant/i'relivnt/ adj. неважен
irreparable /i'reprbl/ adj. непо-
правлив

irresistible /iri'zist∂bl/ adj. неза-
држлив, незапирлив
irresponsible /iri'spansibl/ adj.
неодговорен
irritate /'iriteit/ v. раздразнува,
нервира, иритира
island /'ail∂nd/ n. остров
isle /ail/ n. остров
isolate /ais∂leit/ v. изолира
issue /iSu:/ n. тема, (спорно)
прашење
it /it/ pron. тоа, она
item /'ait∂m/ n. предмет, број,
точка
itself /it'self/ pron. самиот
ivory /'aivri/ n. слонова коска

J

jack /d3æk/ n. лост, макара
jacket /'d3ækit/ n. сако, џакет
jam /d3æm/ n. метеж, турка-
ница, застој, мармалад
jasmine /'d3æsmin/ n. јасмин
jazz /d3æz/ n. џез
jealous /'d3æl∂s/ adj. љубоморен, завидлив
jeep /d3i:p/ n. џип
jelly /'d3æli/ n. желе
jeopardy /'d3ep∂di/ n. опасност, ризик
jerk /"d33:k/ n. глупчо, шут-
рак, влечење

jet /'d3et/ n. авион на млазен
погон, ахат
Jew /'d3u:/ n. евреин
jewel /'d3u:∂l/ n. скапоцен-
/бесценет камен
jingle /'d3ingl/ v. свони, суни
job /'d3ab/ n. работа, служба
jockey /"d3aki/ n. џокеј
jog /'d3ag/ v. трчка, напредува, потрчува, поттурнува
join /'d3oin/ v. спојува, сврзува, се зачленува во (друштво, клуб)
joke /'d3∂uk/ n. шега, виц

journal /'dɜː:nl/ *n.* дневник, списание
journey /'dɜː:ni/ *n.* патување, пат
joy /'dɜoi/ *n.* среќа, радост, веселост
judge /'dʒʌ'dʒ/ *n.* судија, експерт
juggle /'dʒʌgl/ *n.* жонглирање
jumbo /'dʒʌmb∂u/ *adj.* голем
jump /'dʒʌmp/ *v.* скока, скокнува
junction /'dʒʌnkSn/ *n.* спој, слив
jungle /'dʒʌngl/ *n.* џунгла

junior /'dʒu:ni∂/ *adj.* помлад
junk /'dʒʌnk/ *n.* стари предмети, отпад
jurisdiction /'dʒuris'dikSn/ *n.* судство, јурисдикција
jury /'dʒuri/ *n.* жири, суд, порота
just / dʒʌst/ 1. *adj.* праведен, точен, основан; 2. *adv.* токму, баш, тукушто, точно
justice /'dʒʌstis/ *n.* правда, право, оправданост, судство
justify /'dʒʌstifai/ *v.* оправдува
juvenile /'dʒu:v∂лолетен

К

kangaroo /'kæ̃ђg∂'ru:/ *n.* кенгур
keen /ki:n/ *adj.* остар, жесток
keep /ki:p/ *v.* држи, задржува, продолжува
kettle /ketl/ *n.* чајник, котле
key /ki:/ *n.* клуч, решение
kick /kik/ *v.* удира, рита, отфрла
kidnap /'kidnæp/ *v.* киднапира
kidney /'kidni/ *n.* бубрег
kill /kil/ *v.* убива, усмртува, коле
kilogram /'kil∂græm/ *n.* килограм
kilometer /ki'lamit∂/ *n.* километар

kind /kaind/ 1. *adj.* љубезен, услужлив; 2. *n.* род, сорта, раса, карактер
kindle /kindl/ *v.* (се) пали, (се) разгорува
king /kiђ/ *n.* крал
kiosk /'ki:ask/ *n.* киоск
kiss /kis/ *v.* бакнува
kitchen /'kitSin/ *n.* кујна
kitten /'kitn/ *n.* маче
knack /næk/ *n.* трик, умеење
knead /ni:d/ *v.* меси, замесува
knee /ni:/ *n.* колено
knife /naif/ *n.* нож
knight /nait/ *n.* рицар
knit /nit/ *v.* плете

knock /nak/ v. тропа, чука; ~
down соборува; ~ out
нокаутира
knot /nat/ n. јазол, клупче
know /n∂u/ v. знае, познава, се
разбира
knowledge /'nalidЗ/ n. знаење,
познавање
knuckle /'nʌkl/ n. зглоб (на
прст)

L

label /'leibl/ n. етикета, натпис
labor /'leib∂l/ n. работа, труд,
работна рака
laboratory /'læbr∂tori/ n. лабораторија
labyrinth /'læb∂rinθ/ n. лавиринт
lack /læk/ v. недостига, нема,
има потреба
lady /'leidi/ n. леди, дама, госпоѓа
lake /leik/ n. езеро
lamb /læm/ n. јагне, јагнешко
lamp /læmp/ n. ламба
lance /læns/ n. копје
land /lænd/ n. земја, територија, имот; ~ lord /lænlord/ n.
сто-пан
language /'længwidЗ/ n. јазик,
говор
lantern /'lænt∂n/ n. фенер
lap /'læp/ n. скут
lapse /læps/ n. пропуст
large /lardЗ/ adj. голем, простран, опсежен, широк
lash /læS/ 1. n. камшик, клепка; 2. v. шиба, бие, удира
last /læst/ 1. adj./adv. заден,
краен, минат; 2. v. трае, из-
држува
late /leit/ adj./adv. доцен, за-
доцнет, недамнешен, пос-
леден, покоен
lath /læθ/ n. летва
latitude /'lætitu:d/ n. географска ширина
latter /'læt∂l/ adj./adv. последен, краен
lattice /'lætis/ n. дрвена
решетка/ограда
laugh /læf/ v. се смее, се
потсмева
laughter /'læft∂l/ n. смеа, смее
ње
laundry /'lo:ndri/ n. пералница,
перење
lavatory /'læv∂tori/ n. клозет
law /lo:/ n. закон, право

lay /lei/ *v.* става, поставува, положува, мегнува, снесува, несе; ~ off престанува да работи, напушта работа, отпушта од работа

lazy /'leizi/ *adj.* мрзлив, неработен, пропаднат

lead /led/ *n.* олово, графит; /li:d/ водство, водечка идеја, пример

leaf /li:f/ *n.* (*pl.* leaves) лист

leak /li:k/ *n.* пукнатина

learn /lɜ:n/ *v.* учи, дознава, разбира

lease /li:s/ *n.* закуп, наем

least /li:st/ *adj.* најмал, најнезначен

leave /li:v/ *v.* остава, напушта

lecture /'lektʃə/ *n.* лекција

left /left/ *adj.* лев

leg /leg/ *n.* нога, бут

legal /'li:gl/ *adj.* законски, законодавен, правен

legend /'ledʒnd/ *n.* легенда, предание

legislative /'ledʒisleitiv/ *adj.* законодавен, законски

legitimate /li'dʒitimit/ *adj.* законски, озаконет, разумен

leisure /'li:ʒ:/ *n.* слободно време, одмор

lemon /'lemən/ *n.* лимон

lend /lend/ *v.* дава на заем

less /les/ *adj.* помал, помалку

lesson /'lesn/ *n.* лекција, урок, поука

let /let/ *v.* дозволува, (до)-пушта

letter /'letə/ *n.* буква, писмо

lettuce /'letis/ *n.* зелена салата

level /'levl/ *n.* ниво, рамниште

liable /'laiəbl/ *adj.* одговорен

liberal /'librəl/ *adj.* либерален, дарежлив, великодушен

liberate /'libəreit/ *v.* ослободува

library /'laibrəri/ *n.* библиотека

license /'laisns/ *n.* дозвола, овластување, лиценца

lick /lik/ *v.* лиже

lie /lai/ 1. *n.* лага; 2. *v.* лаже, мами

lie /lai/ *v.* межи, легнува, се простира

lieutenant /lu:tenant/ *n.* подофицер

lift /lift/ *v.* (се) дига, укинува (бокада/мерки)

light /lait/ 1. *n.* светлина, виделина, ламба; 2. *adj.* лесен, несериозен

like /laik/ 1. *adj.* еднаков, сличен; 2; *v.* се допаѓа, сака

likely /'laikli/ 1. *adj.* веројатен, соодветен; 2. *adv.* most/very ~ веројатно

lily /'lili/ *n.* лилија

lime /laim/ *n.* лепило, вар, липа

limit /'limit/ *n.* лемет, граница

limp /limp/ *v.* куца, поткуцнува

linden /'limdən/ *n.* липа

line /lain/ *n.* црта, линија, ред,
редица, низа, раб, граница,
телефонска линија

link /link/ *n.* врска, алка (од)
верига

lion /laiðn/ *n.* лав

lip /lip/ *n.* усна

liqueur /li'kз:r/ *n.* ликер

liquor /likðl/ *n.* алкохол

list /list/ *n.* список, попис, лис-
та

listen /'lisn/ *v.* слуша, послушува, наслушува

literal /'litrðl/ *adj.* буквален,
пишан

literature /'litrðtSðr/ *n.* литература, книжевност

little /'litl/ *adj.* мал, ситен, дро-
бен, незначителен

live /liv/ 1. *v.* живее, преживува; 2. /laiv/ *adj.* жив, енергичен

liver /'livðl/ *n.* црн дроб

load /lðud/ *n.* товар, тежина

loan /lðun/ 1. *n.* заем; 2. *v.* по-
зајмува

local /'lðukl/ *adj.* локален,
месен

lock /lak/ *n.* брава, катинар

logic /'ladʒik/ *n.* логика

logical /'ladʒikðl/ *adj.* логичен

lone /lðun/ *adj.* осамен, сам

loneliness /'lðunlinis/ *n.* осаме-
ност, самотија

long /loђ/ *adj.* долг, дол-
готраен

look /luk/ *v.* гледа, погледнува, разгледува

loose /lu:s/ 1. *adj.* лабав

lord /lord/ *n.* Господ, господар, стопан, лорд

lose /lu:z/ *v.* губи, загубува

lottery /latri/ *n.* лотарија

loud /laud/ *adj.* гласен, силен,
бучен

louse /laus/ *n.* вошка

love /lʌv/ 1. *n.* љубов,либе
миличок; 2. *v.* љуби, милува

low /lðu/ *adj.* низок, долен,
прост

loyal /'loiðl/ *adj.* верен, лојален

luck /lʌk/ *n.* судба, среќа, кос-
мет

luggage /'lʌgidʒ/ *n.* багаж

lunch /lʌntS/ *n.* ручек

lung /lʌђ/ *n.* бел дроб

lurk /lз:k/ *v.* дебне, чека во
засада

lush /lʌS/ *adj.* буен, сочен

lust /lʌst/ *n.* страст, похота

lynch /lintS/ *v.* линчува

lyre /laið/ *n.* лира, лутња

lyrical /'lirikl/ *adj.* лирски, ли-
ричен

machine /məˈSiːn/ n. машина, уред

mad /mæd/ adj. улав, луд, бесен

madam /ˈmædəm/ n. госпоѓа, господарка

magazine /mægəˈziːn/ n. списание, магацин, складиште

magic /ˈmædʒik/ n. магија, убавина

magnet /ˈmægnit/ n. магнет

magnificent /mægˈnifisnt/ adj. прекрасен, величествен

maid /ˈmeid/ n. девојка, слугинка

maiden /ˈmeidn/ n. девојка, немажена мома

mail /meil/ 1. n. потша; 2. n. испраќа по пошта; ~ box /meilbaks/ n. поштенско сандаче; ~ man /ˈmeilmən/ n. поштар

main /mein/ adj. главен, најважен

maintain /meinˈtein/ v. подржува, држи; застапува, тврди

majesty /ˈmædʒisti/ n. височество, величество, достоинство

major /ˈmeidʒə/ adj. важен, главен, водечки; ~ general / meidʒə genrəl/ генерал мајор

make /meik/ v. прави, твори, гради, создава, приготува, произведува, постигнува, успева, принудува

male /meil/ adj. машки

malice /ˈmælis/ n. злоба, омраза, злонамера

man /mæn/ pl. men n. маж, човек, човечки род

manage /ˈmænidʒ/ v. управува, раководи, стопанисува

management /ˈmænidʒmənt/ n. раководство, управа, вештина

manager /ˈmænidʒə/ n. раководител, директор, шеф

mandate /ˈmændeit/ n. мандат, овластување

maniac /ˈmeiniæk/ n. манијак, лудак

manipulate /məˈnipəleit/ v. манипулира, искористува, управува, (зло)употребува

manner /ˈmænə/ n. начин, манир, стил

manual /ˈmænjuəl/ adj. рачен, физически

manufacture /mænjəˈfæktSə/ v. произведува, изработува, прави

manuscript /ˈmænjəskript/ n. ракопис

many /ˈmeni/ pron. многу

map /mæp/ n. географска карта

marathon /'mærθan/ n. маратон

marble /'marbl/ n. мермер, мрамор

March /martS/ 1. n. март

march v. маршира, напредува

marine /mɑri:n/ n. морнар, маринец

marital /'mæritl/ adj. брачен

mark /mark/ n. знак, белег, отпечаток

market /'markit/ n. пазар

marriage /'mærid3/ n. брак, женидба

marry /mæri/ v. (се) жени, (се) мажи, оженува, омажува

marvelous adj. чудесен, прекрасен

masculine /'mæskjɑlin/ adj. мажествен, силен, смел, јак

massacre /'mæsɑkɑ/ n. масовно убивање, колеж

massage /mɑsa:3/ n. масажа

master /'mæstɑ/ n. мајстор, стопан, управник (на уцилиште)

match /mætS/ n. игра, натпревар; добра прилика

mate /meit/ n. пријател, другар, колега

material /mɑtiriɑl/ 1.n. материјал, материја; 2. adj. физички, материјален

maternal /mɑ'tɜ:nl/ adj. мајчин, мајчински

mathematics /mæθimætiks/ (math /mæθs/ n. математика

matrix /'meitriks/ n. матрица

matter /'mætɑ/ n. материја, работа, предмет, суштина, важност; as a ~ of fact всушност; no ~ what/where/who бело што/каде/кој; Does it ~? важно ли е?

mattress /'mætris/ n. душек

mature /mɑ'tSuɑ/ adj. зрел, созреан, развиен, израстен

maximum /'mæksimɑm/ n. најголемо количество, највисок степен

may /mei/ v. mod. може, би можел, смее

mayor /meiɑr/ n. градоначалник

me /mi:/ pron. (мене) ме, (мене) ми

meadow /'medɑu/ n. ливада, пасиште

meal /mi:l/ n. јадење

mean /mi:n/ 1. adj. зол, подол, нечесен; 2. v. значи, намерава

measure /'me3ɑ/ n. мера, степен

meat /mi:t/ n. месо

medical /'medikl/ adj. медицински, лекарски

medicine /'medisn/ n. медицина, лекарство

Mediterranean /medit∂reni∂n/ n. Средоземно море

meet /mi:t/ v. (се) среќава, (се) запознава

melody /'mel∂di/ n. мелодија, напев

melt /melt/ v. (се) топи, (се) растопува

member /'memb∂/ n. член

memory /'memri/ n. памтење, спомен

mental /'mentl/ adj. интелектуален, душевен

mention /'menSn/ v. спомнува, напомнува

merchant /m3:tSnt/ n. трговец

merchandise /'m3:tSndaiz/ n. (трговска) стока

mercy /'m3:si/ n. милост, сожаление

merry /'meri/ adj. весел, радосен, забавен

mess /mes/ n. растуреност, збрка, неуредност

message /'mesid3/ n. вест

metal /'metl/ n. метал

method /'meθ∂d/ n. метод

microscope /'maikr∂sk∂up/ n. микроскоп

mid /mid/ adj. среден

middle /'midl/ n. средина, среден дел, половина

migrate /'maigreit/ v. се отселува, мигрира

mild /maild/ adj. нежен, кроток, благ

mile /mail/ n. милја

military /'militri/ adj. ваен, војнички

milk /milk/ n. млеко

mill /mil/ n. мерница, воденица, фабрика

million /'mili∂n/ num. милион

mind /maind/ n. памет, разум, мнение, свест, мисла

mine /main/ 1. pron. мој; 2. n. рудник, мина

mineral /'minr∂l/ adj. минерален, руден

minimum /'minim∂m/ n. минимум

minister /'minist∂/ 1. v. служи, помага; 2. n. министер, свештеник

minute /minit/ n. минута

miracle /'mir∂kl/ n. чудо

mirror /mir∂/ n. огледалс

misbehave /misbi'heiv/ v. недолично постапува

miscarry /mis'kæri/ v. пометнува

miscellaneous /mis∂'leini∂s/ adj. мешан, мешовит

miserable /'mizr∂bl/ adj. мизерен, беден, несреќен

misery /'misri/ n. беда, невола,

misinterpret /misin'tɜ:prit/ v. погрешно толкува

miss /mis/ 1. v. пропушта, испушта, не забележува, недостига; 2. n. госпожица

mistake /mi'steik/ n. грешка, погрешка

mister /'mist∂/ n. господин

misunderstand /misʌnd∂'stænd/ v. погрешно разбира

misuse /mis'ju:z/ v. злоупотребува

mix /miks/ v. (се) меша

mobile /'m∂ubi:l/ adj. подвижен

model /'madl/ n. модел, примерок, манекен

modern /'madern/ adj. модерен, современ, денешен

modest /'madist/ adj. скромен

modify /'madifai/ v. променува, преиначува, модифицира

molecule /'malikju:l/ n. молекула

moment /'m∂ument/ m. момент, миг

monarchy /'man∂rki/ n. монархија

monastery /'man∂steri/ n. манастир

money /'mʌni/ n. пари

monitor /'manit∂r/ n. монитор

monkey /'mʌnki/ n. мајмун

monopoly /m∂'napli/ n. монопол

monster /'manst∂/ n. чудовиште, ѕвер

month /mʌnθ/ n. месец

monument /'manj∂m∂nt/ n. споменик

mood /mu:d/ n. расположение, табиет

moon /mu:n/ n. луна, месечина

moral /'mor∂l/ adj. морален, поучен

more /mor/ pron. повеќе, уште

morgue /morg/ n. мртвачница

morning /'morniŋ/ n. утро, претпладне

mortal /'mortl/ adj. смртен, смртоносен

mortgage /'morgid3/ n. замог, заложен имот, хипотека

Moslem /'mazlim/, **Muslim** /'muzlim/ 1. adj. муслимански; 2. n. муслиман

mosque /mosk/ n. џамија

moss /mas/ n. маховина

mother /mʌ∂∂/ n. мајка

motion /'m∂uSn/ n. движение

motive /'m∂utiv/ n. мотив, поттик, повод, побуда

motor /'m∂ut∂/ n. мотор

mountain /mauntin/ n. планина, гора

mourn /morn/ v. оплакува, тажи

mouse /maus/ n. (pl. mice) глушец

mouth /mauθ/ n. уста, устие

move /muːv/ v. движи, помрднува, предизвикува, преселува, преместува, превезува, напредува, тече
mow /ˈməʊ/ v. коси
much /mʌtS/ pron. многу
mud /mʌd/ n. кал, блато, нечистотија
muggy /ˈmʌgi/ adj. спарен, влажен
multiple /ˈmʌltipl/ adj. многукратен
multitude /ˈmʌltitjuːd/ n. множество, маса
mummy /mʌmi/ n. мумија
murder /ˈmɜːdər/ n. убиство
murderer /ˈmɜːdrər/ n. убиец
muscle /ˈmʌsl/ n. мускул
museum /mjuːˈziːəm/ n. музеј

mushroom /ˈmʌSrum/ n. печурка, шампињон
music /ˈmjuːzik/ n. музика, ноти
must /mʌst/ mod. мора, треба
mustard /ˈmʌstəd/ n. сенф
mutate /mjuːteit/ v. мутира
mute /mjuːt/ adj. нем
mutual /ˈmjuːtSuəl/ adj. заемен, меѓусебен
my /mai/ pron. мој
myself /maiself/ pron. (себе) си, (себе) се
mystery /ˈmistri/ n. загатка, мистерија, тајна, загадочност
mystic, mystical /ˈmistik(l)/ adj. мистичен, таинствен
myth /miθ/ n. мит, легенда
mythology /miθaləðʒi/ n. митологија

N

nail /neil/ n. нокт
naive /naˈiːv/ adj. наивен, простодушен
naked /ˈneikid/ adj. гол, необлечен
name /neim/ n. име, назив
nap /næp/ n. краток сон, дремка
napkin /ˈnæpkin/ n. салфетка
narcotic /narˈkatik/ n. дрога, наркотик, опојно средство

narrate /ˈnæreit/ v. раскажува
narrow /ˈnærəu/ adj. тесен, слаб
nasty /ˈnæsti/ adj. одвратен, гаден, непријатен
nation /ˈneiSn/ n. народ, нација
native /ˈneitiv/ adj. роден, домашен, домородечки
nature /ˈneitSə/ n. природа, карактер, состав
navigate /ˈnæviˈgeit/ v. плови,

управува (со авион), води

navy /'neivi/ *n.* воена флота/морнарица

Nazi /'natsi/ 1. *n.* нацист; 2. *adj.* нацистички

near /ni∂/ *adv.* блиску, во близина, речиси

necessary /'nesiseri/ *adj.* нужен, потребен, неопходен

neck /nek/ *n.* врат, гуша, шија

need /ni:d/ *n.* нужда, потреба, неопходност

needle /'ni:dl/ *n.* игла

negate /ni'geit/ *v.* одрекнува, негира

neglect /ni'glekt/ *v.* пренебрегнува, омалова-жува

negotiate /ni'g∂uSieit/ *v.* преговара, се спогодува, се договара

neighbor /'neib∂/ *n.* сосед

nephew /'nefku:/ *n.* внук

nerve /n3:v/ *n.* нерв, живец

nest /nest/ *n.* гнездо, засолниште

net /net/ 1. *n.* мрежа; 2. *adj.* нето, чист

neutral /'nu:tr∂l/ *adj.* неутрален, неопределен

never /'nev∂/ *adv.* никогаш, ниеднаш

new /nu:/ *adj.* нов, модерен

news /nu:z/ *n.* вест, новост, вести

next /nekst/ *adj.* следен, иден, нареден

nice /nais/ *adj.* убав, мил, приј атен

niche /nitS/ *n.* ниша

nickname /'nikneim/ *n.* прекар, надиме

niece /ni:s/ *n.* внука

night /nait/ *n.* ноќ, вечер, мрак

nine /nain/ *num.* девет

no /n∂u/ 1. *adv.* не; 2. *pron.* никој, никаков

nobody /'n∂u'b∂di/ *pron.* ниедин, никој

noble /n∂ubl/ *adj.* благороден, прекрасен

noise /noiz/ *n.* врева, бука, сензација

none /nʌn/ *pron.* ниеден, никој

nonsense /'nans∂ns/ *n.* глупост, бесмислица

noodle /nu:dl/ *n.* фиде, тестенина

noon /nu:n/ *n.* пладне

nor /nor/ *conj.* ниту, исто така не

norm /norm/ *n.* норма, правило

normal /norml/ *adj.* нормален, обичен

north /norθ/ *n.* север

nose /n∂uz/ *n.* нос, клун

not /nat/ *adv.* не

notary /n∂ut∂ri/ *n.* нотар

note /nʌut/ *n.* белешка, забелешка, прибелешка
nothing /'nʌθiŋ/ *pron.* ништо; ~ but само, единствено
notice /'nʌutis/ 1. *n.* соопштение, известување, објава; 2. *v.* забележува, истакнува, спомнува
notify /'nʌutifai/ *v.* известува, информира
notion /'nʌuSn/ *n.* поим, идеја, замисла
nourish /'nʌriS/ *v.* храни, одгледува

novel /'navl/ *n.* роман
now /nau/ *adv.* сега
nuclear /'nu:kli∂r/ *adj.* нуклеарен
nude /nu:d/ *adj.* гол, разголен
numb /nʌm/ *adj.* вкочанет, неосетлив, умртвен, тап
number /'nʌmb∂r/ *n.* број, бројка
nun /nʌn/ *n.* калугерка
nurse /nɜ:s/ *n.* медицинска сестра
nut /nʌt/ *n.* орев, лешник
nymph /nimf/ *n.* нимфа

O

oak /∂uk/ *n.* даб, дабово дрво
oat /∂ut/ *n.* овес, зоб
oath /∂uθ/ *n.* клетва
obedience /'∂bi:di∂ns/ *n.* покорност, послушност, зависност
obey /∂'bei/ *v.* слуша, се покорува
object /'abd3ikt/ 1. *n.* предмет, цел, мотив, граматически предмет; 2. *v.* приговара, се противставува, се противи
obligate /'abligeit/ *v.* обварзува, принудува
obligation /abligeiSn/ *n.* задолженост, обврзаност, благодарност

oblige /∂'blaid3/ *v.* обврзува, врзува, услужува
obnoxious /∂b'nakS∂l/ *adj.* одвратен, гаден, непријатен
obscene /∂b'si:n/ *adj.* непристоен, срамотен
obscure /∂b'skju∂l/ *adj.* мрачен, темен, матен
observe /∂b'zɜ:v/ *v.* набљудува, забележува
obsess /∂b'ses/ *v.* обзема, опседнува
obstacle /'abst∂kl/ *n.* пречка
obtain /∂btein/ *v.* добива, набавува, постигнува

obvious /'abviɒs/ adj. очигледен, очебиен

occasion /ɒ'kei3n/ n. можност, случај, згода

occupy /'akjupai/ v. запоседнува, зазема, окупира

occur /ɒkз:/ v. се (по)јавува, се случува

ocean /'ɒuSn/ n. океан

o'clock /ɒ'klak/ adv. точно; 8/15 ~ точно 8/15 часот

odd /ad/ adj. чуден, необичен

of /ɒv/ prep. од

off /ɒf/ adv. одонде, оттаму, понатаму

offend /ɒ'fend/ v. навредува

offense /ɒ'fens/ n. навреда, напад, атак

offensive /ɒ'fensiv/ n. напад, офанзива

offer /'ofɒr/ v. предлага, дава, поднесува

office /'ofis/ n. канцеларија, кабинет, служба

official /ɒfiSl/ adj. официјален, службен

often /'oftn/, /'ofn/ adv. често

oil /oil/ n. масло, нафта, петролеј, газја

old /ɒuld/ adj. стар, древен, износен, изветвен, претходен, бивш, старомоден

olive /'aliv/ n. маслинка, маслиново дрво

on /on/ prep. на, врз, при, кон, до, крај

once /wʌns/ adv. еднаш, некогаш

one /wʌn/ pron. еден, некој, некаков, некој си, кој било, ист, единствен

oneself /wʌn'self/ pron. (себе) се, (себе) си, сам(иот)

onion /'ʌniɒn/ n. кромид

only /'ɒunli/ 1. adj. единствен; 2. adv. само, единствено, само што

open /'ɒupɒn/ adj. отворен, незаштитен, неврзан, јавен, искрен

opera /'aprɒ/ n. опера

operate /'apɒreit/ v. оперира, работи, функционира

opinion /ɒ'piniɒn/ n. мнение, становиште, гледиште

opportunity /apɒr'tu:niti/ n. згода, можност, водможност

oppose /ɒ'pɒus/ v. се спротиставува на, се противи на

opposite /apɒzit/ adj. спротивен

oppress /ɒ'pres/ v. угнетува, притиска, мачи, измачува

optimism /'aptimism/ n. оптимизам

or /or/ conj. или; either ... ~ ... или ...

orange /'arind3/ *n.* портокал, портокалово дрво

orbit /'orbit/ *n.* орбита

orchestra /'orkistr∂/ *n.* оркестар

order /'ord∂r/ 1. *n.* ред, поредок, одредба, правило, пропис, орден; 2. *v.* наре-дува, одредува, порачува, заповеда

ordinary /ordneri/ *adj.* вообичаен, обичен, секојдневен

organ /'org∂n/ *n.* орган; орудие, средство, носител, тело, органа

organization /org∂niseiSn/ *n.* организација

organize /'org∂naiz/ *v.* организира, уредува

orientation /ori∂nteiSn/ *n.* ориентација

origin /'orid3in/ *n.* потекло, происход, зачеток, почеток, род

original /∂rid3inl/ *adj.* оригинален, изворен, вистинит

orphan /'orfin/ *n.* сирак, сираче

other /'∧9∂/ *pron.* дру; each ~ еден на друг; every ~ секој втор

ought /o:t/ *v. mod.* мора, треба (to да)

our /au∂/ *pron.* наш

out /aut/ *adv.* надвор, вон; be ~ of something потрошен/

распродаден

outbreak /'autbreik/ *n.* излив, избивање

outcome /'autk∧m/ *n.* исход, резултат, последица

outdoor /aut'dor/ *adj.* надворешен

outfit /'autfit/ *n.* опрема

outgoing /aut'g∂uiħ/ *adj.* што заминува, отворен, екстровертен

outlet /'autlit/ *n.* излез, отвор, одлевање

outline /'autlain/ *n.* краток преглед, кратка содржина

outlook /'autluk/ *n.* поглед, глетка, перспектива

output /'autput/ *n.* производство, продукција

outrageous /'autreid3∂s/ *adj.* жесток, суров, подмолен, нечуен, срамотен, шокантен, скандалозен

outreach /aut'ri:tS/ *v.* достигнува подалеку од, надминува, надвишува

outside /'autsaid/ *n.* надворешност, надворешна страна

outspoken /aut'sp∂uk∂n/ *adj.* отворен, искрен

outstanding /aut'stændiħ/ *adj.* истакнат, извонреден, ненаплатен, непрокриен

outturn /autt3:n/ *n.* продукт,

резултат
over /ʊvə/ adv. над, овде, онаму, таму, одозгора
overcoat /'ʊvəkəut/ n. палто
overcome /ʊvə'kʌm/ v. совладува, победува, надминува
overflow /ʊvə'fləu/ v. прелева, претечува
overload /ʊvə'ləud/ v. претоварува
overlook /ʊvə'luk/ v. не забележува, пропушта
overnight /ʊvə'nait/ adv. преку ноќ
oversea(s) /ʊvə'si:z/ adj. прекуморски, прекуокеански

oversee /ʊvə'si:/ v. надгледува, надсира
oversleep /ʊvə'sli:p/ v. се успива, преспива
overture /ʊvər'tʃə/ n. увертира
overweight /ʊvə'weit/ 1. v. пренатоварува; 2. n. преголема тежина
owe /əu/ v. должи
own /əun/ 1. pron. сопствен; 2. v. поседува, потврдува (сопствеништво)
owner /əunər/ n. сопственик, стопан
ox /aks/ n. вол
oxygen /'aksidʒən/ n. кислород

P

pacific /pə'sifik/ adj. мирољубив; the Pacific Пацификот, Тихиот Океан
pack /pæk/ n. торба, бовча, пакет
pagan /'peigən/ adj. пагански, безбожен
page /peidʒ/ n. страница, лист
pain /pein/ n. болка, мака, страдање
paint /peint/ n. боја
pair /peə/ n. пар, двојка
palace /'pælis/ n. дворец

pale /peil/ 1. adj. блед, слаб, бледолик; 2. n. кол
palm /palm/ n. палма, дланка; ~tree палмово дрво
pan /pæn/ n. тава, тиган
panel /'pænl/ n. (панел-плоча), одбор, панел (дискутанти)
panic /'pænik/ n. паника
panorama /pænə'ræmə/ n. панорама
panther /'pænθə/ n. пантер
papa /'papə/ n. тате
paper /'peipə/ n. хартија, труд,

[. *n.* пластика
[..]eit/ *n.* чинија, паница,
[..]а) плоча
[..] /'plætform/ *n.* плат-
[..] подиум, перон, го-
[..]а
[..]ei/ 1. *n.* игра, забава,
[..]рама, глума; 2. *v.*
[..]ири, глуми
[..]/ *n.* молба (за ми-
[..]ростување,
[..] /'pleznt/ *adj.* пријатен,
[..] мил, радосен
[..]li:z/ *v.* задоволува,
[..], радува, сака
[..] /'ple3[∂]/ *n.* задо-
[..], радост, веселие
[..]pled3/ *n.* заклетва, за-
[..]р, обврска
[..]lenti/ 1. *pron.* многу,
[..] 2. *n.* обилство
[..] /n заплет, фабула
[..]а), завера, интрига
[..]nk/ *n.* кубење, трагање
[..]g/ *n.* приклучник,

[..]
[..]m/ *n.* слива
[..]'pl∧nd[∂]/ *v.* ограбува,
[..]сува
[..]lur[∂]/ 1. *adj.* мно-
[..] 2. *n.* множина
[..]s/ *prep.* плус
[..]ia /nu'm[∂]uni[∂]/ *n.* пнеу-

pocket /'pakit/ *n.* џеп, дупка,
отвор
poem /'p[□]uim/ *n.* спев, поема
poet /'p[∂]uit/ *n.* поет
point /point/ *n.* точка, запирка,
степен, пункт, место,
момент, поента, цел, при-
чина
poison /'poizn/ *n.* отров
pole /p[∂]ul/ *n.* пол, спро-
тивност
police /p[∂]'li:s/ *n.* полиција
policy /'polisi/ *n.* политика,
насочница, директива
polish /'paliS/ *v.* полира
polite /p[∂]lait/ *adj.* учтив, вос-
питан, фин
politics /'palitiks/ *n.* политика
poll /p[∂]ul/ *n.* гласање, број
гласови
pollution /p[∂]lju:Sn/ *n.* загаде-
ност, затруеност
polyglot /'paliglat/ *n.* полиглот
pomp /pamp/ *n.* помпа
pond /pand/ *n.* рибник
pool /pu:l/ *n.* бара, базен
poor /pu[∂]/ *adj.* сиромашен,
беден
poverty /'pav∂rti/ *n.* сиромаш-
тво
pope /p[∂]up/ *n.* папа
poppy /'papi/ *n.* афион, мак
popular /'papj[∂]l[∂]/ *adj.* попу-

напис, писмена задача
paprika /'pæprik[∂]/ *n.* пиперка,
пипер
parachute /'pær[∂]Su:t/ *n.* падо-
бран
parade /p[∂]reid/ *n.* парада
paradise /'pær[∂]dais/ *n.* рај
paradox /'pær[∂]doks/ *n.* пара-
докс
paragraph /'pær[∂]græf/ *n.* параграф, став, извадок
parallel /'pær[∂]l[∂]l/ *adj.* пара-
лелен, аналоген, споредлив
paralysis /p[∂]rælisis/ *n.* пара-
лиза
parameter /'p[∂]ræmit[∂]/ *n.* пара-
метар
parcel /'parsl/ *n.* пакет, пратка
pardon /'pardn/ *v.* простува,
помилува
parent /'per[∂]nt/ *n.* родител
parenthesis /p[∂]'renθisis/ *n.* до-
датна мисла, вметната ре-
ченица
park /park/ *n.* парк
parliament /'parl[∂]m[∂]nt/ *n.* парламент, собрание
parrot /'pær[∂]t/ *n.* папагал
parsley /'parsli/ *n.* магданос
part /part/ *n.* дел, парче, член,
рата, страна, рола, пар-
титура
partake /par'teik/ *v.* учествува

partial /parSl/ *adj.* непотполн,
делумен, пристрасен
participate /par'tisipeit/ *v.* учествува, зема учество
participle /'partisipl/ *n.* парти-
цип
particle /'partikl/ *n.* честичка
particular /p∂r'tikj[∂]l[∂]r/ *adj.* на-
рочен, специален, посебен,
точен, определен
partner /'partn[∂]/ *n.* соработ-
ник, партнер, ортак
party /'parti/ *n.* забава, веселба, вечеринка, група, партија
pass /'pæs/ *v.* минува, преминува, надвишува, прелетува,
пропушта, предава
passion /'pæSn/ *n.* страст, лам-
теж
past /pæst/ 1. *n.* минато; 2. *adj.*
минат, бивш, последен; 3.
prep. по, после, зад
paste /peist/ *n.* паста, тесто
pasture /'pæstS[∂]/ *n.* пасиште,
ливада
paternal /p[∂]'t3:nl/ *adj.* татков,
татковски
path /pæθ/ *n.* патека, патче
patient /'peiSnt/ 1. *n.* пациент;
2. *adj.* трпелив
patriarch /'peitriark/ *n.* патриј
арх, глава на фамилијата
patriot /'peitri[∂]t/ *n.* патриот
pattern /'pæt∂rn/ *n.* шара, ша-

блон, мустра, пример

pause /'po:z/ *n.* прекин, пауза

pay /pei/ *v.* плаќа, уплатува, страда

pea /pi:/ *n.* грашок

peacock /'pi:kak/ *n.* паун

peace /pi:s/ *n.* мир, тишина, смиреност, рамнотежа

peach /pi:tS/ *n.* праска

peak /pi:k/ *n.* врв, врхол, нај висока точка

pearl /pɜ:l/ *n.* бисер, седеф

peculiar /pi'kju:liə/ *adj.* необичен, чуден, настран

pedestrian /pi'destriən/ *adj.* пешачки

peel /pi:l/ 1. *v.* (се) лупи; 2. *n.* лушпа, кора

pen /pen/ *n.* перо, пенкало

pencil /'pensil/ *n.* молив

penetrate /'penetreit/ *v.* (се) пробива, проникнува

peninsula /pi'ninsələ/ *n.* полуостров

penny /'peni/ *n.* пени, пара

pension /'penSn/ *n.* пензија

pentagon /'pentəgan/ *n.* петоаголник; the P~ Главниот штаб на Американската армија

people /'pi:pl/ *n.* народ, нација, племе, луѓе, жители, поданици, роднини

pepper /'pepə/ *n.* пипер, пи-

перка

perceive /pə'si:v/ *v.* осека, сфаќа, сознава, разбира

perfect /'pɜ:fikt/ *adj.* совршен, беспрекорен, перфектен

perforate /'pɜ:fəreit/ *v.* продупчува, пробива, перфорира

perform /pər'form/ *v.* спроведува, исполнува, игра, глуми, свири

perhaps /pə'hæps/ *adv.* можеби

period /'piriəd/ *n.* период, епоха, ера

permanent /'pɜ:mənənt/ *adj.* постојанен, траен, непрекинат

permit /'pə'mit/ *v.* дозволува, допушта, дава можност

perpetrate /'pɜ:pitreit/ *v.* прави, (ис)конструисува

persecute /'pɜ:sikju:t/ *v.* преследува, гони, измачува

persist /pə'sist/ *v.* настајува, упорен е, не попушта

person /'pɜ:sn/ *n.* лице, личност, човек

personal /pɜ:sənl/ *adj.* личен

personel /pɜ:sə'nel/ *n.* персонал

perspective /pə'spektiv/ *n.* перспектива

persuade /pə'sweid/ *v.* убедува, уверува

perverse /pə'vɜ:s/ *adj.* изопачен, перверзен

pessimism /'pesimizm/ *n.* песимизам

petition /pi'tiSn/ *n.* (писмена) молба, петиција

pharaoh /'ferəu/ *n.* фараон

pharmacy /'farməsi/ *n.* фармација, аптека

phenomenon /fi'naminən/ *n.* феномен

philharmonic /filhar'manik/ *adj.* филхармониски

philology /fi'laləd3i/ *n.* филологија

philosophy /fi'lasəfi/ *n.* философија

phone /fəun/ *n.* телефон

photo /'fəutək/ *n.* слика, фотографија

phrase /freiz/ *n.* израз, фраза

physical /'fizikl/ *adj.* материјален, природен, телесен, физички

piano /pi'a:nəu/ *n.* пијано, клавир

pick /pik/ *v.* избира, бере, чепка; ~ off отстрелува; ~ out избира, истакнува; ~ up сабира, зема

pickle /'pikl/ *n.* кисели краставчиња, туршија

picnic /'piknik/ *n.* пикник, излет

picture /'piktSə/ *n.* слика, портрет, цртеж

piece /pi:s/ *n.* парче, дел

pier /piə/ *n.*

pig /pig/ *n.*

pigeon /'pi...*

pile /pail/ ...

кол, стол...

pillar /'pilə...*

pilot /'pail...* кормилар...

play /...* шега,
игра, ...

plea /...* лост,

pinch /pint...* лост,

pine /pain...* please...
угоде...

pineapple ...* please...
угоду...

pipe /paip...* pleasu...
кавал волст...

pirate /'p...* pledge...
вет, зе...

piss /pis/ ...

pity /'piti...* plenty ...
чуство, м...* полно ...

place /ple...* plot /p...
стор, пло...* (во др...

plague /p...* pluck ...
сурија

plain /plei...* plug /p...
чен, прос...* штеке...
2. *n.* рам...* plum /...

plan /plæn...* plunde...
мапа пљачк...

plane /ple...* plural ...
скан, пла...* жинск...

planet /'p...* plus /p...

plant /pla...* pneuma...
дува, зас...* монид...

plastic /'p...*

ларен, сакан, обичен

porch /portS/ *n.* предворје, трем

pork /pork/ *n.* свинско месо

port/port/ *n.* порта, пристаниште

portion /'porSn/ *n.* дел, порција

portrait /portrit/ *n.* портрет, слика

position /pƏ'ziSn/ *n.* место, позиција

positive /'pazitiv/ *adj.* позитивен, сигурен, опре-делен, утврден, точен

possess /pƏ'zes/ *v.* поседува, има

possible /'pasibl/ *adj.* возможен, веројатен, поднослив

post /pƏust/ *n.* кол, столб, служба, должност, пошта, поштенска пратка

postpone /pƏus'pƏun/ *v.* одлага, одложува

pot /pat/ *n.* тенџере, чајник, саксија

potato /pƏ'teitƏu/ *n.* компир

potential /pƏ'tenSl/ *adj.* потенцијален, возможен, условен

pound /paund/ *n.* фунта (тежина)

pour /por/ *v.* (се) излива, истекува

powder /'paudƏ/ *n.* прав, прашок, пудра, барут

power /'paudƏ/ *n.* сила, моќ, власт

practical /'præktikl/ *adj.* практичен

practice /'præktis/ 1. *n.* пракса, стварност, практика, обичај; **practice** *v.* тренира, спроведува, се придржува кон

prairie /'preƏri/ *n.* прерија

praise /preiz/ *v.* фали, пофалува, велича

praxis /'pæksis/ *n.* пракса

pray /prei/ *v.* се моли

preach /pri:tS/ *v.* проповеда

precaution /pri'co:Sn/ *n.* претпазливост

precious /'preSƏs/ *adj.* скап, драг, мил, скапоцен

precise /pri'sais/ *adj.* точен, прецизен

predicate /'predikit/ *n.* предикат

predict /pri'dikt/ *v.* предвидува

preface /'prefƏs/ *n.* предговор

prefer /pri'f3:/ *v.* претпочита

pregnant /'pregnƏnt/ *adj.* бремена, трудна

prejudice /'pred3Ədis/ *n.* предубедување, предрасуда

premature /pri'mƏtSud/ *adj.* преран, недораснат, несозреан

premise /'premis/ *n.* претпоставка, премиса

prepare /pri'peə/ v. (се) готви, (се) подготвува

preposition /prepə'ziSn/ n. предлог

prescribe /pri'skraib/ v. препишува

present /preznt/ 1. adj. присутен, сегашен, даден; 2. n. подарок, дар

preserve /pri'zз:v/ v. пази, запазува

press /pres/ 1. v. притиска, стиска; 2. n. преса, печатарска машина, печат, весници, новинари

pressure /preSə/ n. притисок

presume /pri:'zu:m/ v. (се) претпоставува (основано), (се) смета (врз основа на факти)

pretend /pri'tend/ v. се преправа, се прави, претендира

pretty /'priti/ adj. убавичок, сладок

prevent /pri'vent/ v. спречува, оневозможува

previous /'pri:viəs/ adj. претходен, поранешен

price /prais/ n. цена, награда

priest /pri:st/ n. свештеник

primitive /'primitiv/ adj. првобитен, примитивен

prince /prins/ n. принц

principal /'prinsipl/ n. директор, управител (на школа)

principle /prinsipl/ n. принцип

print /print/ n. отпечаток, печат

prior /praiə/ adj. претходен, поранешен

prison /'prizn/ n. затвор

private /'praivit/ adj. личен, приватен

privilege /'privilid3/ n. привилегија

probably /'probəbli/ adv. веројатно

problem /'probləm/ n. проблем

proceed /prə'si:d/ v. следи, продолжува

process /prəuses/ n. процес

proclaim /prə'kleim/ v. прогласува, објавува, прокламира

produce /prə'du:s/ v. произведува, ствара

profit /'prafit/ n. профит, полза

profound /prə'faund/ adj. длабок, продлабочен

prognosis /prag'nəusis/ n. прогноза

program /'prəugræm/ n. програма

progress /'pragres/ n. прогрес, напредок

prohibit /pr'ðibit/ v. забранува

project /'prадЗekt/ n. проект, план

prolong /prɔ'loŋ/ v. оддолжува

prominent /'praminɔnt/ adj. истакнат, значаен

promise /'promis/ v. ветува

promote /prɔ'mɔut/ v. напредува, промовира

pronounce /prɔ'nauns/ v. изговара, прогласува

proof /pru:f/ n. доказ, потврда

proper /'prapɔr/ adj. точен, прав, погоден

property /'prapɔrti/ n. сопственост, имот

propose /prɔ'pɔuz/ v. предлага, предлага брак

prosecute /'prasikju:t/ v. гони (судски), поднесува тужба

prosper /'praspɔr/ v. напредува, успева, просперира

protect /prɔ'tekt/ v. заштитува, брани

protest /'prɔtest/ n. протест

proud /praud/ adj. горд

provide /prɔ'vaid/ v. набавува, снабдува, се грижи

provoke /prɔ'vɔuk/ v. дразни, провоцира

psyche /'saiki/ n. психа, душа

public /'pʌblik/ adj. општ, народен, општествен, државен

publish /'pʌbliS/ v. издава, публикува

puddle /'pʌdl/ n. локва, бара

pull /pul/ v. влече, трга, тегне

pulse /pʌls/ n. пулс

pump /pʌmp/ n. пумпа

pumpkin /'pʌmpkin/ n. тиква

punish /'pʌniS/ v. казнува, малтретира

purchase /'pɜ:tSis/ v. купува

pure /pjuʊ/ adj. чист, непознат

purpose /'pɜ:pɔs/ n. налера, цел, накана

pursue /pɔr'su:/ v. преследува, следи, се стреми кон

push /puS/ v. (се) бутка, (се) турка

put /put/ v. става, поставува

puzzle /'pʌzl/ n. загатка, збуна, проблем

Q

quadrate /'kwadreit/ n. квадрат

quaint /kweint/ adj. необичен, старински

quake /kweik/ 1. v. се тресе; 2.

n. потрес, земјотрес

qualify /'kwalifai/ v. (се) квалификува

quality /'kwaliti/ n. квалитет,

добра особина
quantity /'kwantiti/ *n.* количина, квантитет
quarrel /'kwor∂l/ *n.* кавга, караница
quarter /'kwo:t∂/ *n.* четвртина, четврт, квартал
quartz /kworts/ *n.* кварц
queen /kwi:n/ *n.* кралица
queer /kwi∂/ *adj.* чуден, необичен
quell /kwel/ *v.* потиснува, задушува
query /kwiri/ *n.* прашалник
quest /kwest/ *n.* потрага, барање
question /kwestSn/ *n.* прашање, проблем, сомнение
queue /kju:/ *n.* опашка, перчин, редица, плетенка
quick /kwik/ *adj.* брз, бистер, онтелигентен
quiet /'kwai∂t/ *adj.* мирен, тих, кроток
quit /kwit/ *v.* остава, напушта, престанува со
quite /kwait/ *adv.* токму, сосема, наполно
quiz /kwiz/ *n.* тест, испит, квиз
quote /kw∂ut/ *v.* цитира

R

rabbit /ræbit/ *n.* зајак
race /reis/ *n.* раса, вид; натпревар
radiate /'reidieit/ *v.* зрачи се
radical /'rædikl/ *adj.* радикален
radio /'reidi∂u/ *n.* радио
radish /'rædish/ *n.* цвекло
rag /ræg/ *n.* партал, парче, перде
rage /reid3/ *n.* бес, гнев
rail /reil/ *n.* шина, железница
rain /rein/ *n.* дожд
raise /reiz/ *v.* повишува, зголемува, стасува
rally /ræli/ *n.* собир, средба, авторели
ramble /'ræmbl/ *v.* скита, застранува
ramp /ræmp/ *n.* рампа, косина
ranch /ræntS/ *n.* сточарска фарма
random /'rænd∂m/ *adj.* случаен, непредвиден
range /reind3/ *n.* синџир, низа, опсег
rank /rænk/ *n.* степен, чин, ранк
rankle /'rænkl/ *v.* јаде, гризе
ransom /'rænsm/ *n.* откуп, спас
rape /reip/ *n.* силување

rapid /'ræpid/ *adj.* брз, ненадеен

rare /reθ/ *adj.* недопечен, редок, извонреден

rash /ræS/ *adj.* непромислен, избрзан

raspberry /'ra:zbri/ *n.* малина

rat /ræt/ *n.* стаорец

rate /reit/ *n.* тарифа, такса, цена

rather /ra:θθ/ *adv.* поточно речено, доста, повеќе би сакал

ration /'ræSn/ *n.* порција, оброк

rational /'ræSnθl/ *adj.* разумен, паметен, умен

ravage /'rævidЗ/ *v.* уништува, разорува

rave /reiv/ *v.* беснее, пустоши

raven /reivn/ *n.* гавран

ravish /'ræviS/ *v.* граби, ограбува

raw /ro:/ *adj.* суров, непреработен

ray /rei/ *n.* зрак

raze /'reiz/ *v.* наполно уништува

reach /ri:tS/ *v.* подава, испружува (рака), доживува, посегнува (for за), се протега

read /ri:d/ *v.* чита

ready /'redi/ *adj.* готов, приготвен

real /riθl/ *adj.* вистински, реален

realize /'riθlaiz/ *v.* остварува, риализила, увидува

reap /ri:p/ *v.* жнее, *fig.* собира плодови

rear /riθ/ 1. *n.* заден дел

reason /'ri:zn/ *n.* причина, повод, разум

rebate /'ri:beit/ рабат, попуст

rebellion /ri'belijθn/ *n.* бунт, востание

rebuke /ri'bju:k/ *v.* кори, кара, осудува

recall /ri'kol/ *v.* сеќавање, присеќавање

receive /risi:v/ *v.* прима, добива

recent /'ri:snt/ *adj.* нов, модерен

recess /'ri:ses/ *n.* одмор, распуст, пауза, прекин

recognize /'rekθgnaiz/ *v.* познава, признава, сфаќа

recommend /rekθ'mend/ *v.* препорачува

record /ri'kord/ *n.* регистрирање, документ, досие

recover /ri'kʌvθ/ *v.* оздравува, се оправува, закрепнува

recreation /rikrieiSn/ *n.* одмор

red /red/ *adj.* црвен

reduce /ri'du:s/ *v.* снижува, намалува

reel /ri:l/ *n.* ролна (филм), макара

refer /ri'fз:/ *v.* упатува, препорачува, укажува

reflect /ri'flekt/ *v.* одразува,
изразува

reform /ri'form/ *n.* реформа

refresh /ri'freʃ/ *v.* освежува

refrigerator /ri'fridʒəreitə/ *n.* ладилник

refuge /'refju:dʒ/ *n.* засолниште, азил

refund /ri'fʌnd/ *v.* исплатува,
рефундира

refuse /ri'fju:z/ *v.* отфрла, одбива

regard /ri'ga:rd/ *n.* почит,
внимание, однос

regime /rei'ʒi:m/ *n.* режим, поредок

region /'ri:dʒn/ *n.* предел, област

regret /ri'gret/ *n.* сожалување

regular /'regjələ/ *adj.* редовен,
регуларен

reign /rein/ *n.* власт, управу-
вање

reject /ridʒekt/ *v.* отфрла,
отстранува, не признава

relate /ri'leit/ *v.* се однесува,
во сооднос, поврзува

relative /'relətiv/ *adj.* односен,
релативен

relax /ri'læks/ *v.* олабавува

release /ri'li:s/ *v.* ослободува,
спасува

relief /ri'li:f/ *n.* олеснување,
спас

relish /'reliʃ/ *n.* вкус, мирис

rely /ri'lai/ *v.* се потпира, има
доверба

remain /ri'mein/ *v.* останува

remark /ri'mark/ *n.* забелешка

remember /ri'membə/ *v.* се сек
ава, си спомнува

remind /ri'maind/ *v.* потсетува

remit /ri'mit/ *v.* ослободува (од
долгови), сопира, одлага

remorse /ri'mors/ *n.* каење

remove /ri'mu:v/ *v.* отстранува,
однесува, преместува

render /'rendə/ *v.* прави, чини,
врши, толкува, претвора

rent /rent/ *n.* наем, наемнина

repair /ri'peə/ *v.* поправа,
врши ремонт

repeat /ri'pi:t/ *v.* повторува,
прави уште еднаш

replace /ri'pleis/ *v.* заменува

reply /ri'plai/ *v.* одговара

represent /repri'zent/ *v.* претставува, опишува

republic /ri'pʌblik/ *n.* републ-
лика

request /ri'kwest/ *n.* молба, барање

require /ri'kwaid/ *v.* бара, изискува

rescue /'reskju:/ v. спасува, ослободува

research /ri'sɜ:tʃ/ n. научно, истражување

reside /ri'zaid/ v. живее, престојува

resident /'rezidnt/ n. жител

resign /ri'zain/ v. (се) откажува, дава оставка

resist /ri'zist/ v. дава отпор, се спротивставува

resolve /ri'zalv/ v. решава

resort /ri'zort/ n. засолниште

resource /ri'sors/ n. средство, природни богатства

respond /ri'spand/ v. одговара

responsibility /ri'spansə'biliti/ n. одговорност

rest /rest/ n. одмор, починка; остаток, ресто

restrict /ri'strikt/ v. ограничува

result /ri'zʌlt/ n. резултат

retain /ri'tein/ v. држи, чува

retire /ri'taiə/ v. пензионира

return /rit3:n/ v. (се) враќа

reveal /ri'vi:l/ v. открива, покажува

revenge /ri'vendʒ/ n. одмазда

review /ri'vju:/ n. преглед, ревија

revise /ri'vaiz/ v. ревидира, преиспитува

revolution /revə'lu:ʃn/ n. револуција

reward /ri'word/ n. награда

rib /rib/ n. ребро

rice /rais/ n. ориз

rich /ritʃ/ adj. богат

rid /rid/ v. (се) спасува; get ~ се ослободува (of од)

ride /raid/ v. јава (коњ), се движи, плива, вози

right /rait/ adj. прав, исправен, точен

rigorous /'rigərəs/ adj. суров, немилосрден

rill /ril/ n. поток, поточе, рекичка

rind /raind/ n. кора, лушпа

ring /riŋ/ 1. n. прстен, круг, обрач; 2. v. свони, телефонира

rinse /rins/ v. плакне

ripe /raip/ adj. зрел, созреан

rise /raiz/ v. се издига, се качува, се крева

risk /risk/ n. опасност, ризик

rival /'raivl/ n. соперник, ривал

river /'rivə/ n. река

road /rəud/ n. пат, друм

roast /rəust/ v. (се) пече, (се) пржи

rob /rab/ n. краде, пљачка

rock /rak/ n. камен, карпа, стена

roll /rəul/ v. тркала, валка, вози

roof /ru:f/ n. покрив, таван

room /rum/ *n.* соба, простор, место

root /ru:t/ *n.* корен, жила, основа, причина

rope /rɒup/ *n.* јаже, канап, низа

rose /rɒuz/ *n.* роза, трендафил

rough /rʌf/ *adj.* груб, суров, прост

round /raund/ *adj.* заоблен, во вид на круг, полн

route /ru:t/ *n.* друм, пат

row /rɒu/ *n.* ред, редица

royal /'roiðl/ *adj.* кралски

rub /rʌb/ *v.* (се) трие, (се) брише

rubbish /'rʌbiS/ *n.* смет, отпадоци

rude /ru:d/ *adj.* груб, прост

rug /rʌg/ *n.* килим

ruin /ru:in/ *v.* уништува, разорува, пустоши

rule /ru:l/ *n.* правило, одредба

rumor /ru:mðl/ *n.* гласина

run /rʌn/ *v.* трча, брза

rush /rʌS/ *v.* трча, брза

rust /rʌst/ *n.* плесен

rye /rai/ *n.* рж

S

sacrifice /'sækrifais/ 1. *v.* жртвува; 2. *n.* жртва

sad /sæd/ *adj.* тажен, нажален

safe /seif/ *adj.* сигурен, безопасен

sail /seil/ 1. *n.* едро; 2. *v.* едри, плови

salad /'sælðd/ *n.* салата

salary /'sælðri/ *n.* плата

saliva /sðlaivðl/ *n.* плунка

salt /so:lt/ *n.* сол

salute /sðlu:t/ *n.* поздрав

same /seim/ *adj.* ист

sample /'sæmpl/ *n.* мостра, примерок

sand /sænd/ *n.* песок, песочина

sandwich /'sændwitS/ *n.* сендвич

sane /sein/ *adj.* нормален, здрав

satisfy /'sætisfai/ *v.* задоволува

Saturday /'sætðdi/ *n.* сабота

sauce /so:s/ *n.* сос

sausage /'sosid3/ *n.* колбас

savage /'sævid3/ *adj.* примитивен, див

save /seiv/ *v.* спасува, заштитува, поштедува

say /sei/ *v.* вели, искажува

scale /skeil/ *n.* скала, таблица, размер, лушпа, мемрбана, *pl.* вага

scamp /skæmp/ n. ѓавол, не-
ранимајко

scant /skænt/ adj. скуден, не-
достаточен

scare /ske∂/ v. (се) плаши

scarf /skarf/ n. шал

scent /sent/ v. надушува, на-
мирисува

schedule /'sked3ul/ n. програма, распоред

school /sku:l/ n. училиште

science /'sai∂ns/ n. наука,
умешност

scissor /'siz∂l/ 1. v. сече, пресе-
чува; 2. pl. ножици

score /skor/ n. збир, резултат

scourge /sk3:d3/ n. камшик,
бич

scramble /'skræmbl/ v. меша,
измешува

scrape /skreip/ v. чисти, струга

scream /skri:m/ v. вика, вреска,
се дере

screen /skri:n/ n. параван,
екран

screw /skru:/ n. завртка, винт,
шраф

script /skript/ n. ракопис, писмо

scrub /skrʌb/ v. жули, трие

sculpture /'skʌlptS∂/ n. скулптура, статуа

sea /si:/ n. море

seal /si:l/ n. печат

search /s3:tS/ v. пребарува,
испитува

season /'si:zn/ n. годишно
време

seat /si:t/ n. место, седиште

second /'sek∂nd/ pron. втор,
друг, вторичен, второстепен

secret /'si:krit/ adj. таен, потаен

secure /si'kju∂l/ adj. сигурен,
безбеден

seduce /si'dju:s/ v. заведува,
наведува

see /si:/ v. гледа, разбира

seed /si:d/ n. семе, семка

seek /si:k/ v. бара, изискува

seem /si:m/ v. се чини, изгледа

seize /si:z/ v. одзема,
грабнува

seldom /'seld∂m/ adv. ретко

select /si'lekt/ v. одбира,
избира

self /self/ pron. себе, сам

sell /sel/ n. продава, изигрува,
убедува

senate /'senit/ n. сенат

send /send/ v. праќа, испраќа

sense /sens/ n. сетиво, чувство,
смисла

sensible /'sens∂bl/ adj. чувствителен

sensitive /'sensitiv/ adj. осетлив,
чувствителен

sentence /'sent∂ns/ n. реченица,
пресуда

separate /'seprit/ *adj.* одделен, посебен
sequence /'si:kw∂ns/ *n.* редица, низа
serious /'siri∂s/ *adj.* сериозен, значаен
serve /s3:v/ *v.* служи, работи
service /s3:vis/ *n.* служба, сервис
set /set/ *v.* мести, наместува, определува
settle /'setl/ *v.* населува, договара, средува, се наместува
seven /'sevn/ *num.* седум
several /'sevr∂l/ *pron.* неколку
severe /si'vi∂/ *adj.* суров, жесток, тежок
sew /s∂u/ *v.* шие, зашива
sex /seks/ *n.* пол, секс
shabby /'Sæbi/ *adj.* парталав, издрпан, ефтин
shade /Seid/ *n.* сенка
shadow /'Sæd∂u/ *n.* сенка
shake /Seik/ *v.* (се) затресува, потресува, тресе, трепери
shallow /'Sæl∂u/ *adj.* плиток
shame /Seim/ *n.* срам(ота)
shape /Seip/ *n.* облик, форма
share /Se∂/ дел, придонес, акција
shark /Sark/ *n.* ајкула
sharp /Sarp/ *adj.* остер, наострен, остроумен
shave /Seiv/ *v.* бричи
she /Si/ *pron.* таа
sheep /Si:p/ *n.* овца
sheet /Si:t/ *n.* чаршаф
sight /sait/ *n.* глетка, поглед, вид
sign /sain/ *n.* знак, белег, симбол
signature /'sign∂tS∂/ *n.* потпис
significant /sig'nific∂nt/ *adj.* значителен, значаен
silent /sail∂nt/ *adj.* тих, мирен
silk /silk/ *n.* коприна, свила
silly /'sili/ *adj.* глупав
silver /'silv∂/ *n.* сребро
similar /'simil∂/ *adj.* сличен
simple /'simpl/ *adj.* прост, наивен, обичен, скромен
sin /sin/ *n.* грев
since /sins/ 1. *adv.* оттогаш; 2. *prep.* од
sincere /sin'si∂/ *adj.* искрен, верен
sing /siŋ/ *v.* пее
single /'singl/ *adj.* единствен, еден, единичен, одделен
sink /sink/ *v.* тоне, потонува
sister /'sist∂/ *n.* сестра, калуѓерка
sit /sit/ *v.* седнува, седи
six /siks/ *num.* шест
size /sais/ *n.* размер

skate /skeit/ *n.* лизгалка

ski /ski:/ *n.* скија

skill /skil/ *n.* вештина, умешност

skin /skin/ *n.* кожа

skirt /skɜ:t/ *n.* сукња,
здолниште

sky /skai/ *n.* небо, небеса

slam /slæm/ *v.* треснува, удира

slander /ˈslændər/ *n.* клевета

slap /slæp/ *v.* шлакнува

slash /slæʃ/ *v.* расекува, сече,
расцепува

slaughter /ˈslo:tər/ *n.* колење

slave /sleiv/ *n.* роб

sleep /sli:p/ *v.* спие

slender /ˈslendər/ *adj.* тенок,
слаб, строен

slice /slais/ *n.* резанка, парче

slide /slaid/ *v.* (се) лизга

slight /slait/ *adj.* слаб, мал,
незначителен

slim /slim/ *adj.* тенок, строен,
слаб

slip /slip/ *v.* се лизнува

slow /sloʊ/ *adj.* бавен, заос-
танат

smack /smæk/ *n.* целувка, цмок

small /smo:l/ *adj.* мар, ситен

smart /sma:t/ *adj.* бистер,
умен, паметен

smash /smæʃ/ *v.* (се) разбива,
(се) скршува

smell /smel/ *v.* мириса,
помириснува

smile /smail/ *n.* насмевка

smoke /smoʊk/ 1. *n.* чад, дим;
2. *v.* пуши

smooth /smu:ð/ *adj.* мек, благ,
рамен

smuggle /ˈsmʌgl/ *v.* шверцува

snack /snæk/ *n.* закуска

snail /sneil/ *n.* полжав

snake /sneik/ *n.* змија

sneak /ˈsni:k/ *v.* се прикрадува

sneeze /sni:z/ *v.* кива

sniff /snif/ *v.* шмрка, шмркнува

sniffle /ˈsnifl/, snuffle /snʌfl/ *v.*
шмрка, липа

snore /snor/ *v.* рка

snow /snoʊ/ *n.* снег

so /soʊ/ *adv.* вака, така

soak /soʊk/ *v.* кисне,
накиснува, кваси, наквасува

soap /soʊp/ *n.* сапун

sober /ˈsoʊbər/ *adj.* трезен,
здржан

society /səˈsaiiti/ *n.* општество,
здружение

sock /sak/ *n.* кус чорап

soft /soft/ *adj.* мек, благ,
нежен

soil /soil/ *n.* почва, земја

soldier /ˈsoʊldʒər/ *n.* војник

sole /soʊl/ *adj.* единствен

solid /ˈsalid/ *adj.* едар,
масивен, тврд

solution /səˈlu:ʃn/ *n.* раствор,

решение

solve /salv/ *v.* решава, разрешува

some /sʌm/ *pron.* некој, некаков, малку, нешто

somebody /'sʌmbadi/ *pron.* некој, нешто

something /'sʌmθiŋ/ *pron.* нешто

son /sʌn/ *n.* син; ~ in law зет

song /soŋ/ *n.* песна

soon /su:n/ *adv.* наскоро, брзо

sore /sor/ *adj.* болен, воспален

sorrow /so'rɔu/ *n.* тага, болка, жал

sorry /'sari/ *adj.* жалосен, жален

soul /sɔul/ *n.* душа

sound /saund/ *n.* звук, шум, проток

soup /su:p/ *n.* супа

sour /sauɔ/ *adj.* кисел

source /sors/ *n.* извор

south /sauθ/ *n.* југ

sow /sɔu/ *v.* сее

space /speis/ *n.* простор, место, вселенски простор

spare /speɔ/ *v.* штеди, поштедува

spark /spark/ *n.* искра

sparrow /'spærɔu/ *n.* врапче

speak /spi:k/ *v.* говори, зборува

specify /'spesifai/ *v.* определува, одредува

speculate /'spekjɔleit/ *v.* мисли, смета

speed /spi:d/ *n.* брзина

spend /spend/ *v.* арчи, троши

spider /'spaidɔ/ *n.* пајак

spill /spil/ *v.* прелива, издава (тајна)

spirit /'spirit/ *n.* дух, душа, карактер

spit /spit/ *n.* плука

splash /'splæS/ *v.* (се) прска, (се) плиска

split /'split/ *v.* (се) цепи, (се) дели

spoil /spoil/ *v.* (се) расипува, уништува

spook /spu:k/ *n.* дух, привидение

spoon /spu:n/ *n.* лажица

spot /spat/ *n.* дамка, петно, место

spread /spred/ *v.* (се) шири, (се) протега

spring /spriŋ/ *n.* извор, пролет

square /skweɔ/ *n.* квадрат, четириаголник, плоштад

squeeze /skwi:z/ *v.* стиснува, смачкува

squirrel /'skwirɔl/ *n.* ве(р)верица

stab /stæb/ *v.* прободува

staff /stæf/ *n.* персонал, колегиум

stage /steid3/ *n.* сцена, бина,

подиум

stalk /stɔ:k/ *n.* стебленце, страк

stamp /stæmp/ *v.* тапка, тропа, отпечатува, става печат/марка

stand /stænd/ *v.* стои, заданува, се наоѓа, става, поставува, трпи

star /star/ *n.* звезда, орден

stare /steðr/ *v.* зјапа

start /start/ *v.* тргнува, почнува, стартува

starve /starv/ *v.* умира од глад, изгладнува

state /steit/ 1. *n.* држава; 2. *adj.* службен; 3. *v.* соопштува, кажува, објавува

station /ˈsteiʃn/ *n.* станица, статус, сталеж

stay /stei/ *v.* останува, отседнува, престојува

steady /ˈstedi/ *adj.* солиден, постојан

steal /sti:l/ *v.* краде

steam /sti:m/ *n.* пареа

steel /sti:l/ *n.* челик

stem /stem/ *n.* стебло, страк

step /step/ 1. *n.* стапка, степен; 2. *v.* степува, стапнува

stick /stik/ *n.* бастун, палка

still /stil/ *adv.* се уште, сепак

stingy /ˈstindʒi/ *adj.* стиснат

stink /stink/ *v.* смрди

stock /stak/ *n.* стока, добиток, *pl.* акции

stomach /ˈstʌmək/ *n.* стомак

stone /stðun/ *n.* камен, коска, семка

stop /stap/ *v.* (се) запира, (се) сопира

store /stor/ *n.* склад, магацин

storm /storm/ *n.* бура

story /ˈstori/ *n.* приказ(на)

stout /staut/ *adj.* едар, јак

straight /streit/ *adj.* (ис)прав(ен), откровен, искрен

strain /strein/ *v.* оптегнува, истегнува

strange /streindʒ/ *adj.* чуден, необичаен

strangle /ˈstrængl/ *v.* дави, задавува, задушува

straw /strɔ:/ *n.* слама, сламка

strawberry /ˈstrɔ:beri/ *n.* јагода

stream /stri:m/ *n.* поток, река

street /stri:t/ *n.* улица

stretch /stretʃ/ *v.* (се) растегнува, (се) раширува

strike /straik/ *v.* удира, удира (громот)

string /striŋ/ *n.* конец, канап

strong /strɔŋ/ *adj.* силен, снажен, издржлив

struggle /ˈstrʌgl/ *n.* борба, напор

study /ˈstʌdi/ *v.* учи, студира,

проучува

stupid /'stu:pid/ *adj.* глуп(ав)

subject /'sʌbdʒikt/ *n.* тема, предмет, подмет (во граматиката)

submit /sᴧbmit/ *v.* предава, поднесува

subscribe /sᴧb'skraib/ *v.* потпишува, запишува, се претплатува

substitute /'sᴧbstitu:d/ *n.* замена, заменик

suburb /'sᴧbз:b/ *n.* предградие

success /sᴧk'ses/ *n.* успех

such /sᴧtʃ/ *pron.* таков, каков

suddenly /'sᴧdnli/ *adv.* ненадеен, неочекуван

suffer /'sᴧfᴧ/ *v.* страда, се мачи

sugar /ʃugᴧ/ *n.* шекер

suggest /sᴧg'dʒest/ *v.* предлага, предложува

suicide /'su:isaid/ *n.* самоубиство

sullen /'sᴧln/ *adj.* мрзоволен

summer /'sᴧmᴧ/ *n.* лето

sun /sᴧn/ *n.* сонце

Sunday /'sᴧndi/ *n.* недела

superior /su'piriᴧ/ *adj.* подобар, виш, поквалитетен

supply /sᴧ'plai/ *v.* снабдува, задоволува

support /sᴧ'port/ *v.* придржува

suppose /sᴧ'pᴘuz/ *v.* претполага, смета

sure /ʃuᴧ/ *adj.* сигурен, несомнен

surface /'sз:fis/ *n.* површина

surgeon /'sз:dʒᴧn/ *n.* хирург

surprise /sᴧ'praiz/ *n.* изненадување

surrender /sᴧ'rendᴧ/ *v.* (се) предава, отстапува

surround /sᴧ'raund/ *v.* опколува, опкружува

survive /sᴧ'vaiv/ *v.* преживува, надживува

suspect /sᴧ'spekt/ *v.* претполага, се сомнева во, претчувствува

suspend /sᴧ'spend/ *v.* отстранува, суспендира

sustain /sᴧ'stein/ *v.* потпира, поткрепува

swallow /'swalᴧu/ 1. *v.* голта, голтнува, проголтува; 2. *n.* ластовица

swamp /swamp/ *n.* мочуриште

swan /swan/ *n.* лебед

swarm /sworm/ *n.* рој, толпа, мноштво

swear /sweᴧ/ *v.* (се) колне, (се) заколнува

sweat /swet/ *v.* се поти

sweep /swi:p/ *v.* мете, чисти

sweet /swi:t/ *adj.* сладок, мил

swell | tempt

swell /swel/ *v.* отекува, се надувува

swim /swim/ *v.* плива

swine /swain/ *n.* свиња

swing /swiŋ/ *v.* (се) лула, (се) клати

switch /switS/ 1. *v.* разменува; 2. *n.* (електричен) прекинувач

sword /sord/ *n.* меч

symbol /simbl/ *n.* симбол, знак

sympathy /'simpaθi/ *n.* сочувство, *pl.* симпатии

syringe /si'rindʒ/ *n.* шприц, шприца

system /'sistim/ *n.* систем, метод(а)

T

table /'teibl/ *n.* маса, табла

tail /teil/ *n.* опашка, редица (луѓе)

tailor /'teilə/ *n.* шивач

take /teik/ *v.* зема, презема, прима, однесува, води, набавува

tale /teil/ *n.* раскас, сказна

talk /to:k/ *v.* вели, кажува, зборува

tall /to:l/ *adj.* висок, строен

tame /teim/ *adj.* припитомен, кроток

tank /'tænk/ *v.* полни (бензин)

tape /teip/ *n.* лента, касета; ~ recorder касетофон

target /'targit/ *n.* цел, нишан

task /tæsk/ *n.* задача, задаток

taste /teist/ *n.* вкус

tax /tæks/ *n.* данок, намет

tea /ti:/ *n.* чај

teach /ti:tS/ *v.* учи, предава, научува, обучува

teacher /'ti:tSə/ *n.* учител

team /ti:m/ *n.* тим, екипа, колектив

tear /tiə/ 1. *n.* солза; /teə/ *v.* (се) дере, (се) кине, (се) раскинува

tease /ti:z/ *v.* (се) задева, (се) задира

technology /tek'nalədʒi/ *n.* техника, технологија

teenager /'ti:neidʒə/ *n.* тинејџер

tell /tel/ *v.* кажува, вели, зборува

temper /'tempə/ *n.* расположение, карактер

tempest /'tempist/ *n.* бура, виор, невреме

temple /'templ/ *n.* светилиште, храм

tempt /tempt/ *v.* предизвикува, доведува во искушение

ten /ten/ *num.* десет

tenant /'tenənt/ *n.* станар, наемник

tender /'tendə/ *adj.* нежен, деликатен, чувствителен

tense /tens/ *adj.* напрегнат, нервозен

tent /tent/ *n.* шатор

term /tз:m/ *n.* рок, термин, семестар; *pl.* услови

terrible /'teribl/ *adj.* страшен, ужасен, грозен

terrify /'terifai/ *v.* преплашува

terse /tз:s/ *adj.* краток, збиен

test /test/ *n.* проба, тест, опит

than /ðæn/ *conj.* од, отколку, одошто

thank /θæŋk/ *v.* благодари

that /ðæt/ *pron.* тој, оној

their /ðeə/ *pron.* нивен

them /ðem/ *pron.* нив/ги, ним/им

then /ðen/ *adv.* тогаш, во тоа време

there /ðeə/ *adv.* таму, онаму, онде

they /ðei/ *pron.* тие

thick /θik/ *adj.* дебел, матен (вода), близок

thief /θi:f/ *n.* крадец

thin /θin/ *adj.* тенок, слаб

thing /θiŋ/ *n.* предмет, нешто

think /θink/ *v.* мисли, помис-

лува, верува, наумува, намислува

thirst /θз:st/ *n.* жед, голема желба

this /ðis/ *pron.* овој, тој

thorn /θorn/ *n.* трн

though /ðəu/ *conj.* иако, сепак

thousand /'θauznd/ *num.* илјада

threat /θret/ *n.* закана, опасност

three /θri:/ *num.* три

thrill /θril/ *v.* (се) возбудува, (се) трогнува

throat /θrəut/ *n.* грло, врат

throne /θrəun/ *n.* престол, трон

through /θru/ *prep.* низ, преку

throw /θrəu/ *v.* фрла, исфрла, наметнува

thumb /θʌm/ *n.* палец

thunder /'θʌndə/ *n.* гром, грмотевица

Thursday /θз:zdi/ *n.* четврток

thus /ðʌs/ *adv.* вака, на тој начин

ticket /'tikit/ *n.* билет, карта

tidy /'taidi/ *adj.* уреден, чист

tie /tai/ *n.* вратоврска

tighten /'taitn/ *v.* (се) стегнува, (се) затегнува

time /taim/ *n.* време, рок, доба, ера, епоха

timid /'timid/ *adj.* плашлив, страшлив

tired /tai∂rd/ *adj.* уморен, изморен

tissue /'tiSu:/ *n.* фина ткаеница, тенка хартија/

title /'taitl/ *n.* име, наслов, назив

to /tu/ *prep.* кон, во, до

today /t∂'dei/ *adv./n.* денес, денеска

toe /t∂u/ *n.* ножен прст

together /t∂'ge∂∂/ *adv.* заедно, истовремено

token /'t∂uk∂n/ *n.* знак, белег, симбол

tomb /tu:m/ *n.* гробница, могила

tomorrow /t∂'mor∂u/ *adv.* утре

tongue /tʌŋ/ *n.* јазик

tonight /t∂'nait/ *n.* оваанок

too /tu:/ *adv.* премногу, исто, така

tool /tu:l/ *n.* орудие

tooth /tu:θ/ (*pl.* teeth) *n.* заб

top /top/ *n.* врв, највисока точка/степен

torch /tortS/ *n.* факел

torture /'tortS∂r/ *v.* измачува, мачи

total /'t∂utl/ 1. *adj.* цел, севкупен; 2. *n.* сума, сбир

touch /tʌtS/ *v.* (се) допира, (се) добира до, достигнува

tour /tu∂/ *n.* патување, обиколка, турнеја

tow /t∂u/ *v.* влече, тегне

toward(s) /t∂wo:d(z)/ *prep.* кон

towel /'tau∂l/ *n.* пешкир, крпа за бришење

tower /'tau∂/ *n.* кула, тврдина

town /taun/ *n.* град

toy /toi/ *n.* играчка

trace /treis/ *v.* следи, оди по, открива

track /træk/ *n.* трага, патека, пруга, перон

trade /treid/ *n.* трговија, занает, промет

tradition /tr∂diSn/ *n.* предание, традиција

traffic /'træfic/ *n.* промет, превоз, транспорт

train /trein/ 1. *n.* воз, поворка; 2. *v.* (се) тренира, (се) обучава

traitor /'treit∂r/ *n.* предавник, издајник

translate /træn'sleit/ *v.* преведува

transplant /træn'splænt/ *v.* пресадува, трансплантира

trap /træp/ *n.* примка, клопка, стапица

travel /'trævl/ *v.* патува

treasure /'tre3∂/ *n.* богатство, драгоценост

treat /tri:t/ *v.* се однесува со, постапува кон, гости, обработува, третира

tree /tri:/ *n.* дрво
tremendous /tri'mend∂s/ *adj.*
голем, огромен
trend /trend/ *n.* насока, тенденција
trick /trik/ *n.* лукавство, ит-
рина, измама
trigger /'trig∂/ *n.* чкрапец,
шкрапало
trim /trim/ *n.* уредност, под-
реденост
trip /trip/ *n.* патување, излет
trouble /'trʌbl/ *n.* невола, незгода, мака, непријатност,
грижа
truck /trʌk/ *n.* камион, *Br* отворен вагон
true /tru:/ *adj.* вистински, ве-

рен, реален
trunk /trʌnk/ *n.* труп, ковчег,
Am багажник, на автомобил
trust /trʌst/ *v.* верува во, има
верба, доверба во, доверува
truth /tru:θ/ *n.* вистина
try /trai/ *v.* пробува, испро-
бува
Tuesday /'tu:zdi/ *n.* вторник
turn /tɜ:n/ *v.* врте, завртува
turtle /tɜ:tl/ *n.* желка
twelve /twelv/ *num.* дванадесет
twenty /'twenti/ *num.* дваесет
twice /twais/ *adv.* двапати
twin /twin/ *n.* близнак, двојник
twist /twist/ *v.* (се) врти, (се)
вие
two /tu:/ *num.* два, две

U

ugly /'ʌgli/ *adj.* грд, грозен,
не-пријатен
umbrella /ʌm'brel∂/ *n.* чадор,
заштита
unable /ʌn'eibl/ *adj.*
неспособен, не во состојба
unbearable /ʌn'ber∂bl/ *adj.*
неподнослив
uncle /'ʌnkl/ *n.* тетин, старико,
вујко
uncommon /ʌn'kam∂n/ *adj.*
необичен, несекојдневен

unconscious /ʌn'kanS∂s/ *adj.*
несвесен, во бесвест
under /'ʌnd∂/ 1. *adv.* (по)долу,
здола; 2. *prep.* под
undercover /ʌnd∂'cʌv∂/ *adj.* таен, скришен
underground /'ʌnd∂graund/ *adj.*
подземен, таен
undermine /ʌnd∂'main/ *v.* пот-
копува
underneath /ʌnd∂ni:θ/ *adv.* здола, долу

understand /ʌndəˈstænd/ v. разбира, подразбира, сфаќа

undertake /ʌndəˈteik/ v. презема се, се обврзува

underwear /ˈʌndəˈweə/ n. долна облека

undo /ʌnˈduː/ v. одврзува, разлабува

unfortunate /ʌnˈfortSənit/ adj. несреќен

unhappy /ʌnˈhæpi/ adj. незадоволен

unheard /ʌnhɜːd/ adj. неcослушан

unify /ˈjuːnifai/ v. обединува, изедначува

union /juːniən/ n. сојуз, унија, здружение, друштво, синдикат

unique /juːniːk/ adj. единствен, необичен

unit /ˈjuːnit/ n. единица, составен дел

unite /juːnait/ v. (се) обединува, (се) соединува

universe /ˈjuːnivɜːs/ n. семир, вселена, универзум

university /juːniˈvɜːsiti/ n. универзитет

unjust /ʌnˈdʒʌst/ adj. неправеден

unknown /ʌnˈnəun/ adj. непознат, незнаен

unlawful /ʌnˈloːfl/ adj. незаконит, незаконски

unless /ənˈles/ conj. освен ако, ако не

unlike /ʌnˈlaik/ 1. adj. различен, поинаков; 2. prep. спротивно на, за разлика од

unlikely /ʌnˈlaikli/ adj. неверојатен

unload /ʌnˈləud/ v. растоварува, се ослободува од, испразнува (пушка)

unlock /ʌnˈlak/ v. отклучува

unpack /ʌnˈpæk/ v. распакува, отпакува

unreal /ʌnˈriəl/ adj. неств舂рен

until /ənˈtil/ 1. conj. додека; 2. prep. до

untrue /ʌnˈtruː/ adj. невистинит, неправ

up /ʌp/ adv. (на)горе, исправено

update /ʌpˈdeit/ v. осовременува, модернизира

uphold /ʌpˈhəuld/ v. крепи, поддржува

upon /əˈpon/ prep. на, врз

upright /ʌpˈrait/ adj. изправен

upset /ʌpˈset/ v. вознемирува, нарушува

upstairs /ʌpˈsteəz/ adv. горе, на погорниот кат

urban /ɜːˈbɜːn/ adj. градски

urge /ɜːdʒ/ v. тера, натерува

us /ʌs/ pron. нас (не), нам (ни)

use /ju:s/ *v.* употребува

useful /'ju:sfl/ *adj.* корисен

usual /'ju:ʒuəl/ *adj.* обичен, во-обичаен

utensil /'ju:tensl/ *n.* алат, сад; *pl.* прибор

utility /ju:tiliti/ *n.* полезност, услуга

V

vacant /'veikənt/ *adj.* празен, слободен

vacation /və'keiSn/ *n.* училишен распуст, годишен одмор, ваканција

vague /veig/ *adj.* матен, нејасен

vain /vein/ *adj.* суетен, неважен, напразен

valley /'væli/ *n.* долина

value /'vælju:/ *n.* вредност, корист

vanish /'væniS/ *v.* изчезнува, се губи

various /'veriəs/ *adj.* разен, разноврстен

vary /'veri/ *v.* варира, (се) про-менува

vegetable /'ved3tbl/ *n.* зеленчук

vehicle / 'vi:ikl/ *n.* возило, носи-тел, средство

vein /vein/ *n.* вена, жила

velvet /'velvit/ *n.* кадифе

vend /vend/ *v.* нуди, продава

venture /'ventSə/ *n.* авантура, ризик, смел потфат

verb /vз:b/ *n.* глагол

verdict /'vз:dikt/ *n.* решение на поротата, суд

verify /'verifai/ *v.* проверува, потврдува

verse /vз:s/ *n.* стих

very /'veri/ 1. *adv.* многу, мош-но; 2. *adj.* самиот, токму тој

vicinity /vi'siniti/ *n.* околина

victim /'viktim/ *n.* жртва

victory /'viktəti/ *n.* победа

view /vju:/ *n.* поглед, гледка, гледиште

vinegar /'vinigə/ *n.* оцет

violent /'vaiələnt/ *adj.* насилен, насилнички

violin /vaiə'lin/ *n.* виолина

virtue /'vз:tSu:/ *n.* доблест, предност, вредност

vision /'viʒn/ *n.* вид, поглед, привидение

visit /visit/ *v.* посетува

vital /'vaitl/ *adj.* битен, животен, необходен

vocabulary /və'kæbjuləri/ *n.* лексика, речник

voice /vois/ *n.* глас

volume /'valʃm/ *n.* книга, том,
волумен, опсег

volunteer /valʃn'tiʃ/ *v.* добро-
волно се јавува, волонтира

vote /vʌut/ *n.* глас, гласање

vow /vau/ *n.* клетва, заклетва

vulnerable /'vʌnrʃbl/ *adj.*
чувствителен, ранлив

W

wade /weid/ *v.* цапа, гази

wage /'weidʒ/ *n.* wages /'/'weid
ʒiz/ *n. pl.* надница

wagon /'wægʃn/ *n.* товарен
вагон, запрежна кола

wail /seil/ *v.* (се) оплакува,
реди

waist /weist/ *n.* струк , половина

wait /weit/ *v.* чека

wake /weik/ *v.* (се) буди, (се)
пробудува

walk /wo:k/ *v.* оди пеш, се
шета

wall /wo:l/ *n.* зид, бедем

wallet /'walit/ *n.* портмоне,
машко кесе за пари

wander /'wandʃr/ *v.* скита,
лута

want /want/ *v.* сака, бара

war /wor/ *n.* војна

ware /weʃl/ *n.* стока

warm /worm/ *adj.* топол,
страстен

warn /worn/ *v.* предупредува,
опоменува

warranty /'worʃnti/ *n.* гаранција

wash /woʃ/ *v.* (се) мие, (се)
пере

waste /weist/ *v.* арчи, запустува, попусто троши

watch /wotʃ/ *v.* гледа, пос-
матра, дебне

water /'watʃl/ *n.* вода

wave /weiv/ *n.* бран, кадра (на
коса)

way /wei/ *n.* пат, начин, ме-
тода

we /wi/ *pron.* ние

weak /wi:k/ *adj.* слаб, сла-
бичок

wealth /welθ/ *n.* богатство,
изобилство

weapon /'wepʃn/ *n.* оружие

wear /weʃl/ *v.* носи, има, трае

weather /'weθʃl/ *n.* време

web /web/ *n.* пајажина

wed /wed/ *v.* (се) венчава

wedding /'wediʃ/ *n.* свадба

Wednesday /'wenzdi/ *n.* среда

weed /wi:d/ *n.* плевел, бурјан

week /wi:k/ *n.* недела, седмица

weep /wi:p/ *v.* плаче, липа

weigh /wei/ *v.* мери, измерува, одмерува, вага

weight /weit/ *n.* тежина, тег, мерка

welcome /'welkəm/ 1. *adj.* добредојден; 2. *v.* пожелува добредојде

welfare /'welfeə/ *n.* благосостојба, социална помош

well /wel/ 1. *n.* бунар, извор; 2. *adv.* арно, добро, фино

west /west/ *n.* запад

wet /wet/ *adj.* влажен, мокар, наквасен

whale /weil/ *n.* кит

wharf /worf/ *n.* пристаништен брег

what /wat/ *pron.* кој, што

wheat /wi:t/ *n.* пченица, жито

wheel /wi:l/ *n.* тркало, колце, круг, коло

when /wen/ *adv.* кога

where /weə/ *adv.* каде

which /witS/ *pron.* кој, што

while /wail/ *n.* време, час, извесно време

whim /wim/ *n.* каприц

whip /wip/ *n.* бич, камшик

whirl /wз:l/ *v.* (се) врти бргу

whisk /wisk/ *v.* мавта, замавнува, тера

whisper /'wispə/ *v.* шепоти, прошепотува

whistle /'wisl/ *v.* свири, свирка

white /wait/ *adj.* бел, блед

who /hu:/ *pron.* кој, којшто

whole /həul/ *adj.* цел, сиот

whom /hu:m/ *pron.* кого (го), кому (му)

whose /hu:s/ *pron.* чиј, чијшто

why /wai/ *adv.* зошто

wide /waid/ *adj.* широк

widow /'widəu/ *n.* вдовица

wife /waif/ *n.* (*pl.* wives) сопруга, жен

wild /waild/ *adj.* див, незауздан, бесен

will /wil/ *mod.* 1. *v.* ќе; 2. *n.* волја

willow /'wiləu/ *n.* врба

win /win/ *v.* добива, победува

wince /wins/ *v.* се стресува, се тргнува

wind /wind/ *n.* ветер, здив

window /'windəu/ *n.* прозорец

wine /wain/ *n.* вино

wing

wing /wiђ/ *n.* крило

wink /wink/ *v.* намига

winter /'wint∂/ *n.* зима

wipe /waip/ *v.* брише

wire /waid/ *n.* жица, тел

wise /waiz/ *adj.* мудар, разумен

wish /wiS/ *v.* посакува, пожелува

wit /wit/ *n.* духовитост, бистрина

witch /witS/ *n.* вештерка, маѓесница

with /wiѳ/ *prep.* со, при, од

withdraw /wiѳdro:/ *v.* зема, вади (пари од банка)

withhold /wiѳ'h∂uld/ *v.* задржува, ускратува

within /wi'ѳin/ 1. *adv.* внатре; 2. *prep.* во рок од, во рамките на

without /wiѳaut/ *prep.* без

witness /'witnis/ *n.* сведок, присутен

wizard /'wiz∂d/ *n.* вештер, магесник

wolf /wulf/ *n.* (*pl.* **wolves**) волк

woman /'wum∂n/ *n.* (*pl.* **wimin** /'wimin/) жена

wonder /'wлnd∂/ *v.* се чуди, се прашува

wood /wud/ *n.* дрво, шума

wool /wul/ *n.* волна

word /wз:d/ *n.* збор, слово, вест

work /wз:k/ 1. *n.* работа, дејност, творба; 2. *v.* работи, изработува

world /wз:ld/ *n.* свет

worm /wз:m/ *n.* црв, црвец, глиста

worry /'wзri/ *v.* (се) загрижува, (се) вознемирува

worth /wз:ѳ/ *adj.* што заслужува, што вреди, достоен

wound /wu:nd/ *n.* рана

wrap /ræp/ *v.* завива, завиткува

wrestle /resl/ *v.* се бори

wring /riђ/ *v.* витка, врти, стиска

wrinkle /'rinkl/ 1. *v.* се брчка; 2. *n.* брчка

wrist /rist/ *n.* рачен зглоб

write /rait/ *v.* пишува, запишува, забележува

wrong /roђ/ *adj.* погрешен, неточен, неправ

X

xerox /'ziraks/ v. фотокопира
xenon /'zinan/ n. ксенон
xenophobia /zenðfðubiðl/ n.
ксенофобија

xylography /zai'lagrðfi/ n.
резбарство
xylophone /zailðfðun/ n. кси-
лофон

Y

yacht /jat/ n. јахта
yard /ja:d/ n. јарда, двор
yawn /jo:n/ v. се просева
year /jið/ n. година
yearn /jз:n/ v. копнее
yeast /ji:st/ n. квасец, квас
yell /jel/ v. вика, се дере
yellow /jelðu/ adj. жолт
yes /jes/ adv. да
yesterday /'jestðdi/ adv. вчера

yet /jet/ adv. уште, се уште
yield /ji:ld/ v. доз-волува,
отстапува, про-пушта, дава
yoke /jðuk/ n. јарем, ропство
yolk /jðuk/ n. жолчка
you /ju:/ pron. ти, вие
young /jлђ/ adj. млад
your /juðr/ pron. твој, ваш
youth /ju:θ/ n. младост, младеж,

Z

zany /'zeni/ n. глупак, шут
zeal /zi:l/ n. жар, ревност
zebra /'zi:brðl/ n. зебра
zenith /'zeniθ/ n. зенит
zero /'zi:rðu/ num. нула, ништо
zest /zest/ n. полет, елан,
страст, занес

zip /zip/ n. зип, полет, елан
zither/'ziθð/ n. цитра
zone /zðun/ n. зона, појас
zoo /zu:/ n. зоолошка градина
zoom /zu:m/ v. прибилжува,
фокусира
zucchini /zuki:ni/ n. тиквички